IMAGES
of America

John F. Kennedy's North Carolina Campaign

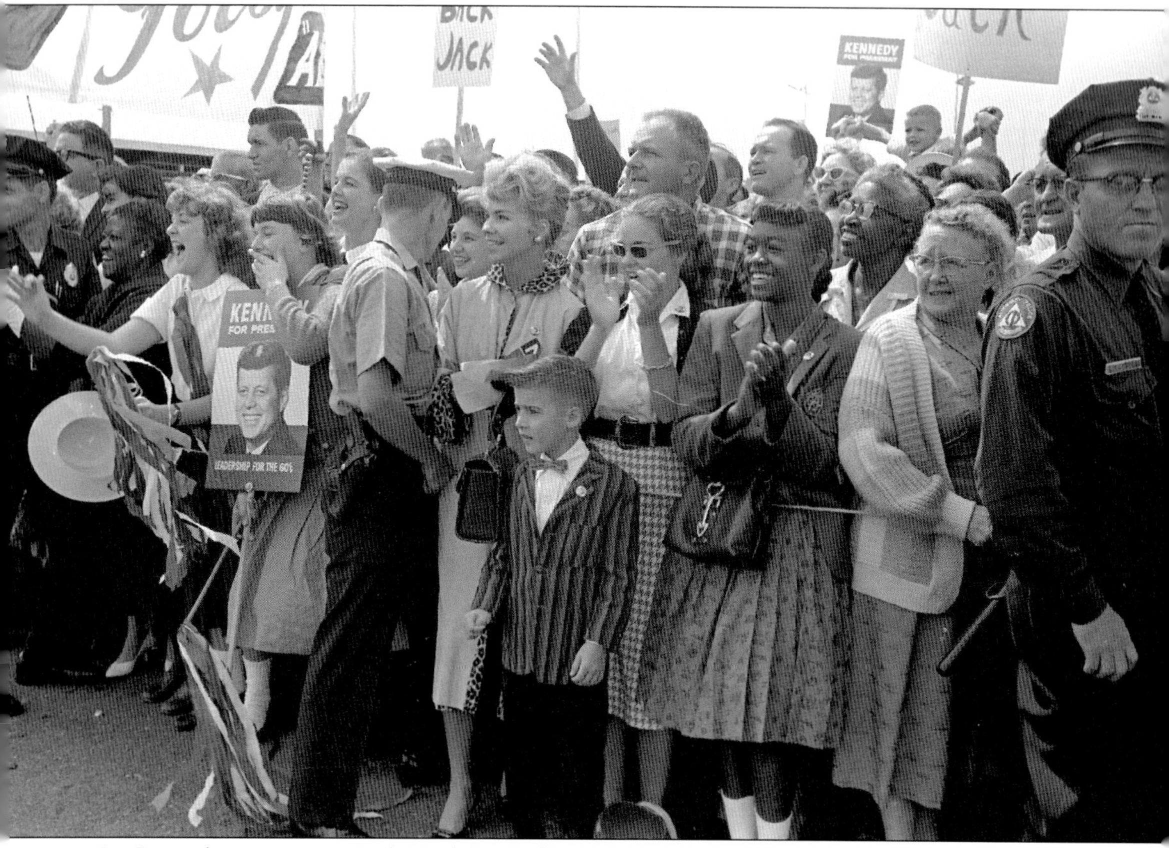

In Greensboro, supporters cheered Sen. John F. Kennedy's arrival. Earlier, Kennedy had staged a successful rally, the first of the day, on the campus of East Carolina College in Greenville. Over 12,000 attended the College Stadium rally, the first by a presidential candidate in eastern North Carolina in the 20th century. (Photograph by Don Sturkey, Wilson Library, University of North Carolina.)

On the Cover: This photograph shows Senator Kennedy leaving Greenville. Shortly after it was taken, the red Mercury Monterey accelerated onward to the Pitt-Greenville Airport. Left of Kennedy are Rep. Herbert C. Bonner (center) and Democratic gubernatorial nominee Terry Sanford. The driver, Henry F. Lawson, was a police detective. Next to Lawson is John G. Clark Jr., chair of the Pitt County Democratic Party. (Photograph by Hugh Morton; courtesy of Wilson Library, University of North Carolina.)

IMAGES
of America

JOHN F. KENNEDY'S NORTH CAROLINA CAMPAIGN

John Allen Tucker

ARCADIA
PUBLISHING

ISBN 978-0-7385-9294-7

Published by Arcadia Publishing
Charleston, South Carolina

Printed in the United States of America

Library of Congress Control Number: 2012935197

For all general information, please contact Arcadia Publishing:
Telephone 843-853-2070
Fax 843-853-0044
E-mail sales@arcadiapublishing.com
For customer service and orders:
Toll-Free 1-888-313-2665

Visit us on the Internet at www.arcadiapublishing.com

To Kate and Kaleigh Tucker

Contents

ACKNOWLEDGMENTS

My thanks to Arcadia Publishing for working with me on this project. I especially want to thank Lindsay Carter, Katie Kellett, and Erin Rocha at Arcadia for their support throughout the submission and development process.

My sincere thanks to Kacy Guill, university archivist, and Arthur Carlson, assistant archivist, at J.Y. Joyner Library, East Carolina University (ECU) for their work in making resources available to me. Also deserving thanks are Joe Barricella and Michael Reece in Digital Collections, Joyner Library. Without their digitization work, this project would have been impossible. Thanks, too, to my graduate assistant, Kate Schnitzer, for help in editing the text. Students in my ECU history class—Chelsey Gunter, Brian Roberts, Samuel Hickman, and Andrew Tagliareni—proofread the text and served as editorial consultants. My sincere thanks to each of them.

I am indebted to Dr. Larry Boyer, dean of Joyner Library; Maury York; Ralph Scott; and the ECU Joyner Library Special Collections staff for their continuing support of the project. Chancellor Steve Ballard, Provost Marilyn Sheerer, and Associate Provost Austin Bunch deserve heartfelt thanks for their support in my role as university historian.

My thanks to the Whichard family of Greenville and the *Daily Reflector* for the images donated to Joyner Library. Without them, the project never would have begun. I also wish to thank Keith Longiotti and staff at the Louis Round Wilson Library, University of North Carolina, Chapel Hill for their help in having negatives digitized. I am grateful to Don Sturkey for his permission to use some of his images. I also am very thankful that the *News and Observer* permitted use of their images. Thanks as well to Kim Cumber of the North Carolina State Archives staff for her help in having those digitized so promptly.

Last, but not least, thanks to my daughter Kaleigh and wife Kate for their patience with me throughout all of this.

INTRODUCTION

Saturday, September 17, 1960, was a red-letter day in the history of presidential campaigns in North Carolina. John F. Kennedy, then the junior senator from Massachusetts and the Democratic Party's nominee for the presidency, barnstormed across the Tar Heel State. Senator Kennedy's campaign blitz began as his personal plane, a Convair-240, landed in Greenville for an eventful 87-minute whirlwind tour of the rural college town.

Never before had a successful presidential candidate bothered to campaign in eastern North Carolina. Admittedly, Pres. George Washington toured the South, including much of the coastal plains, in 1791, but his visit was a statesman's survey of the region, not a political campaign courting locals. Then, in 1896, William Jennings Bryan, the Democratic nominee for president, held whistle-stop rallies statewide. Bryan, however, lost to Republican William McKinley, diminishing memories of his stops in eastern North Carolina. For the next six decades, presidential campaigns ignored eastern North Carolina. The region's loyalty to the Democratic Party allowed candidates to take it for granted, while Republicans simply wrote it off as a lost cause. Senator Kennedy changed that, coming first to eastern North Carolina and making himself a part of life in the region, even if for just one morning.

A group of Alpha Delta Pi sorority sisters wearing white dresses, mock-straw Kennedy hats, and holding a banner reading, "A.D. Pi Welcomes Kennedy," greeted Kennedy on behalf of East Carolina College. A motorcade parade through town followed, with a stop at Farmers Warehouse where Ray Oglesby, the most famous auctioneer of the day, conducted a mock tobacco auction of recently harvested and cured golden leaf. Kennedy's Greenville visit climaxed with a mid-morning rally at East Carolina College's stadium. Reportedly, some 12,000 people drawn from over 30 counties in eastern North Carolina attended.

Before the day ended, Kennedy had flown across most of the state, making stops in Greensboro, Charlotte, and finally Raleigh, where he dined with Gov. Luther H. Hodges before a rally at Reynolds Coliseum. Kennedy's entourage even circled Asheville for a scheduled rally there but had to cancel due to inclement weather. Kennedy's otherwise highly successful air blitz of the state was made possible by his personal plane, the *Caroline*, and charter flights orchestrated by a host of North Carolina Democratic politicians accompanying him. Each of Kennedy's campaign stops was headline news, but the one in Greenville at East Carolina was most especially so. After all, Kennedy had never visited eastern North Carolina. As early as March 1947, he delivered a speech on foreign policy at the University of North Carolina. In October 1956, he was the keynote speaker at the 21st Annual Meeting of the Young Democratic Clubs of North Carolina, held in Winston-Salem. In January 1959, he and his wife, Jacqueline, had flown to Charlotte to address a chamber of commerce banquet including over 1,000 business and political leaders. In December 1959, Kennedy spoke at Duke University. By 1960, the only regions that Kennedy had not visited were the eastern and western parts of the state.

Democratic strength in the coastal plains and the party's comparative weakness in the western part of the state made the decision to open the September 17 rallies in eastern North Carolina an easy one. Greenville, the geographic center of the region with a vibrant, coeducational liberal arts college of over 5,000 students, was also a natural choice. Further recommending the small town was the new leader of East Carolina College, Dr. Leo Jenkins, an early follower of Kennedy and enthusiastic believer in having faculty and students participate in politics. In January 1960, Dr. Jenkins invited Kennedy to speak at East Carolina. Kennedy initially declined, but before the year was over, he accepted the offer in order to advance his presidential campaign. Jenkins, eager to have a strong turnout, encouraged faculty to have their students attend the rally.

Kennedy immersed himself in the life of eastern North Carolina. The outdoor rally at College Stadium in Greenville was the big gathering that morning, but Kennedy pleased locals earlier by stopping at Farmers Warehouse, the largest in a county known for its world-ranking production of flue-cured tobacco. After rubbing shoulders and shaking hands with hundreds of tobacco farmers and their wives and children, Kennedy left Farmers Warehouse perched on the back of a red Mercury Monterey convertible along with Democratic gubernatorial nominee Terry Sanford and US Representative Herbert Bonner.

The Kennedy motorcade proceeded through Greenville to East Carolina's College Stadium. In May 1960, Dr. Jenkins had been inaugurated as the school's new president at College Stadium. However, his later years as an unwavering advocate for East Carolina were underwritten on September 17, 1960, with potent political connections as nearly every Democratic player in the state gathered in little Greenville to kick-start the North Carolina barnstorm, leaving no room for doubt about Democratic solidarity. Still, some voices in the community echoed Norman Vincent Peale and others in declaring that the threat posed by a Catholic president was extreme. In an acerbic letter to Terry Sanford, the senior clergy at Greenville's oldest Methodist church stated that a Catholic president would "surely cut America's head off."

At the East Carolina rally, however, Kennedy's wit and charm were prefaced by an invocation delivered by the Reverend Floyd B. Cherry, senior clergyman at Black Jack Freewill Baptist Church. Some might question whether Cherry voted for Kennedy on Election Day, but Cherry showed, through his own profile in courage, that eastern North Carolinians would not succumb to the worst. That Kennedy gave eastern North Carolina an opportunity to prove it was beyond such bigotry—78 percent of Pitt County voters chose him on Election Day—was one of the most historic consequences of his September 17, 1960, visit.

Greenville might have remained, in some eyes, a "trifling place," as President Washington judged; Kennedy, however, had the political acumen to elevate it as first on his North Carolina campaign and the wisdom to conjure only words of appreciation and respect for the people and their historic region. During his 87-minute encounter with the town, its enormous tobacco warehouse, and its college, Kennedy was gregarious and consistently appreciative of the local people and down-east life. His hour-and-a-half stop in Greenville that climaxed with the rally at College Stadium went a long way toward winning the hearts and minds of eastern North Carolinians who may have harbored misgivings about the Massachusetts senator's politics and religion. Kennedy won the vast majority of their votes in the November election, helping refortify the state's devotion to the Democratic agenda.

For East Carolina College, Kennedy's campaign was equally important in that it brought the campus statewide and even national attention. The small but ambitious college had flawlessly coordinated what was the single-most successful rally of the day, surpassing all other North Carolina stops with its logistical execution and positive publicity. The college's new leader, Dr. Leo Jenkins, emerged as a visible and clearly adroit political figure. He earned considerable respect and substantial political capital for having played a crucial role in orchestrating the rally at East Carolina and, by extension, Kennedy's victory in North Carolina. By cashing in this newly won capital, even while simultaneously building on the momentum it created, Jenkins would preside over a decade of phenomenal growth for both East Carolina and the region. This would give rise to a new incarnation of eastern North Carolina, one in which East Carolina College served as the powerful engine of higher education, driving the region forward in growth, quality of life, and political influence.

The daylong campaign forged a powerful bond between Kennedy and North Carolinians, one reiterated at the 1961 University Day ceremonies in Chapel Hill as then president Kennedy delivered the keynote address. When the tragedy of assassination struck, heartfelt responses reflected the closeness cultivated on September 17, 1960, as memorial services occurred statewide, particularly in places like Greenville and East Carolina, where Kennedy had connected with the people. These climaxed again in Kenan Stadium, marking a solemn conclusion to one dimension of Kennedy's North Carolina campaign.

One

OVERTURES

Well before his campaign tour of the state, John F. Kennedy, the junior senator from Massachusetts, had been courting North Carolina political leaders, especially Gov. Luther H. Hodges (1898–1974) and Sen. B. Everett Jordan (1896–1974). Sen. Samuel J. Ervin, a constitutional defender of segregation, was not as close to Kennedy politically as Hodges and Jordan, the more progressive North Carolinians. Yet more than Hodges or Jordan, Kennedy found political kinship with former state senator Terry Sanford. Sanford's run for governor in 1960 cast his political fortunes in a universe parallel to and eventually intersecting with Kennedy's. With support from Sanford, his political ally, Kennedy made his not entirely unexpected blitz of the state on September 17, 1960.

Helping mediate things was Dr. Leo Warren Jenkins, a New Jersey native who rose to the presidency of East Carolina College following the resignation of Dr. John Messick in late 1959. Shortly after being appointed interim and then president of East Carolina, Jenkins wrote to Kennedy inviting him to speak on campus. Although Kennedy declined, the idea of an eastern visit into the Democratic heartland of North Carolina had been sown. It came to fruition nine months later, in unexpected ways.

Complicating the realization of Dr. Jenkins's dream, however, was highly destructive Hurricane Donna just days before Kennedy's visit. Although a frightening disaster, eastern North Carolina quickly recovered and apparently found the young senator from Massachusetts a much more welcome visitor.

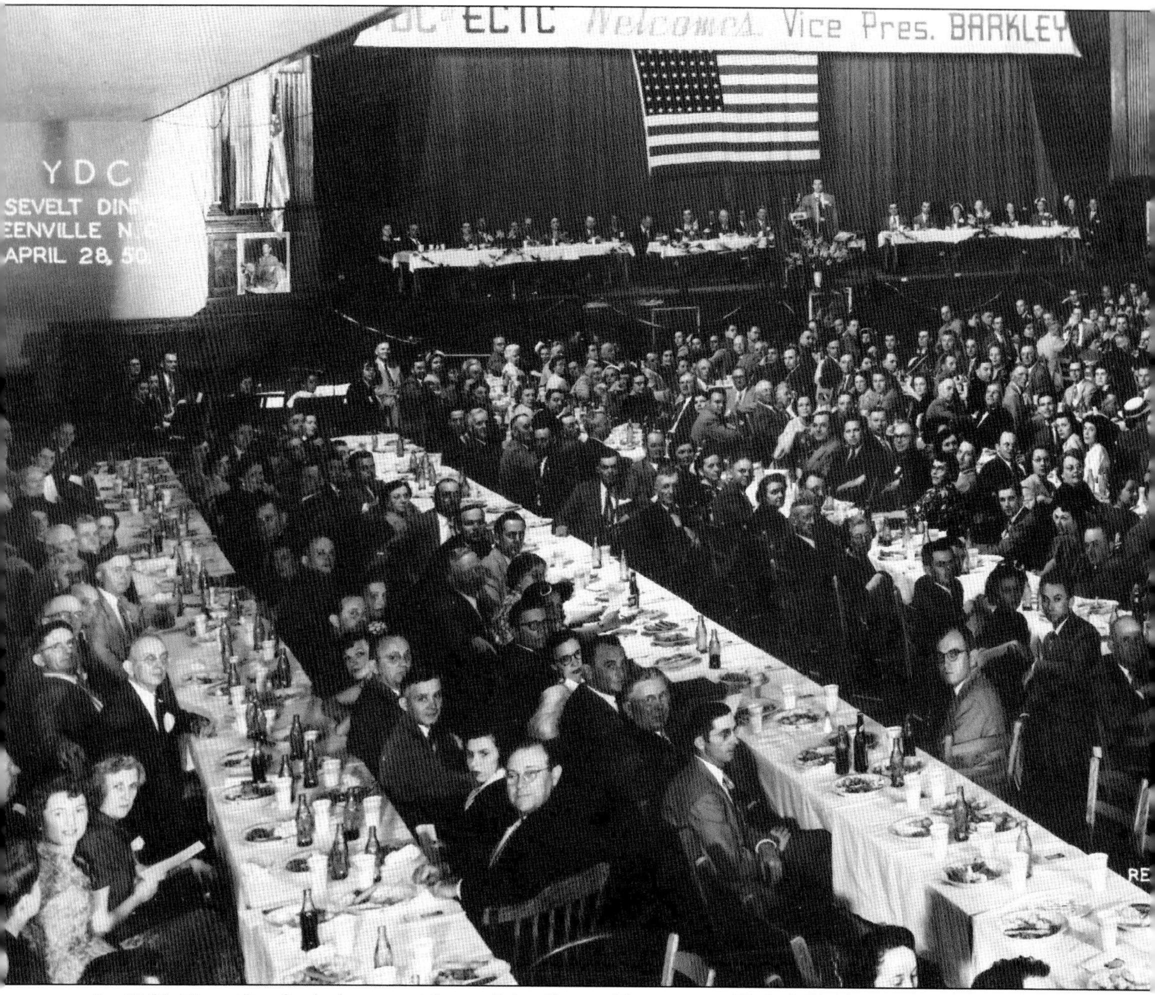

In 1950, Terry Sanford, then president of the Young Democrats Club (YDC), organized a Roosevelt Day Dinner fundraiser for Democratic candidates. The guest speaker was Vice Pres. Alben W. Barkley, and the venue was Wright Auditorium, located on the campus of East Carolina Teachers' College (ECTC). Assisting Sanford was Dr. Leo Warren Jenkins, a New Jersey native serving ECTC as dean of students. On stage was Sen. Franklin Graham, incumbent candidate in the Democratic Party's senatorial primary against conservative Willis Smith. Graham, former president of the University of North Carolina and a significant influence on Sanford, was targeted by the Smith forces as a communist who supported the mixing of the races. By bringing Vice President Barkley

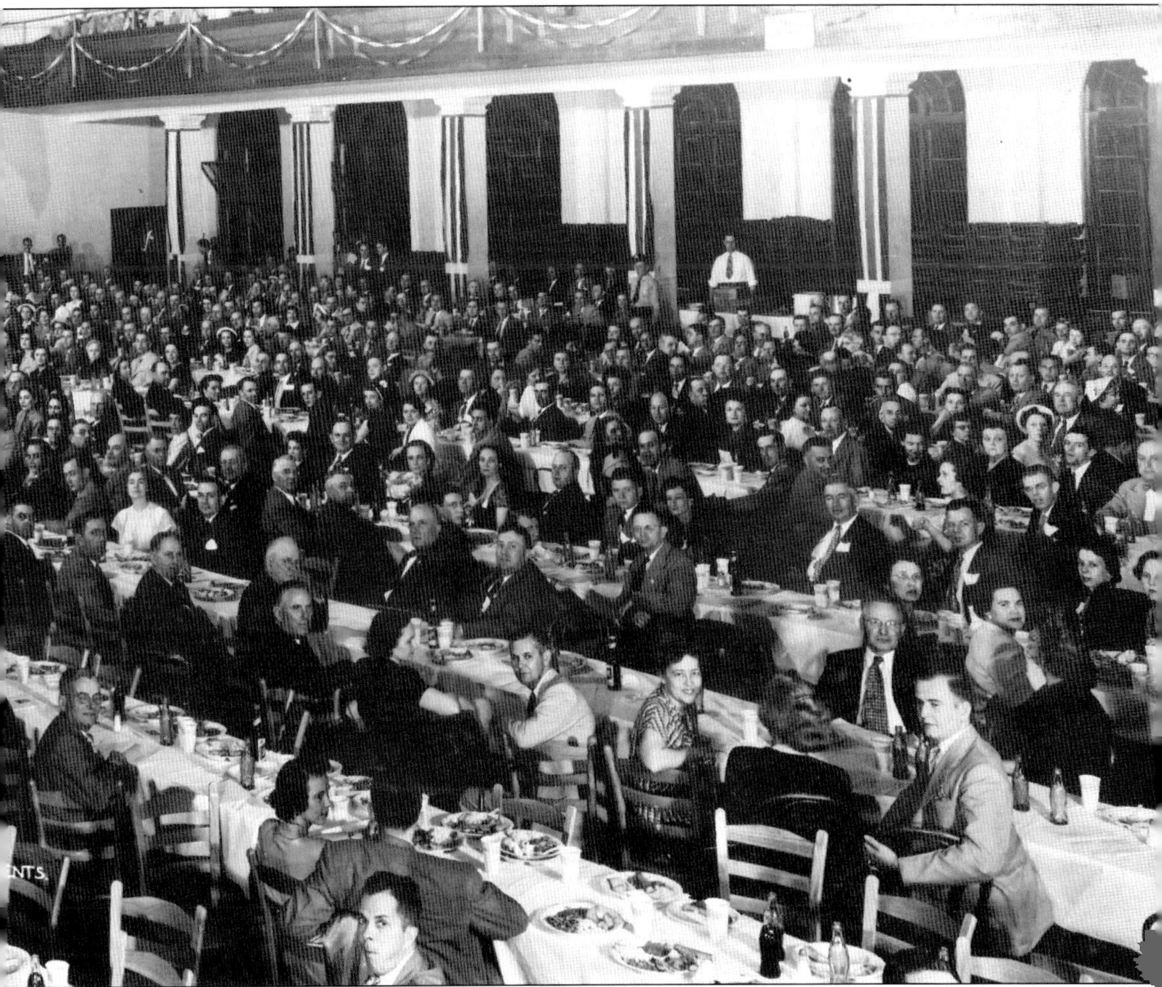

to East Carolina for the Roosevelt dinner and including Graham on stage with him, Sanford hoped to help Graham in the upcoming primary. Nevertheless, Graham was defeated and Sanford was profoundly disappointed. More positively, the YDC Roosevelt Day Dinner at ECTC marked the beginning of a collaboration between Sanford and Jenkins in support of Democratic causes. Wherever possible, Jenkins mobilized East Carolina for political action. A decade later, in 1960, this teamwork resulted in the Kennedy rally at College Stadium. (Courtesy of Betty Speirs and J.Y. Joyner Library, East Carolina University.)

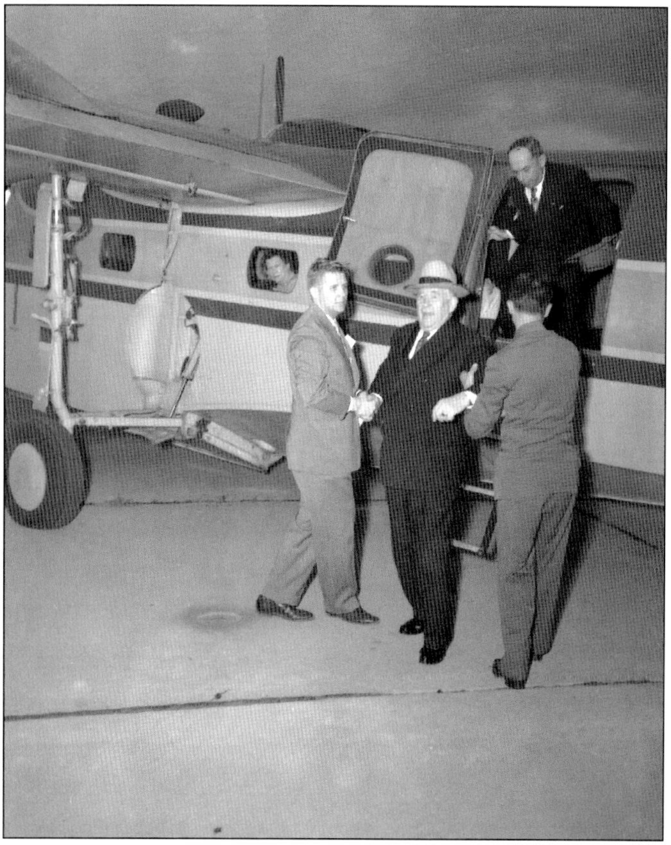

Sanford helps Vice President Barkley disembark his plane at Pitt-Greenville Airport. Also disembarking is Rep. Herbert C. Bonner. A decade later, Sanford greeted Sen. John Kennedy at the same airport when Kennedy arrived in North Carolina for his opening rally at East Carolina College. (Courtesy of J.Y. Joyner Library, East Carolina University.)

From left to right are (first row) Richard Taft, Hoover Taft III, Charles Taft, and Tom Taft; (second row) Vice President Barkley, Rep. Harold D. Cooley, Hoover Taft Jr., and Rep. Herbert C. Bonner. (Courtesy J.Y. Joyner Library, East Carolina University.)

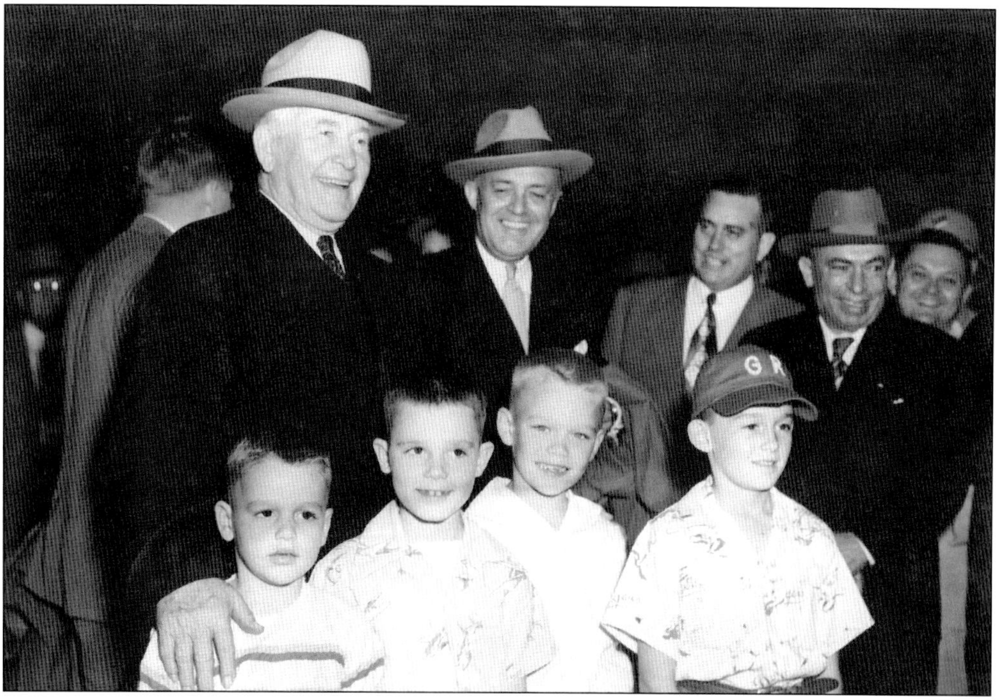

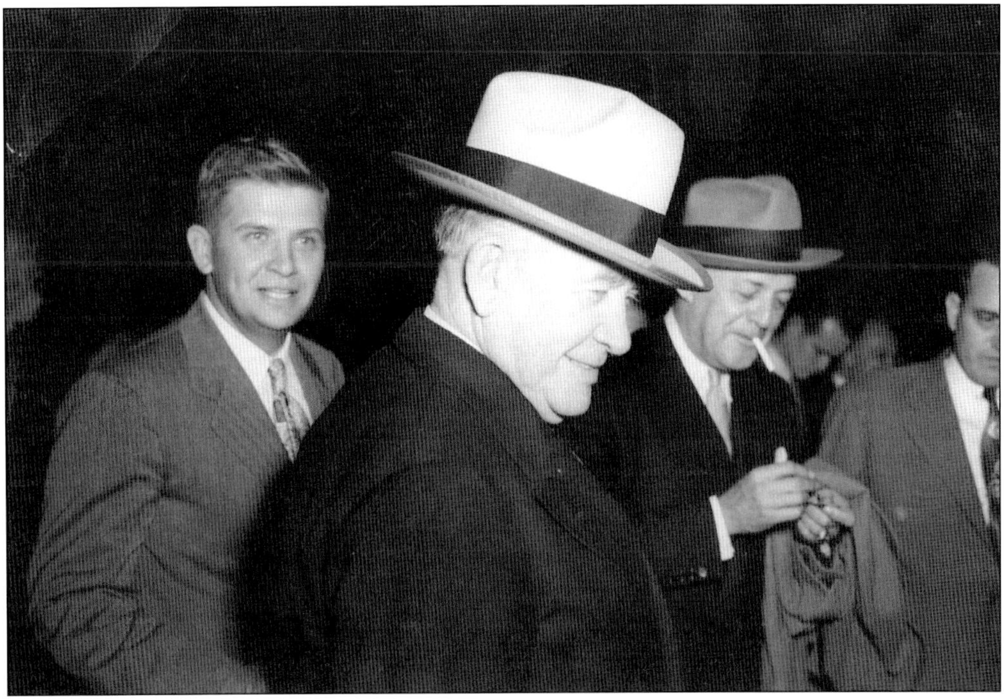

In Greenville for the Roosevelt Day Dinner at East Carolina Teacher's College, young Terry Sanford escorts Vice President Barkley, Representative Cooley, and Hoover Taft. (Courtesy J.Y. Joyner Library, East Carolina University.)

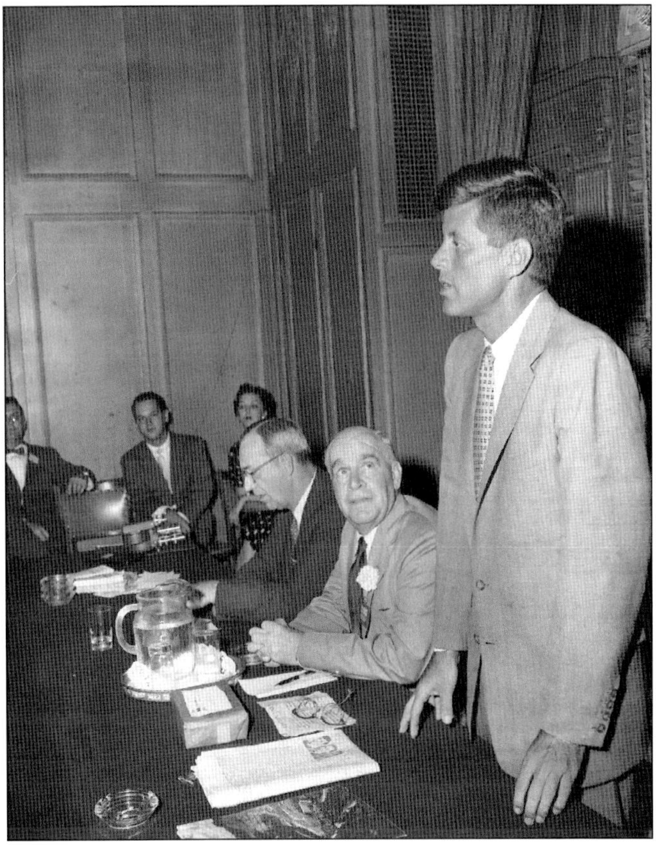

Senator Kennedy's ties to North Carolina trace back to his address before the North Carolina caucus at the Democratic National Convention in Chicago in August 1956. Next to Kennedy are Gov. Luther H. Hodges and Sen. B. Everett Jordan. In 1956, Kennedy ran second to Sen. Estes Kefauver for the vice presidency. (Photograph by Hugh Morton; courtesy of Wilson Library, University of North Carolina.)

JOHN F. KENNEDY
MASSACHUSETTS

COMMITTEES:
FOREIGN RELATIONS
LABOR AND PUBLIC WELFARE
JOINT ECONOMIC COMMITTEE

United States Senate
WASHINGTON, D.C.

January 19, 1960

Dr. Leo W. Jenkins
President
East Carolina College
Greenville, North Carolina

Dear Dr. Jenkins:

Congressman Bonner has spoken to me concerning your kind invitation for me to speak at the 7th Annual World Affairs Day at East Carolina College.

I certainly appreciate this invitation, but my decision to seek the Democratic nomination for the Presidency makes it necessary for me in the coming months to devote all my time away from Washington to those states in which I am likely to run in the primaries. I regret, therefore, that I must decline your very kind invitation.

I am extremely sorry about this, particularly because of the interest expressed by Congressman Bonner in this invitation.

Thanking you for thinking of me and with every good wish, I am

Sincerely yours,

John Kennedy

John F. Kennedy

JFK:el

Dr. Leo W. Jenkins, newly appointed president of East Carolina College in Greenville, wrote Senator Kennedy inviting him to speak at the 7th Annual World Affairs Day. Kennedy's response expresses his appreciation for Jenkins's invitation, but adds that his decision to run for the Democratic nomination for the presidency required that he devote himself to campaigning. Jenkins's letter shows that efforts from within East Carolina College to bring Kennedy to campus were under way as of early 1960. (Courtesy of J.Y. Joyner Library, East Carolina University.)

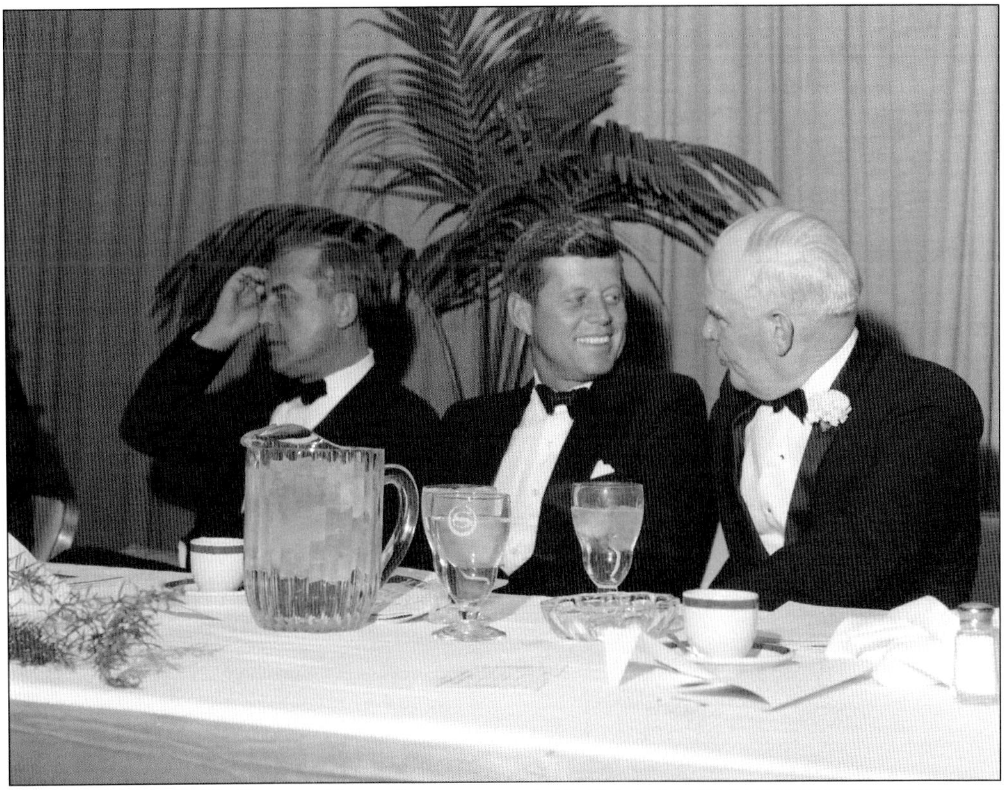

On January 23, 1960, Senator Kennedy attended a $100-a-plate fundraiser held at the Washington Sheraton Park Hotel. The event, sponsored by the Democratic National Committee, gave prospective candidates a public forum. Kennedy talks with North Carolina governor Luther H. Hodges. To the left of Kennedy is Rep. Chester Bowles of Connecticut. (Photograph by Hugh Morton; courtesy of Wilson Library, University of North Carolina.)

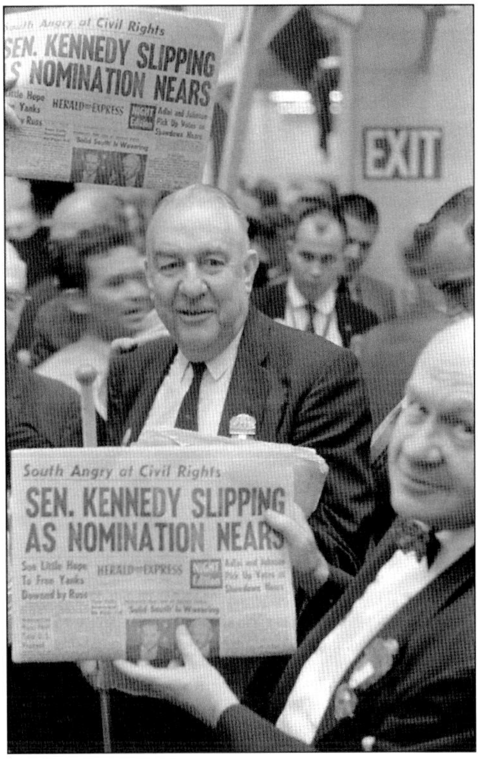

At the 1960 Democratic National Convention held in Los Angeles at the Memorial Sports Arena from July 11 to 15, the North Carolina delegation largely supported Sen. Lyndon Baines Johnson, the Senate majority leader from Texas. When the *Los Angeles Herald and Express* reported that Senator Kennedy's fortunes were slipping and the South was "angry" over the civil rights platform, Sen. Samuel J. Ervin, standing behind the newspaper, looked on with satisfaction. (Photograph by Hugh Morton; courtesy of Wilson Library, University of North Carolina.)

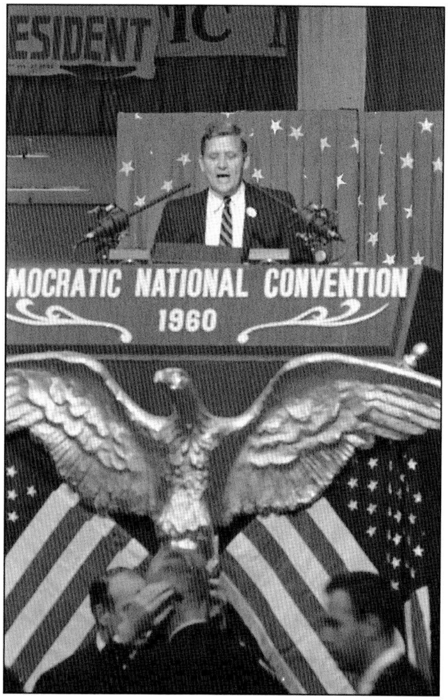

At the 1960 Democratic National Convention, Senator Kennedy needed a Southerner to endorse his nomination publicly. Terry Sanford, though only a gubernatorial candidate, agreed to do so. Many North Carolina delegates were upset that Sanford did this without briefing them. Sanford's speech, televised nationally, prompted a backlash from many North Carolina Protestants who sent Sanford telegrams condemning him. For Sanford's sake and his own, Kennedy agreed to a day of campaigning in North Carolina to convince skeptics that he was a trustworthy candidate and that Sanford had made the right decision. (Photograph by Hugh Morton; courtesy of Wilson Library, University of North Carolina.)

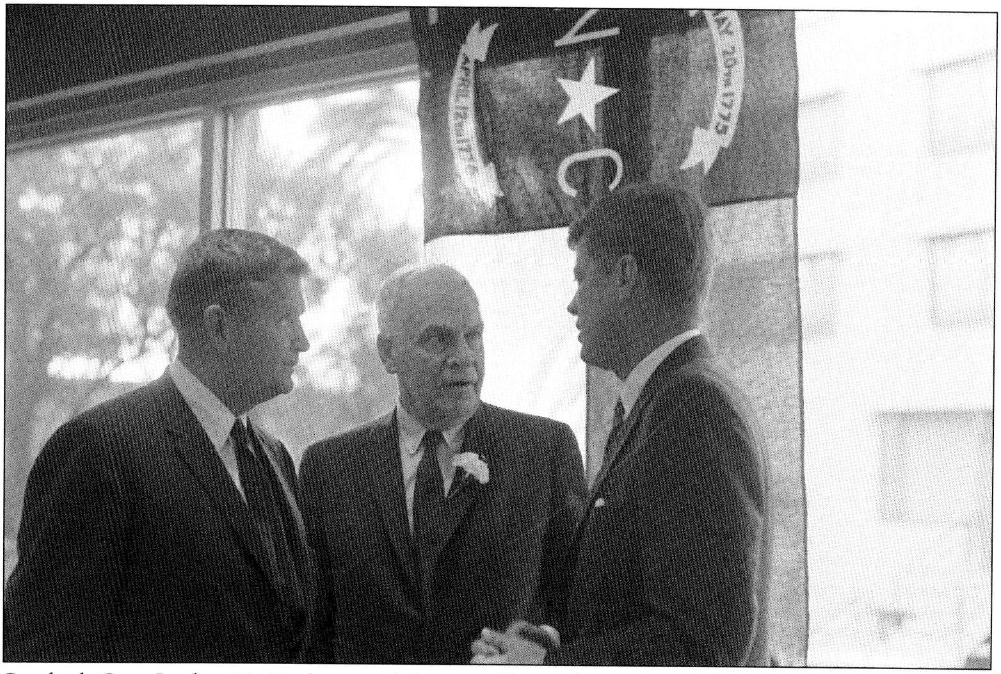

Sanford, Gov. Luther H. Hodges, and Senator Kennedy confer at the North Carolina caucus during the 1960 Democratic National Convention in Los Angeles. Hodges had been a supporter of Lyndon B. Johnson but quickly realigned himself with Kennedy after the Massachusetts senator won the nomination on the first ballot. Following his election, Kennedy appointed Hodges as secretary of commerce. (Photograph by Hugh Morton; courtesy of Wilson Library, University of North Carolina.)

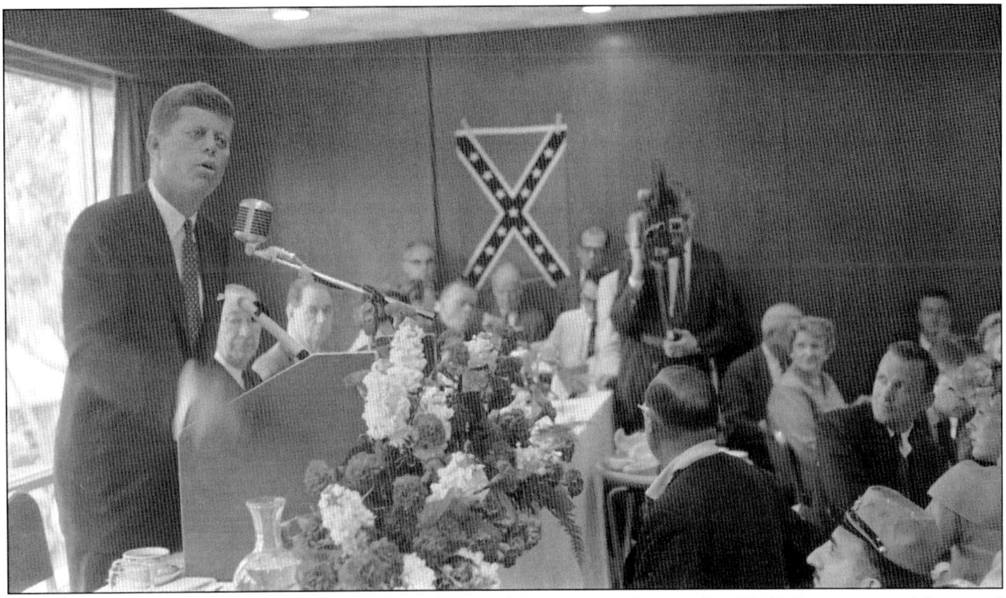

Here, Senator Kennedy addresses the North Carolina caucus during the 1960 Democratic National Convention. A Confederate flag has been taped to the far wall, and in the lower right-hand corner, a man is wearing a Confederate hat. To Kennedy's right is North Carolina senator B. Everett Jordan. Although a liberal, Kennedy was also a politician who understood the importance of gaining broad-based support and so overlooked the icons of the Old South. (Photograph by Hugh Morton; courtesy of Wilson Library, University of North Carolina.)

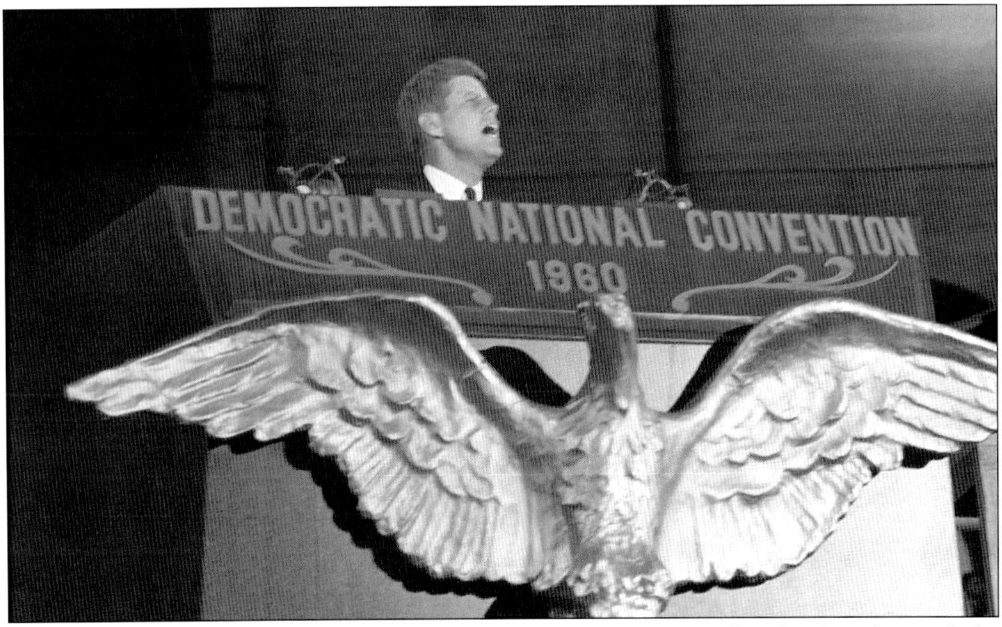

Senator Kennedy delivered his acceptance speech on July 15, 1960. After thanking his rivals for their support and praising Democratic unity, Kennedy emphasized his vision of the "New Frontier," a time when national courage, imagination, and perseverance rather than complacency and mediocrity would characterize the new order. (Photograph by Hugh Morton; courtesy of Wilson Library, University of North Carolina.)

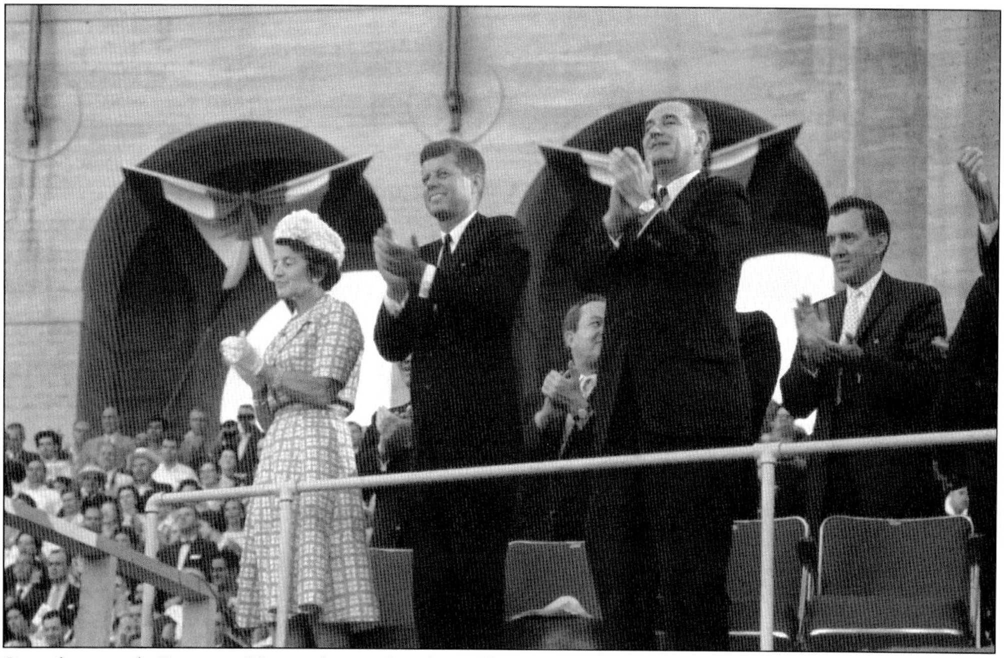

Standing with Senator Kennedy on the day of his acceptance speech at Memorial Coliseum in Los Angeles on July 15 are Kennedy's mother, Rose Kennedy, and the vice presidential nominee, Lyndon Johnson. Behind Johnson's left shoulder is Sen. Edmond Muskie of Maine. (Photograph by Hugh Morton; courtesy of Wilson Library, University of North Carolina.)

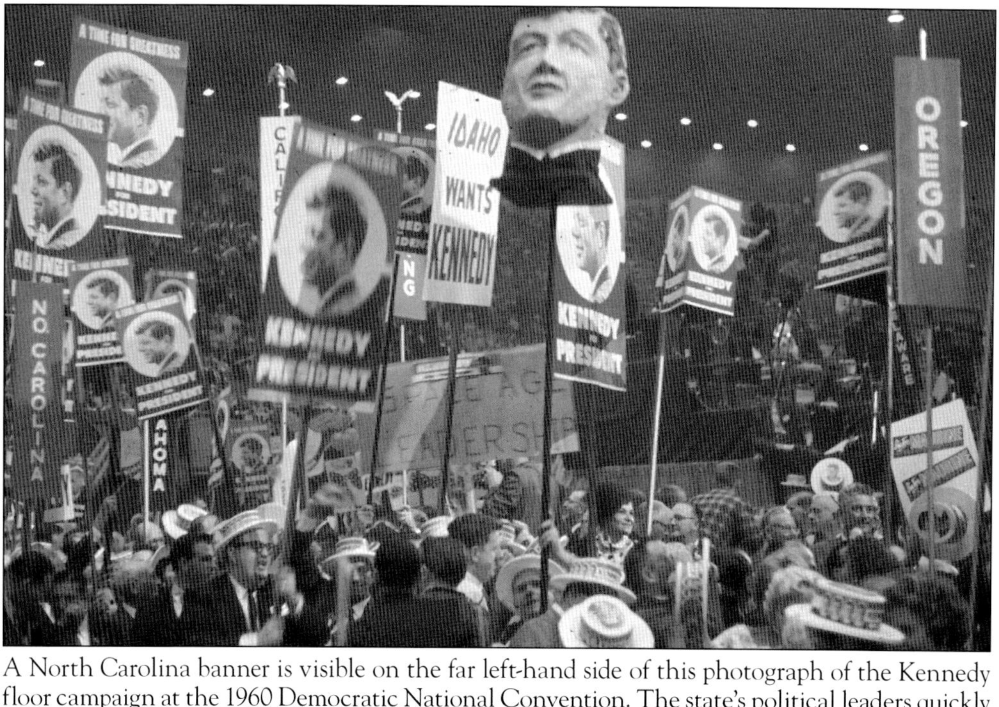

A North Carolina banner is visible on the far left-hand side of this photograph of the Kennedy floor campaign at the 1960 Democratic National Convention. The state's political leaders quickly rallied behind the candidate once he secured the nomination. (Photograph by Hugh Morton; courtesy of Wilson Library, University of North Carolina.)

EAST CAROLINA COLLEGE

GREENVILLE, NORTH CAROLINA

24 August 1960

Honorable John F. Kennedy
Senate Office Building
Washington, D.C.

Dear Senator Kennedy:

I am confident the people of this area will greet you with enthusiasm during the forthcoming campaign. You would be assured maximum television coverage in eastern North Carolina by the Greenville and Washington stations. Some five thousand students and faculty members of East Carolina College would form part of a most enthusiastic audience. We have facilities for a large outdoor rally and there is a convenient local airport.

I believe it would be fitting and appropriate to address the young people of this section of the state. Practically all of the counties of the state are represented in our student body. We have a very active group of Terry Sanford backers among the faculty and students.

Defection from party ranks, acts of political perfidy, assumption of the "conservative" label, appeals to race prejudice and religious bigotry have all made this campaign year memorable for bitterness and hysteria. I hope this state will be true to its liberal tradition in spite of all the ordeals the candidates have had to face. The primary results were encouraging and Kefauver's victory in Tennessee was reassuring. But we are all aware of an uphill fight in the election.

We look forward to greeting you and the other Democratic candidates during the campaign.

Yours very sincerely,

Joseph F. Steelman
Associate Professor of History

Amplifying Dr. Jenkins's earlier letter, Joseph Steelman, a professor of history at East Carolina College, wrote to Senator Kennedy encouraging him to plan a campus rally. Professor Steelman was one of the more politically active faculty at East Carolina. He corresponded often with Terry Sanford and others involved in Democratic Party campaigns. (Courtesy of J.Y. Joyner Library, East Carolina University.)

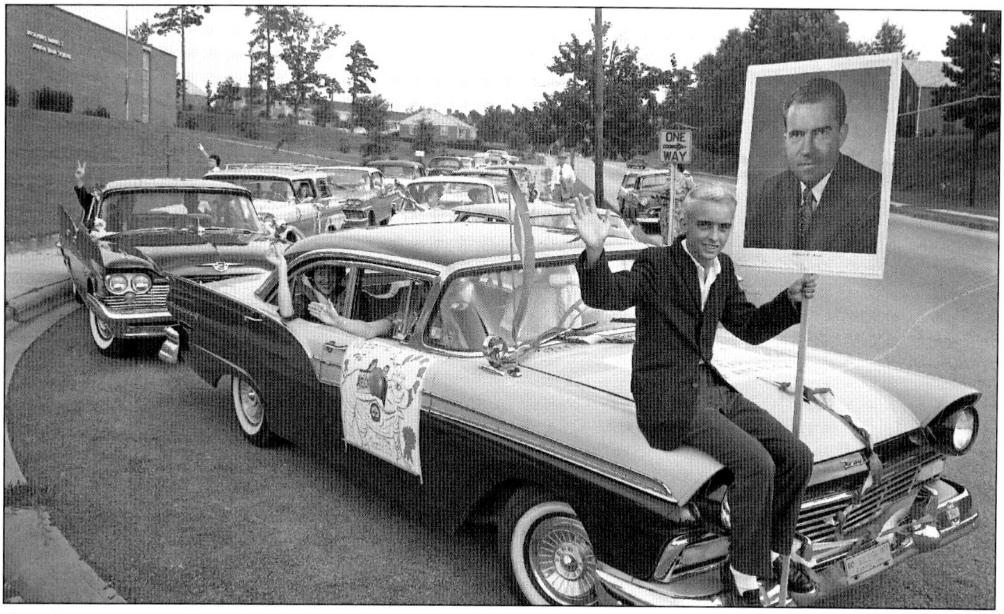

On August 17, 1960, one month before Sen. John Kennedy's statewide campaign, Republican presidential nominee Richard M. Nixon surprised the political world with a highly successful rally that packed Greensboro's new War Memorial Coliseum to overcapacity. Nixon's success in Greensboro also prompted Kennedy to consider devoting serious campaign time to North Carolina, traditionally a safe Democratic state. (Courtesy of the *News and Observer* and the North Carolina State Archives.)

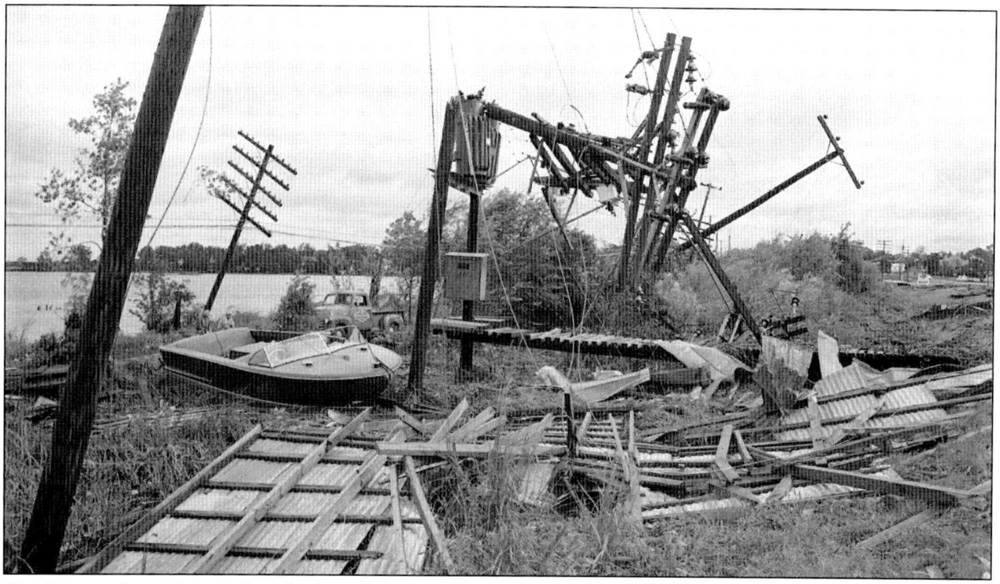

On September 14, just days before Senator Kennedy arrived in Greenville to launch his daylong North Carolina campaign blitz, Hurricane Donna, one of the most destructive storms of the decade, wreaked havoc across the Southeast. Several lives were lost in eastern North Carolina, and millions of dollars in property damage from Morehead City inland resulted. Fortunately for the Kennedy campaign, Greenville was not severely damaged. (Courtesy of the *Daily Reflector* and J.Y. Joyner Library, East Carolina University.)

Hurricane Donna shattered the showroom windows of Bright Leaf Motors. Senator Kennedy's visit gave everyone a reason to clean up the debris as quickly as possible. In Greenville, East Carolina College students were mobilized along with the college grounds crews to ensure the campus was presentable for the College Stadium rally. (Courtesy of the *Daily Reflector* and J.Y. Joyner Library, East Carolina University.)

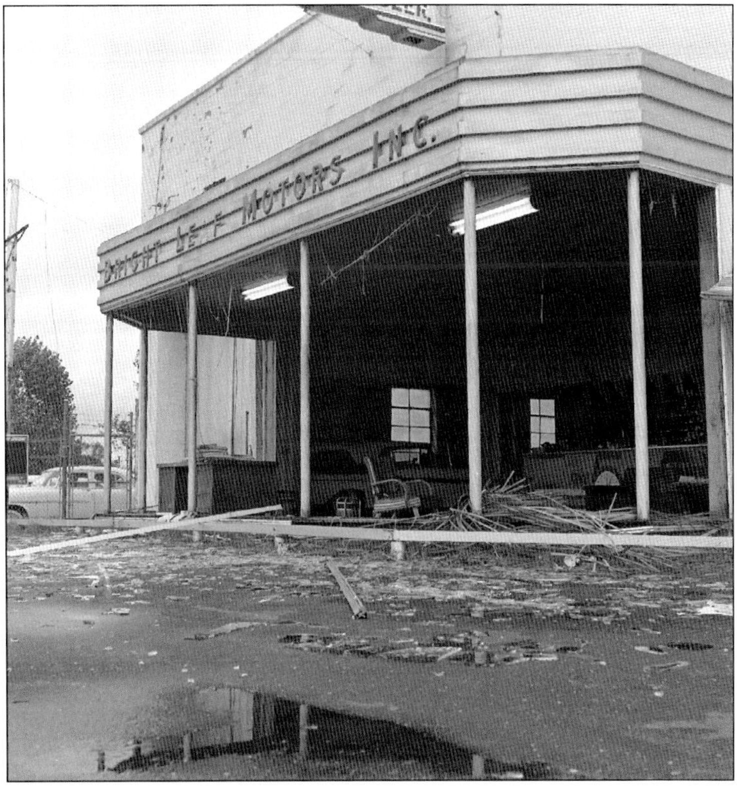

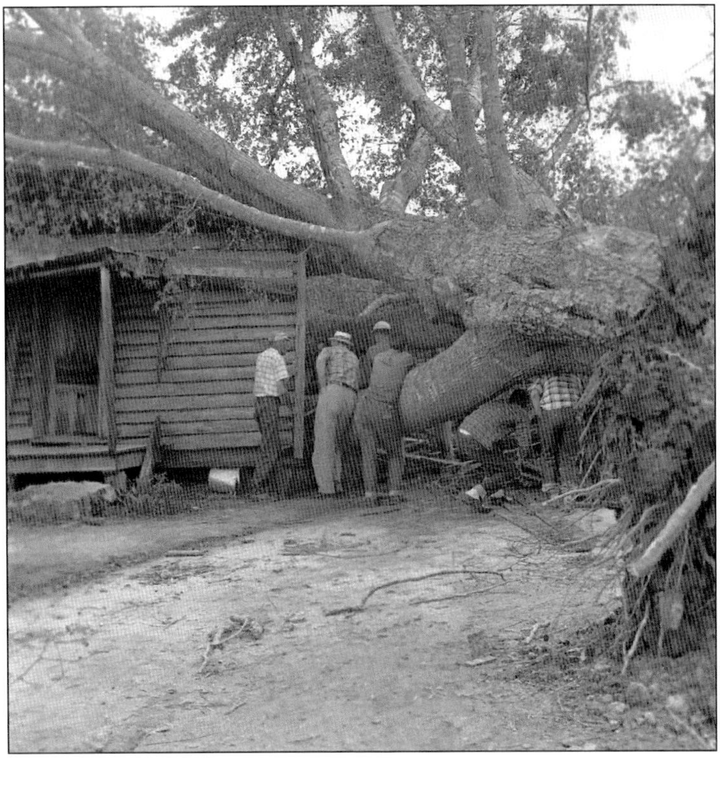

Hurricane Donna left a path of destruction. For many in rural areas, the next two days meant at the very least power outages, intermittent television and radio broadcasts, spotty telephone service, and school closings. (Courtesy of the *Daily Reflector* and J.Y. Joyner Library, East Carolina University.)

U. S. SENATOR . . .

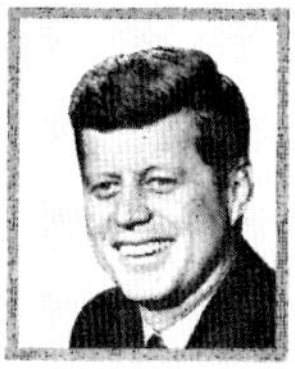

JOHN F. KENNEDY

FOR PRESIDENT

★ ★ ★ ★

HEADQUARTERS · 1106 CONNECTICUT AVE., N.W. · WASHINGTON, D. C. · DISTRICT 7-1717

September 23, 1960

Professor Joseph F. Steelman
East Carolina College
Greenville, North Carolina

Dear Professor Steelman:

Senator Kennedy has asked me to reply to your recent letter and to thank you for the cordial invitation you have extended to him.

The staff has prepared the Senator's national campaign schedule and, at the present time, has comitted the Senator's limited time to previous engagements which precludes his acceptance of your invitation. He regrets this very much, but is grateful for your thoughtfulness in writing to him.

With every good wish,

Sincerely,

Kenneth P. O'Donnell

Kenneth P. O'Donnell

My letter was in August. Kennedy spent the morning in Greenville and the East Carolina Campus on September 17.

The Kennedy campaign was both slickly organized and very confused. This letter from Kenneth O'Donnell, Senator Kennedy's campaign director, to Prof. Joseph Steelman explained that Kennedy would not be able to visit East Carolina College. It was written, as Steelman's handwritten note relates, six days after Kennedy participated in a successful rally on campus. (Courtesy of J.Y. Joyner Library, East Carolina University.)

Two

PITT-GREENVILLE AIRPORT

Senator Kennedy's first stop in his North Carolina campaign was in the eastern portion of the state at Pitt-Greenville Airport. Scheduled to arrive between 9:00 and 9:30 a.m., his plane was approximately 30 minutes late due to unstable weather conditions lingering from Hurricane Donna. Eastern North Carolina was elated to be the first stop on Kennedy's itinerary. "At Last, Recognition For The East" proclaimed Greenville's newspaper, the *Daily Reflector*, in its September 1, 1960, editorial.

Local Democrats made the moment special. Joe Butterworth of Bethel, a PT boat captain who shared a tent with Kennedy during World War II, was present to greet the senator. In a ceremony lasting long enough for photographs, Mayor Eugene West greeted Kennedy and presented him with a key to the town. Gov. Luther H. Hodges, who had arrived earlier, officially welcomed Kennedy to North Carolina. Hodges accompanied Kennedy for the remainder of the day, projecting an indelible image of solidarity. Gubernatorial candidate Terry Sanford, who drove to Greenville for the occasion, predicted that eastern North Carolina would provide "the largest crowd in the state to greet Senator Kennedy." Sen. Sam J. Ervin and Sen. B. Everett Jordan were also present to welcome Kennedy to North Carolina. Representing East Carolina College, a group of Alpha Delta Pi sorority sisters sporting white navy dresses and mock-straw Kennedy hats welcomed the Massachusetts senator. Over 100 journalists and photographers covered the event. A motorcade featuring brand-new convertibles was lined up and ready to whisk Kennedy and the political dignitaries on the parade route through Greenville.

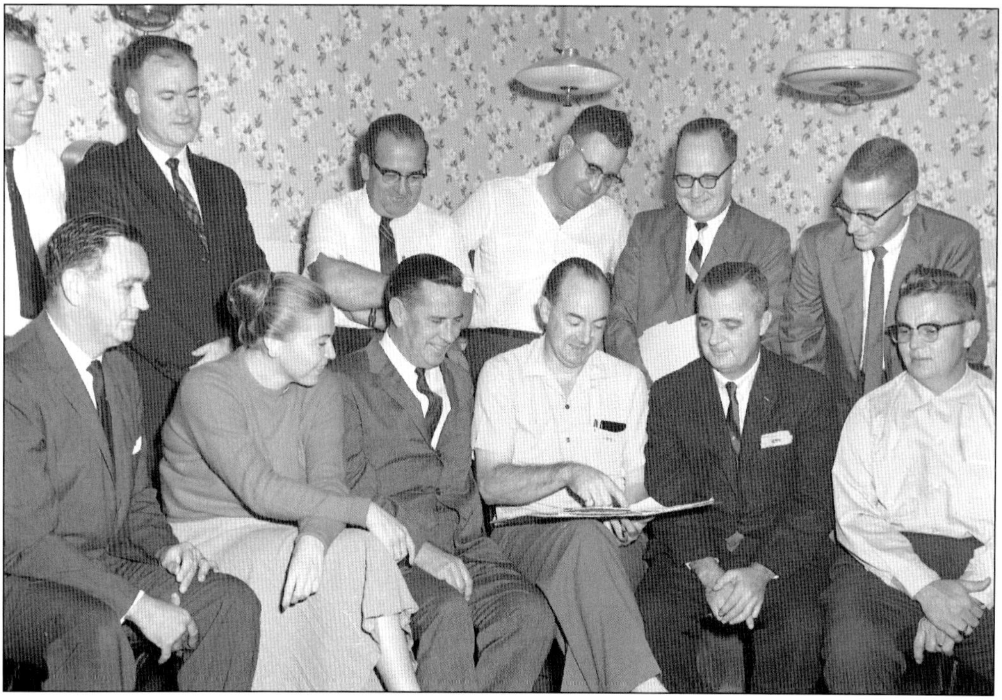

The Eastern Carolina Kennedy Rally Planning Committee included, from left to right, (first row) Walter B. Jones (Farmville), Janice Hardison (instructor, East Carolina College), Jack H. Spain (administrative assistant to Sen. Samuel J. Ervin), Charles Horne (Greenville businessman), Dr. Leo Jenkins (president of East Carolina College), and Marvin Speight (Farmville businessman); (second row) J.B. Spillman Jr. (businessman), Robert Rouse (attorney), Leonard Bloxam (Greenville city manager), Arthur Tripp (co-owner, Farmers Warehouse), Ed Dragon (Kennedy campaign advance staff), and David J. Whichard (editor, *Daily Reflector*). (Courtesy of the *Daily Reflector* and J.Y. Joyner Library, East Carolina University.)

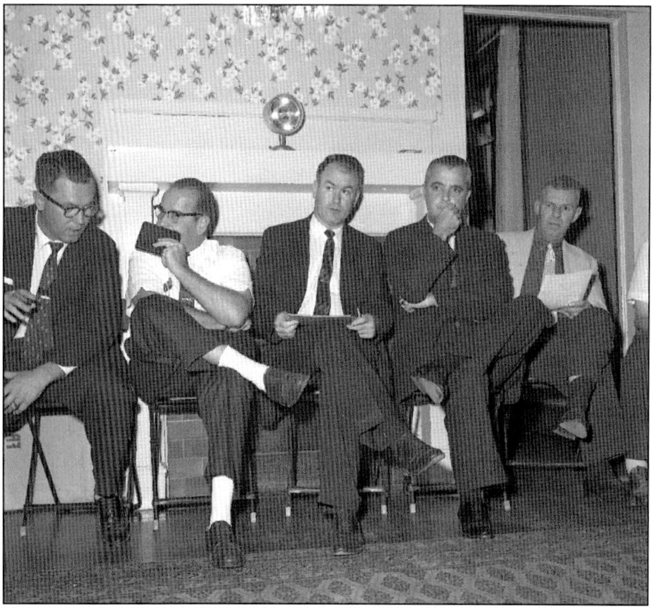

Members of the Eastern Carolina Kennedy Rally Planning Committee deliberate over logistics for the upcoming Greenville leg of Senator Kennedy's North Carolina campaign. Seated from left to right are Greenville police chief Sullivan Gibbs, City Manager Leonard Bloxam, Farmville attorney Robert Rouse, president of East Carolina College Dr. Leo W. Jenkins, and *Washington Daily News* editor Ashley Futrell. (Courtesy of the *Daily Reflector* and J.Y. Joyner Library, East Carolina University.)

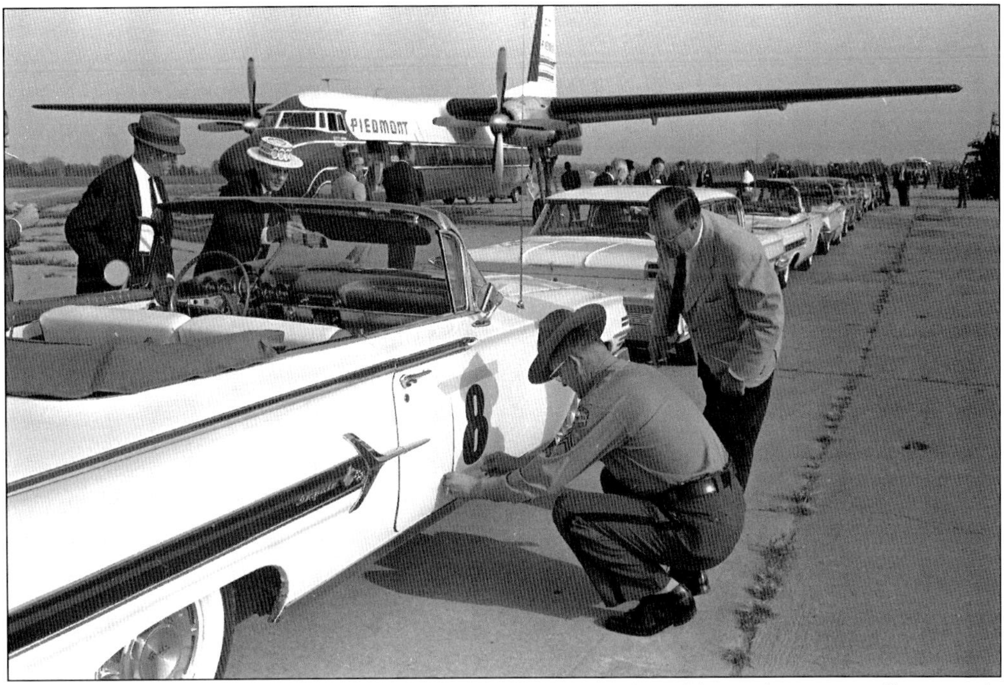

With the Kennedy plane landing soon, local campaign officials and law enforcement officers ready the motorcade. (Photograph by Don Sturkey, Wilson Library, University of North Carolina.)

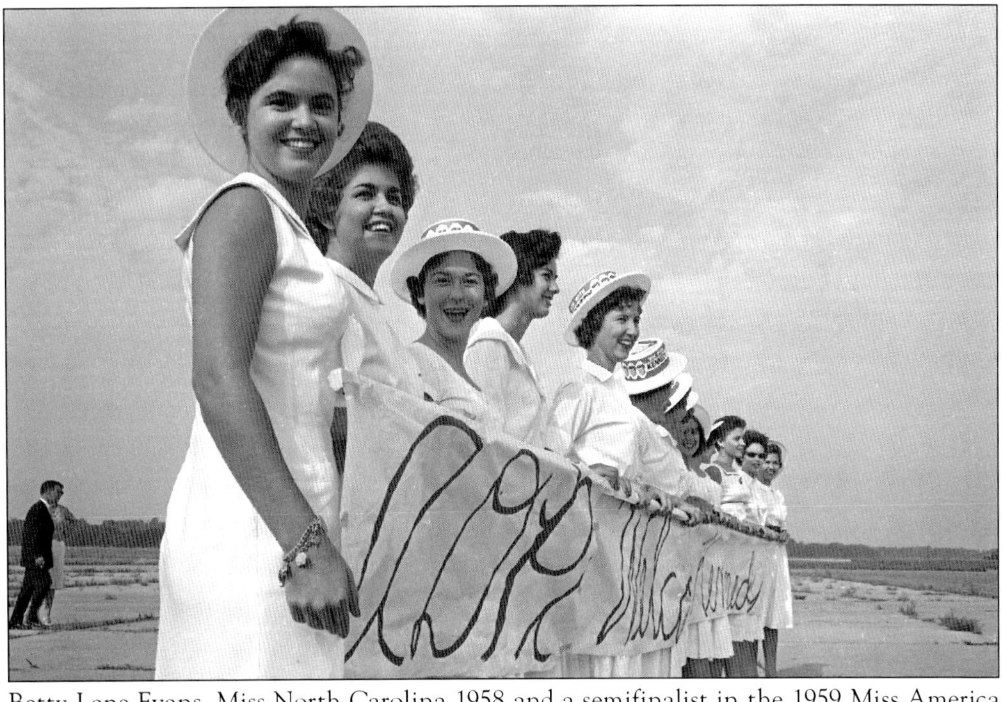

Betty Lane Evans, Miss North Carolina 1958 and a semifinalist in the 1959 Miss America pageant, led the delegation of Alpha Delta Pi sisters welcoming Senator Kennedy to eastern North Carolina on behalf of East Carolina College. (Courtesy of the *News and Observer* and the North Carolina State Archives.)

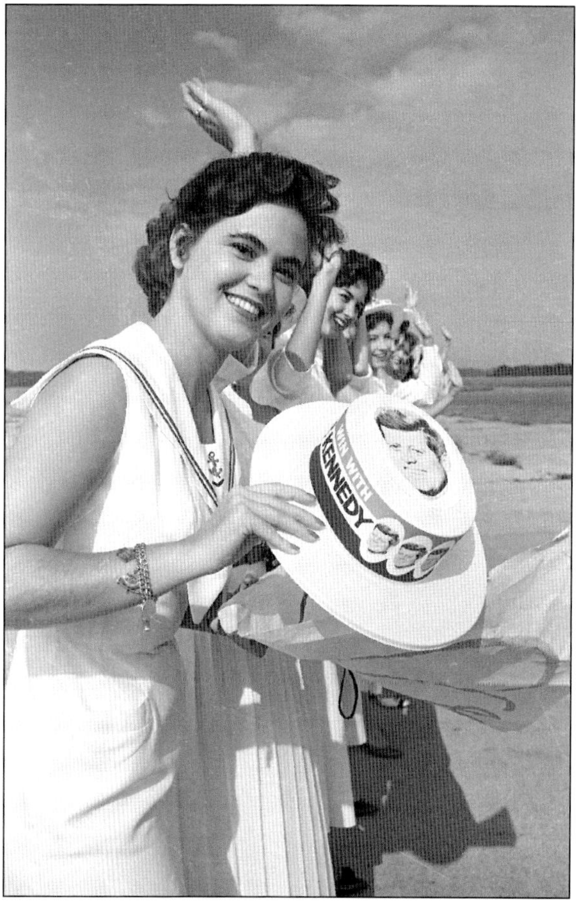

The greeting party included 14 Alpha Delta Pi sorority sisters dressed in white sailor suits recalling Senator Kennedy's service in the Navy. Led by former Miss North Carolina Betty Lane Evans, the coeds presented a banner that read, "A.D. Pi Welcomes Kennedy." Alpha Delta Pi had chartered its ECC chapter, Delta Omicron, earlier the same year on February 6, 1960. (Courtesy of the *News and Observer* and the North Carolina State Archives.)

Featured in the *Buccaneer*, East Carolina College's student yearbook, the grand activity for the Alpha Delta Pi sorority in the 1960 1961 academic year was its role in welcoming Senator Kennedy at the Pitt-Greenville Airport and then hurrying back to campus for the rally at College Stadium. (Courtesy of the *News and Observer* and the North Carolina State Archives.)

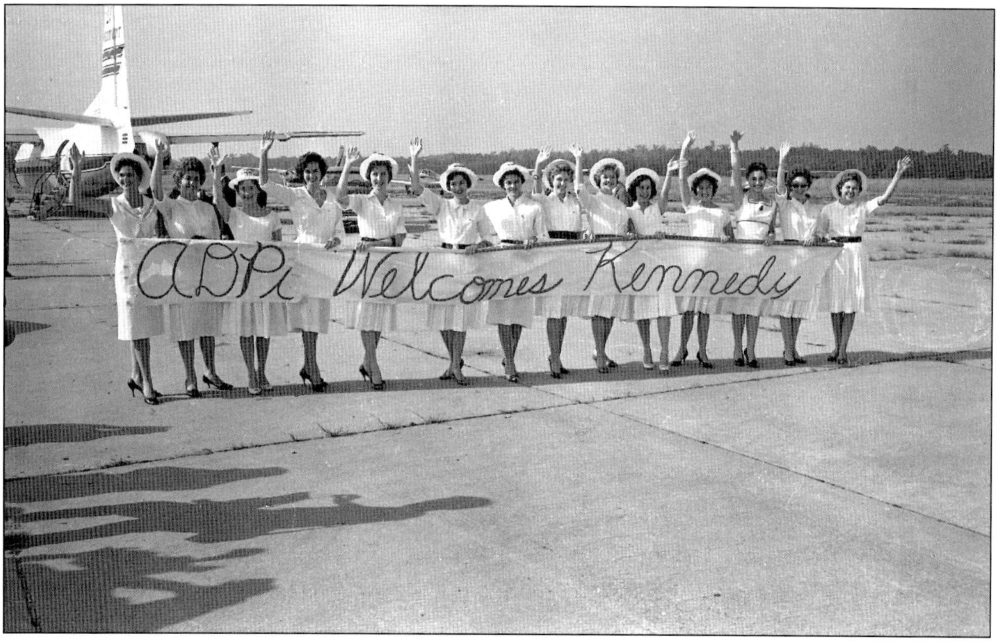

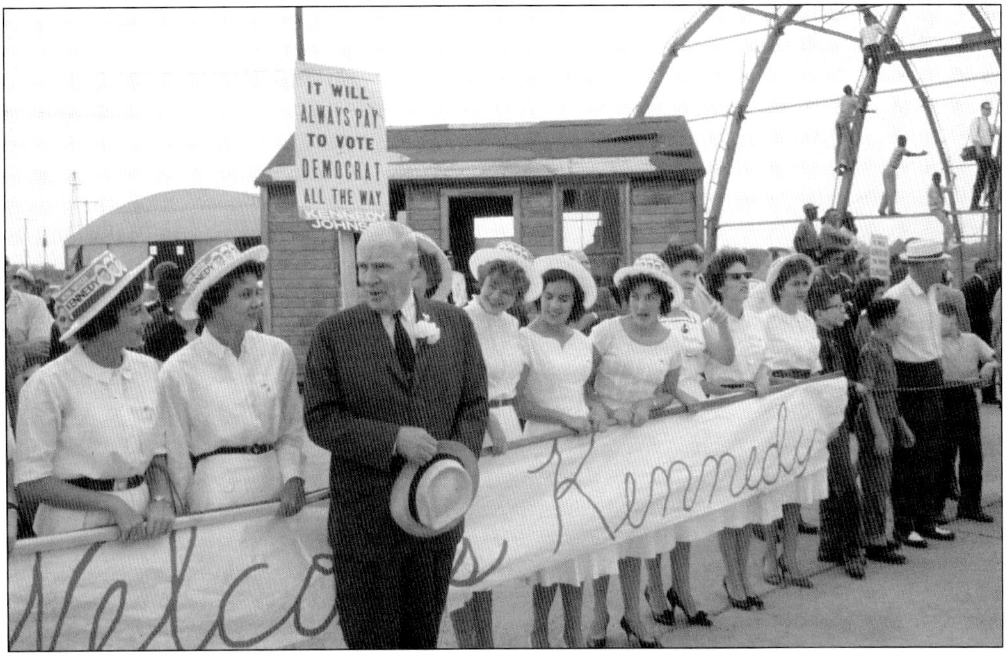

The Alpha Delta Pi sisters attracted all of the photographers, prompting Gov. Luther H. Hodges to join the welcoming committee. Hodges soon found himself discussing politics with the coeds from East Carolina College. (Photograph by Hugh Morton; courtesy of Wilson Library, University of North Carolina.)

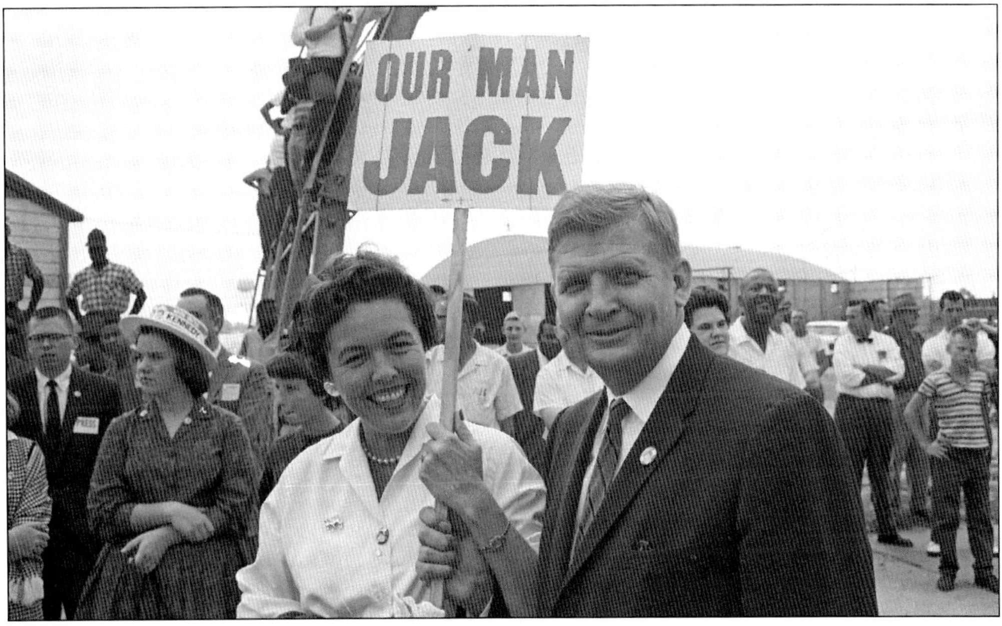

Also welcoming Senator Kennedy at the Pitt-Greenville Airport were Terry Sanford, Democratic gubernatorial nominee, and his wife, Margaret Rose Sanford. Sanford was instrumental in organizing Kennedy's North Carolina campaign tour. Sanford's efforts were fruitful—more voters were impressed by personal attention from Kennedy than by political ideologies and so ended up voting for Kennedy. (Courtesy of the *News and Observer* and the North Carolina State Archives.)

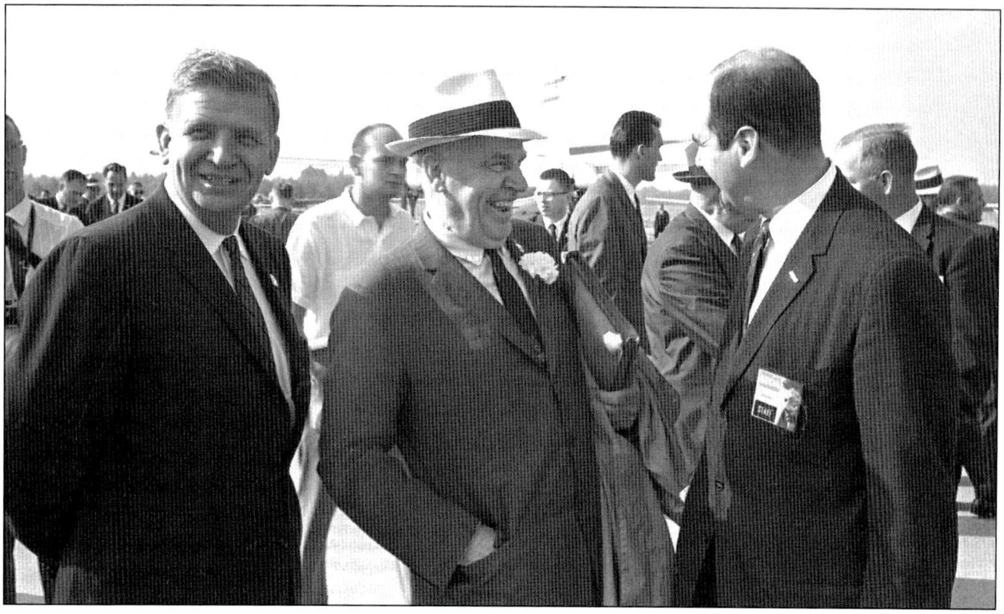

Terry Sanford (left), Gov. Luther H. Hodges (center), and an unidentified advance man from the Kennedy staff enjoy a light moment while waiting for the senator. Advance men would typically review arrangements and itineraries, advise, consult, and coordinate local activities with the central campaign staff. (Courtesy of the *News and Observer* and the North Carolina State Archives.)

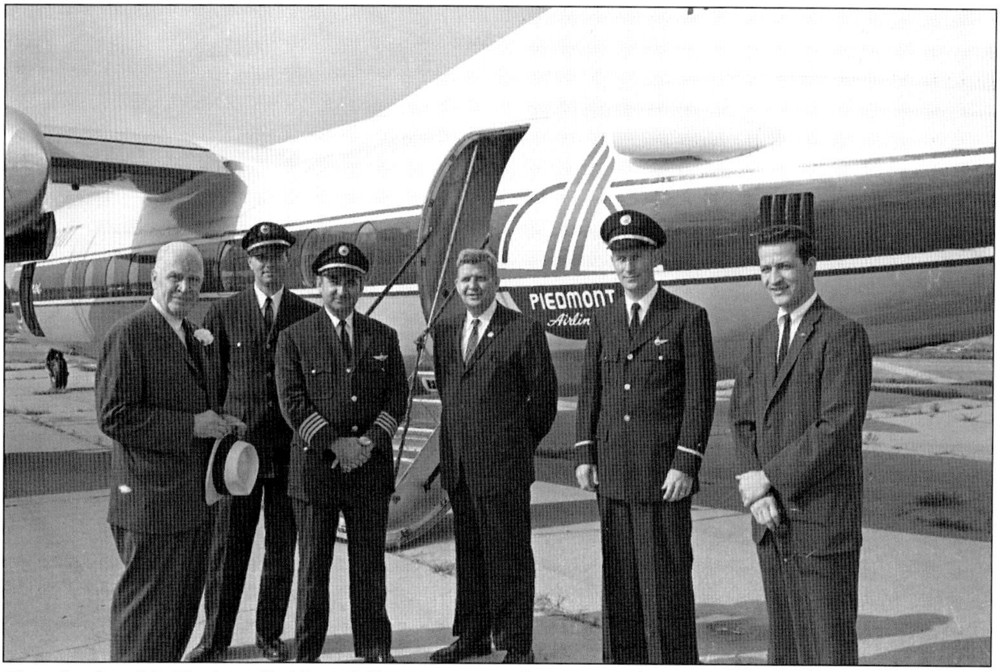

Gov. Luther H. Hodges (left) and Democratic gubernatorial nominee Terry Sanford (center) stand with Piedmont Airlines pilots while waiting for Senator Kennedy's plane to arrive. Weather conditions had been unstable for days after Hurricane Donna swept through eastern North Carolina. Kennedy's plane was 30 minutes late due to bad weather in Washington, DC. (Courtesy of the *News and Observer* and the North Carolina State Archives.)

Margaret Rose Sanford was among the most excited people in the crowd. She wore a pillbox hat, such as those made famous by Jackie Kennedy, who was pregnant and thus could not participate in the North Carolina campaign. (Courtesy of the *News and Observer* and the North Carolina State Archives.)

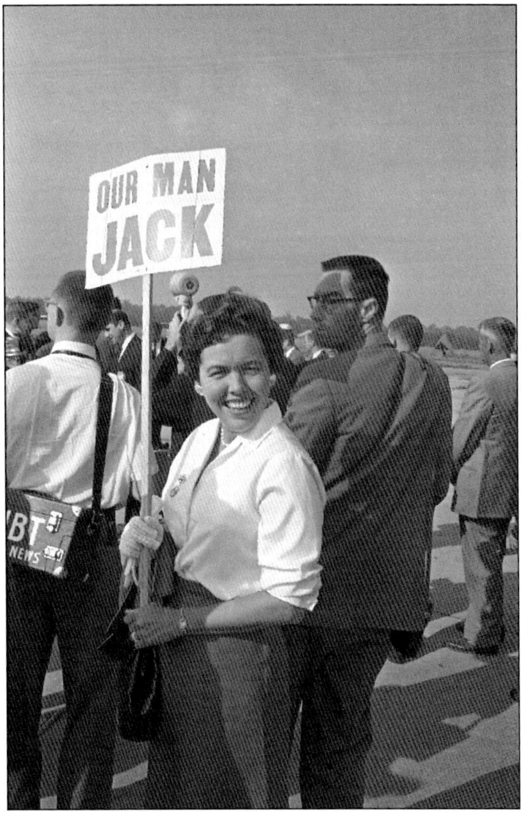

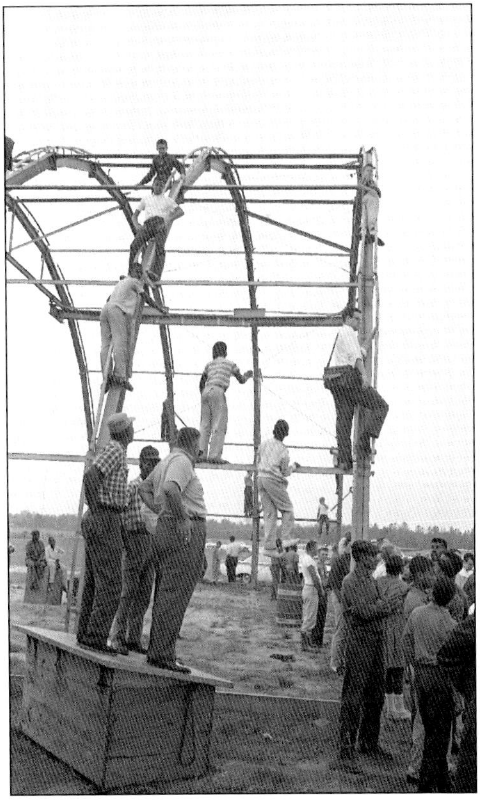

In 1960, the Pitt-Greenville Airport had no commercial service. Built in 1940 by the Works Progress Administration, it served as an outlying field for Marine Corps Air Station Cherry Point during World War II. When Senator Kennedy arrived, Quonset hut shells defined its landscape. (Courtesy of the *New and Observer* and the North Carolina State Archives.)

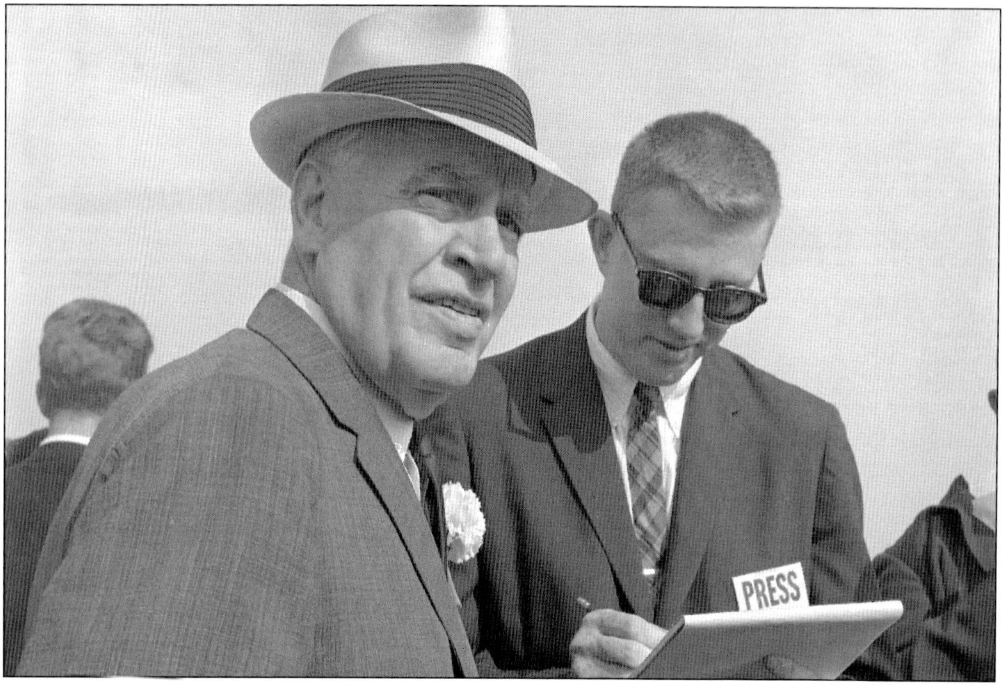

Alvin Taylor, a reporter for the *Daily Reflector*, Greenville's daily newspaper, interviews Gov. Luther H. Hodges while waiting for Kennedy's plane to arrive. The *Daily Reflector* gave the Kennedy campaign extensive advance coverage. Editorials emphasized the historic importance of Kennedy's prospective visit to the East. Editor David Whichard provided advertising for the rally as well. Whichard was a member of the Eastern Carolina Kennedy Rally Planning Committee and had been one of a group of North Carolina newsmen invited to Washington to discuss the prospects for a rally in eastern North Carolina. (Courtesy of the *Daily Reflector* and J.Y. Joyner Library, East Carolina University.)

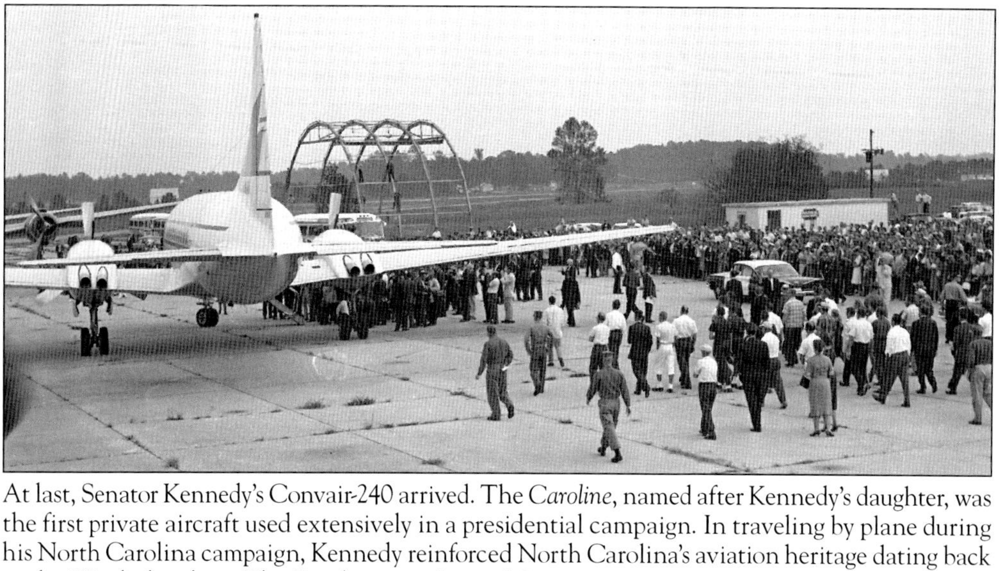

At last, Senator Kennedy's Convair-240 arrived. The *Caroline*, named after Kennedy's daughter, was the first private aircraft used extensively in a presidential campaign. In traveling by plane during his North Carolina campaign, Kennedy reinforced North Carolina's aviation heritage dating back to the Wright brothers. The Smithsonian Air and Space Museum now owns Kennedy's Convair-240. (Courtesy of the *News and Observer* and the North Carolina State Archives.)

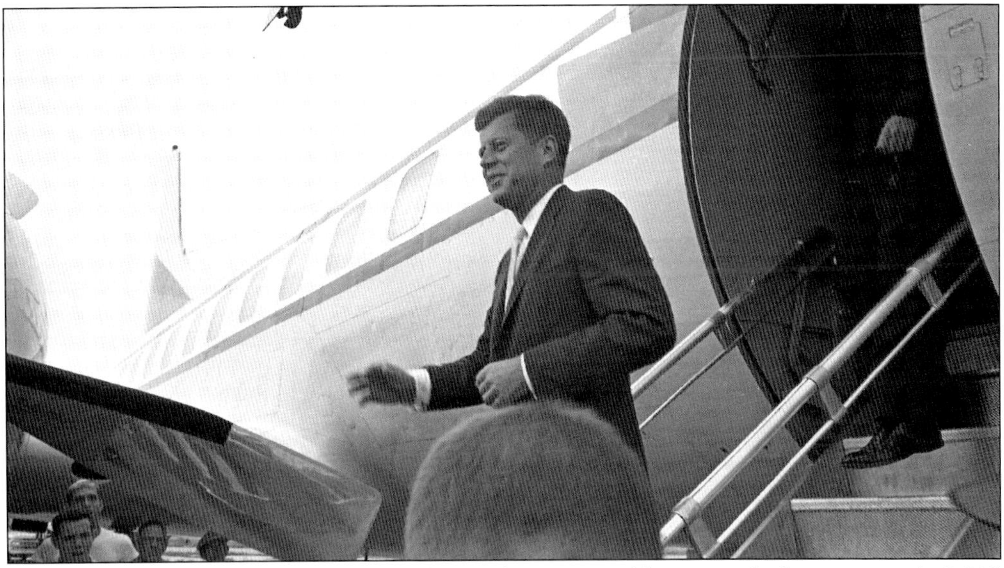

Senator Kennedy disembarked the *Caroline* and was greeted by a crowd of approximately 2,000 people. Kennedy's Greenville visit lasted 87 minutes, precisely three minutes under the tightly planned schedule for Greenville. (Courtesy of the *News and Observer* and the North Carolina State Archives.)

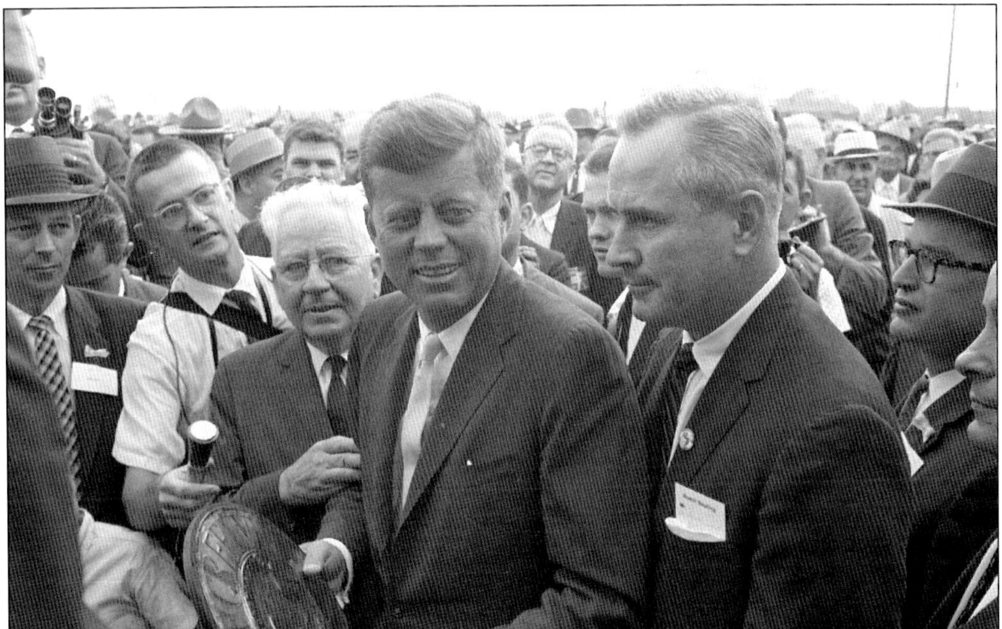

After disembarking, Senator Kennedy received a plaque and a key to the city of Greenville from Mayor Eugene West. Left of Kennedy is John G. Clark. Right of Kennedy is Joe Butterworth, a Bethel businessman who served as a PT boat captain in World War II. Butterworth and Kennedy shared a tent during their tour of duty and corresponded often after the war. Kennedy even sent Butterworth a signed, first edition copy of *Profiles in Courage*. Their airport reunion established a personal tie between Kennedy and eastern North Carolina. (Photograph by Don Sturkey, Wilson Library, University of North Carolina.)

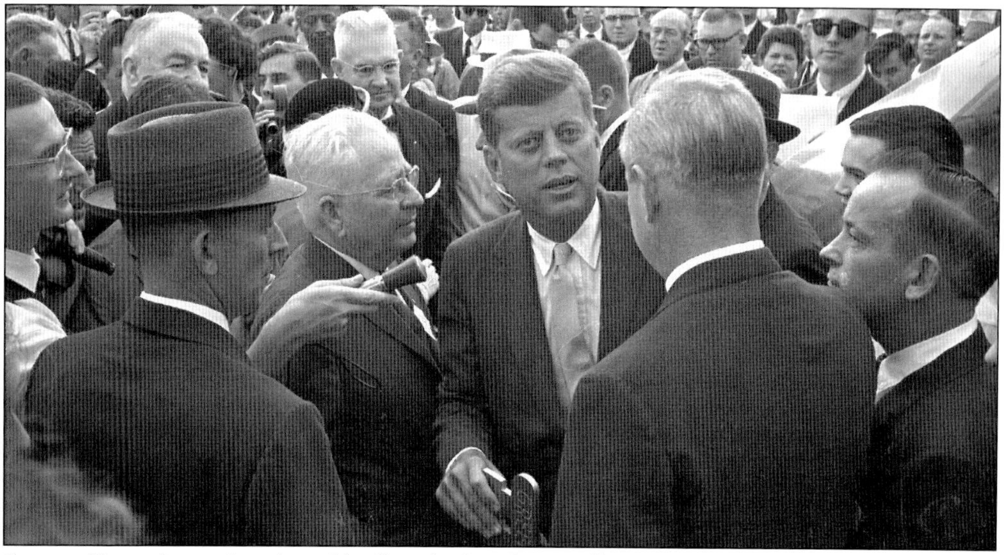

Senator Kennedy was "nearly mobbed" at the Pitt-Greenville Airport. On the far left is a journalist from Charlotte WBGT; the man in the hat is one of Kennedy's bodyguards; just above his hat, Sen. Sam Ervin looks toward Kennedy; and to the left of Kennedy is John G. Clark. Kennedy holds the large key to the city given him by Mayor Eugene West. Facing Kennedy is Joe Butterworth. (Courtesy of the *News and Observer* and the North Carolina State Archives.)

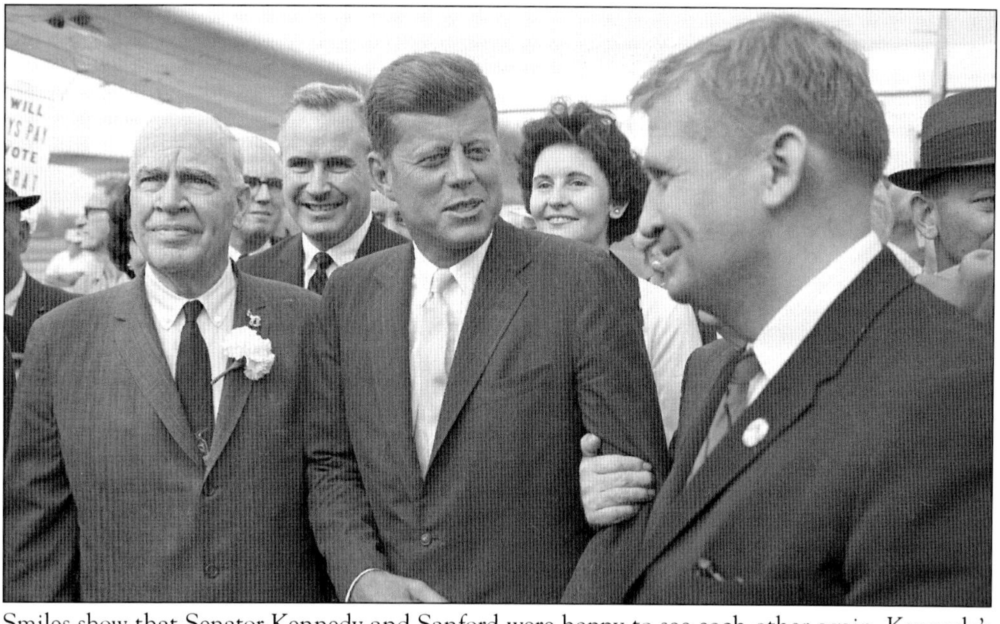

Smiles show that Senator Kennedy and Sanford were happy to see each other again. Kennedy's nomination had been given a more national character with Sanford's speech seconding the nomination. In it, Sanford drew cheers at the Democratic National Convention when he declared that Kennedy was "another Franklin Roosevelt." Sanford was pleased to see Kennedy in part because he knew that North Carolinians would support Kennedy—and by extension, himself—if they had the chance to meet the charismatic senator. Gov. Luther H. Hodges is left of Kennedy. Behind Hodges and Kennedy is Joe Butterworth, Kennedy's World War II buddy. (Courtesy of the *News and Observer* and the North Carolina State Archives.)

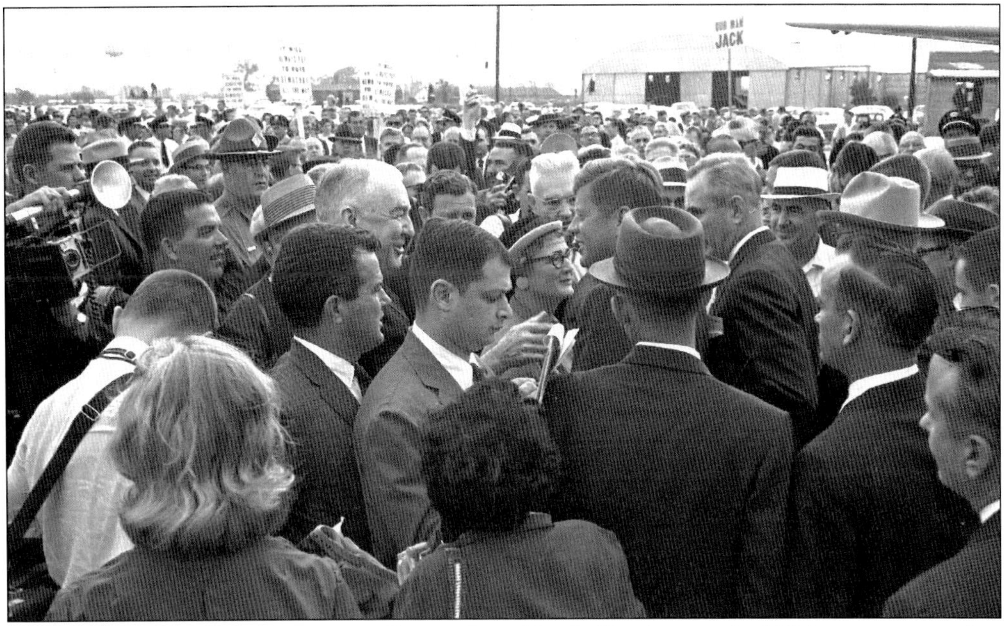

Sen. Sam Ervin, Kennedy's senior colleague from North Carolina in the US Senate, approaches him with a grin, happy to see the young candidate in eastern North Carolina. Although Ervin was from the western part of the state, he understood the electoral power of eastern North Carolina. A strong showing there would counter Republican growth in urban areas like Greensboro and Charlotte. (Courtesy of the *News and Observer* and the North Carolina State Archives.)

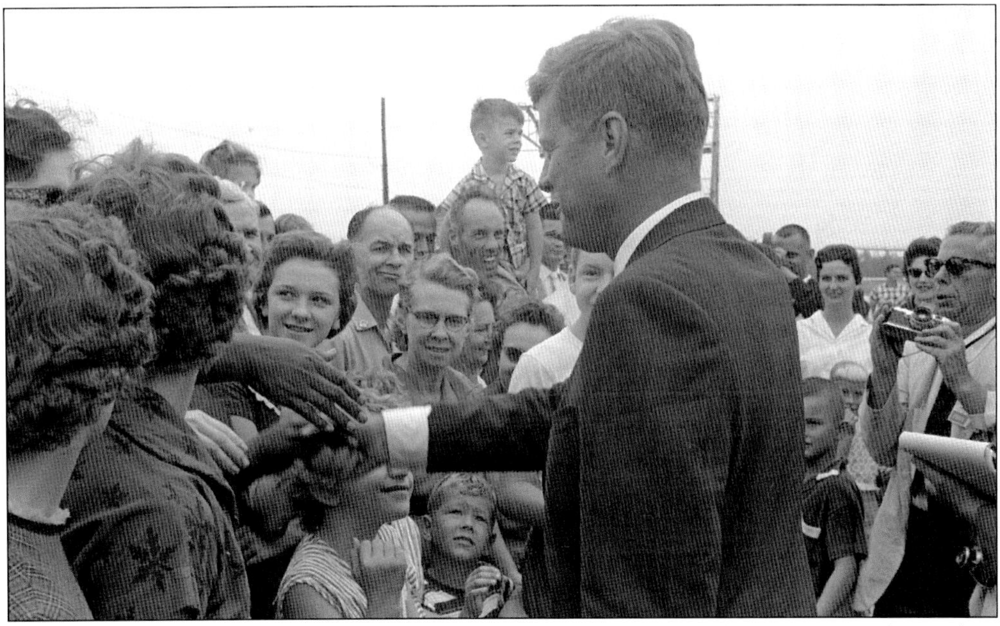

Political rallies in the South were often segregated, but this was not the case in North Carolina on September 17, 1960. Nevertheless, the African American population in the South had yet to embrace Senator Kennedy's candidacy as enthusiastically as it would later. Martin Luther King Jr.'s father, for example, had publicly declared his support for Nixon. (Photograph by Hugh Morton; courtesy of Wilson Library, University of North Carolina.)

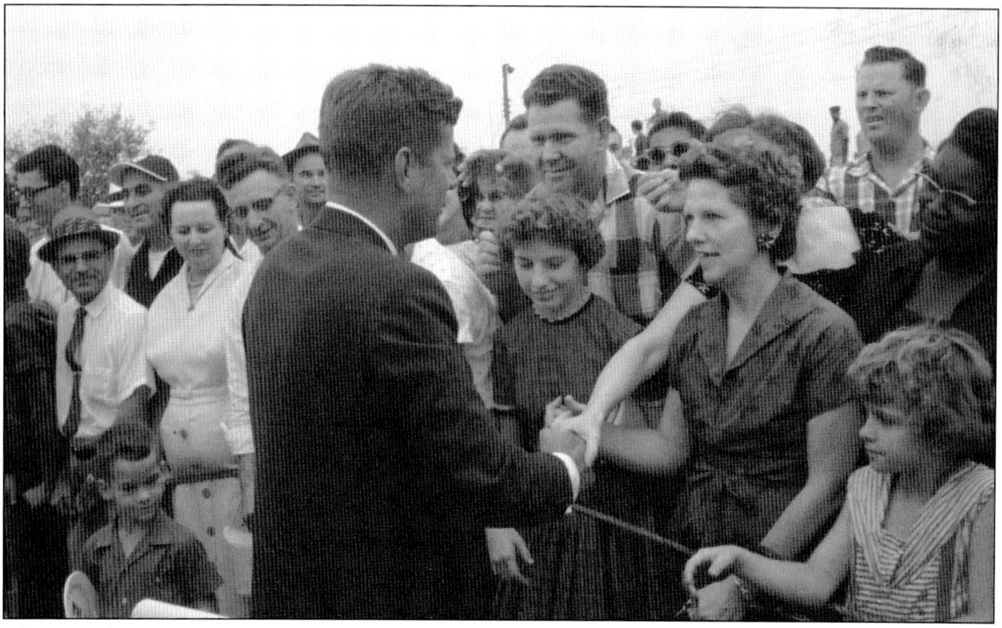

The crowd greeting Senator Kennedy at the Pitt-Greenville Airport was a mixture of politicians, press, and local folk who lived nearby. Kennedy interacted with the crowd, and they greeted him in a manner that many would not have predicted. Whatever notions people had about Kennedy being a Boston Brahmin with an elite Harvard degree were dispelled by his engaging charm and openness. (Photograph by Don Sturkey, Wilson Library, University of North Carolina.)

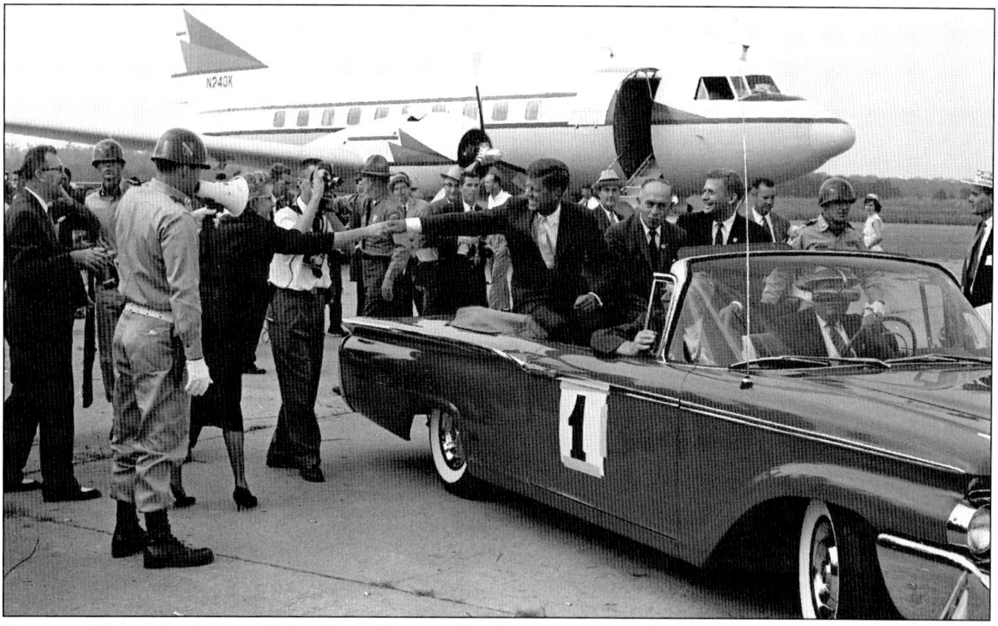

Senator Kennedy departed the Pitt-Greenville Airport in a red Mercury Monterey convertible. The red convertible carried Kennedy, First District Rep. Herbert Bonner, and Terry Sanford. John G. Clark sat in front of Kennedy. The driver was Henry F. Lawson, a local clergyman and Greenville Police Force detective. Kennedy's Convair-240 is in the background. (Photograph by Don Sturkey, Wilson Library, University of North Carolina.)

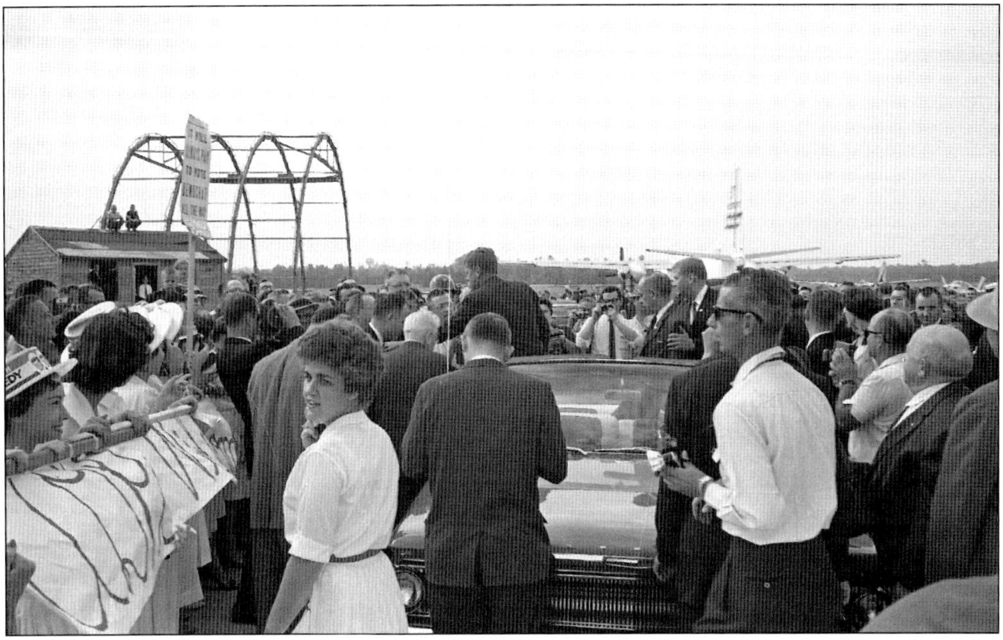

The Kennedy car was overwhelmed with well-wishers reluctant to miss their opportunity to shake the senator's hand. As the motorcade proceeded away from the *Caroline*, one Alpha Delta Pi sister slipped under the rope to secure a picture of Senator Kennedy. At left, Camilla Henderson looks on with a grin. (Courtesy of the *News and Observer* and the North Carolina State Archives.)

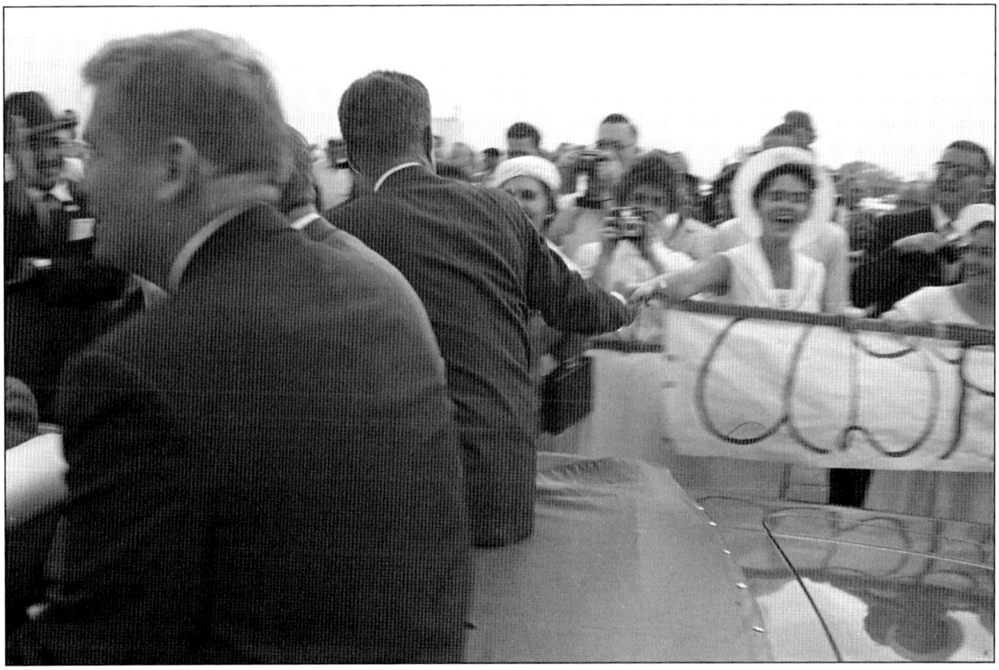

As the Kennedy car passed the Alpha Delta Pi delegation, an ecstatic Betty Lane Evans connected briefly with Senator Kennedy as one sorority sister snapped a picture and another, Camilla Henderson, looked on. (Courtesy of the *News and Observer* Collection and the North Carolina State Archives.)

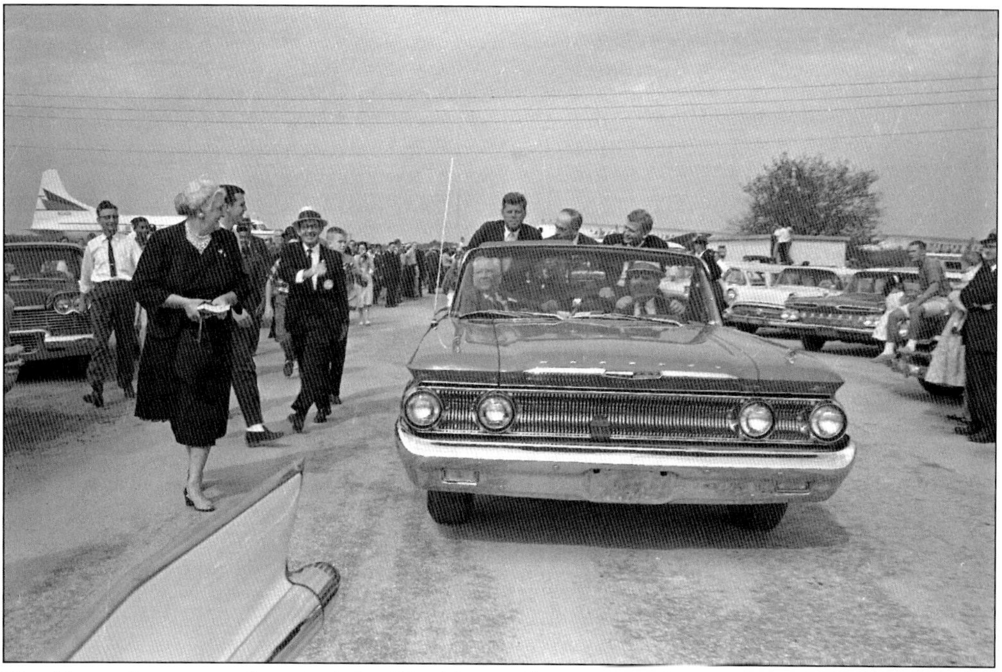

The Kennedy motorcade exited the Pitt-Greenville Airport along a dirt track that provided access to nearby Mumford Road, a paved road connecting the airport to Greene Street. In the background, the tail of the *Caroline* is visible. (Courtesy of the *News and Observer* and the North Carolina State Archives.)

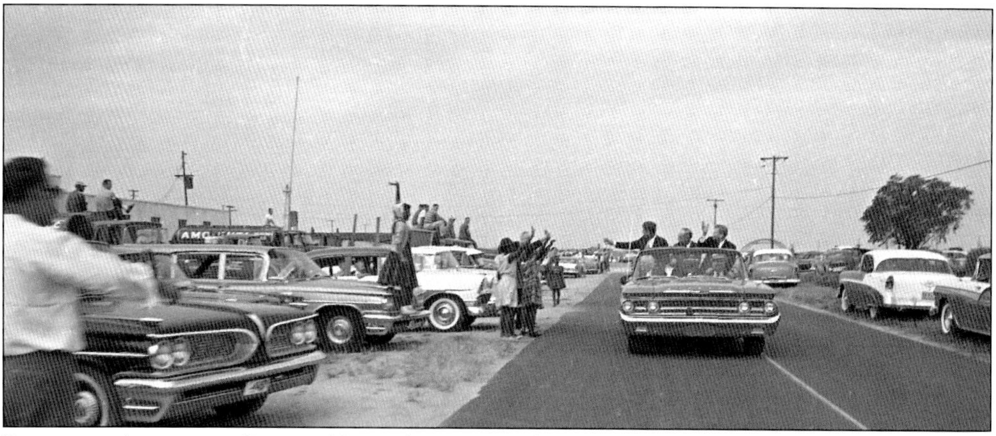

Departing the airport, Senator Kennedy's motorcade greets the first of many groups assembled along the streets of Greenville looking, waving, and wishing the candidate well. (Courtesy of the *News and Observer* and the North Carolina State Archives.)

Three

Farmers Warehouse

Arthur Tripp, co-owner of Farmers Warehouse and a major supporter of the Democratic Party, orchestrated the day's show-stealing moment: a mock auction in "the world's largest flue-cured tobacco warehouse." The auctioneer was Ray Oglesby, renowned for Lucky Strike commercials and appearances on the *Ed Sullivan* show. Billy Clark, an auctioneer of 30 years, assisted Oglesby. The warehouse was packed with long rows of tobacco piles and several thousand people. A "Democratic donkey" on-site reportedly "brayed loudly to herald the senator's arrival in eastern North Carolina." When the motorcade drove in the warehouse, "a tremendous shout went up from the crowd." If anyone wondered whether Senator Kennedy would be well received in eastern North Carolina, the reception at Farmers Warehouse gave an unequivocal answer.

Senator Kennedy affirmed the Democratic farm policy providing price supports for tobacco and controlling market supply through grower quotas. Kennedy emphasized that he was affirming commitments made by North Carolina congressmen Harold Cooley and Herbert Bonner. Before cameras and reporters, Arthur Tripp shook hands with Kennedy and presented him with a plaque commemorating the occasion and a bunch of tobacco, which a delighted Kennedy raised high before the now-adoring crowd. Oglesby added a new line to his auctioneer's chant, "Let's see old Jack to the White House, boys." Before departing, Kennedy thanked all who welcomed him and observed that the experience "added to his education."

The significance of Kennedy's visit was not lost on the crowd. Burney Tucker, mayor of Winterville, noted, "If Kennedy takes time to come to a little place like Greenville, then he's getting to the level of the people. It shows he's interested in people. It shows he's interested in this part of the country and the farmers." G.H. Tucker, also from Winterville, added, "Others fly over us, but Kennedy is stopping here." Kennedy's attention to farmers contrasted markedly with Nixon's "Southern strategy," which targeted big cities such as Greensboro, Birmingham, Atlanta, and Charlotte with quick "in-and-out" rallies.

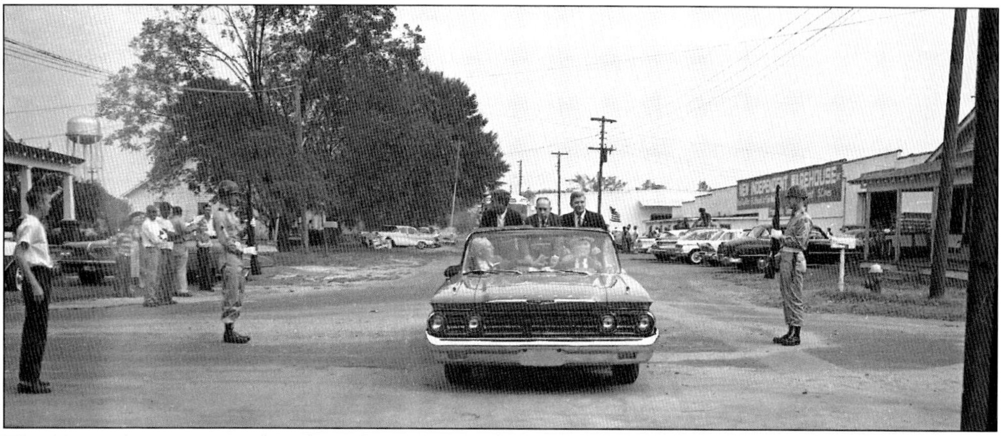

The Kennedy car approaches the side entrance of Farmers Warehouse. By early September, most of the tobacco crop had been harvested, cured, and was ready for sale by auction at tobacco warehouses in eastern North Carolina. Good days would bring sales of over $1 million, infusing substantial capital into the region. To do well in the eastern part of the state, Kennedy needed to bond with the tobacco industry. His visit to Farmers Warehouse, which had been coordinated by Arthur Tripp, co-owner of Farmers Warehouse and a major supporter of the Democratic Party, made this possible. (Courtesy of the *News and Observer* and the North Carolina State Archives.)

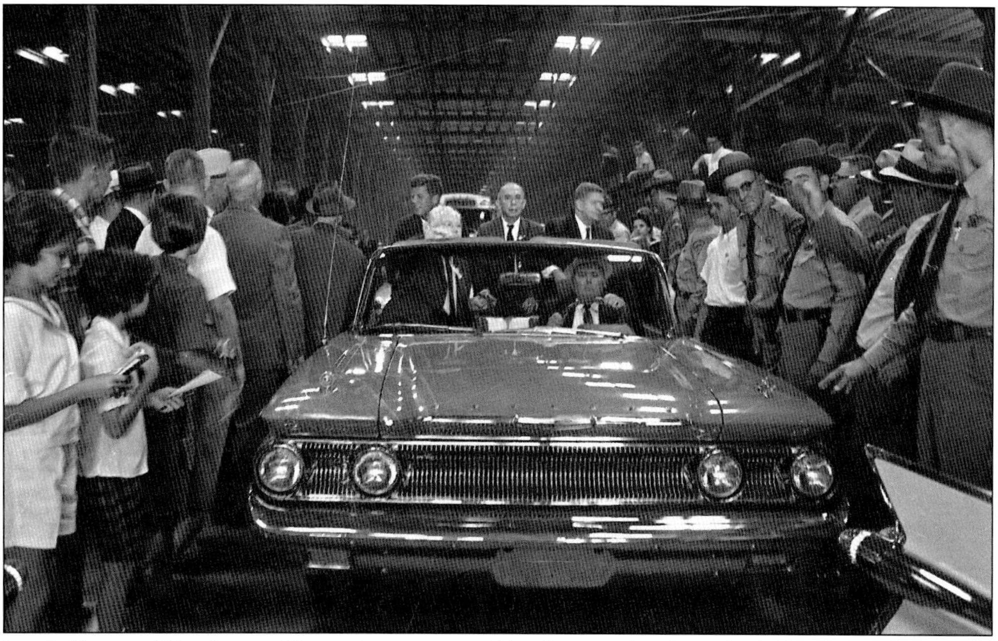

Inside Farmers Warehouse, Kennedy was greeted by thousands of people. Tobacco auctions were typically held Monday through Thursday. Kennedy's visit was on a Saturday, making a mock auction necessary. Kennedy could have had various reactions to all of this. That he appeared thrilled by the experience endeared him to eastern North Carolinians. (Courtesy of the *News and Observer* and the North Carolina State Archives.)

Warehousemen and tobacconists as well as farmers, tobacco hands, and sharecroppers attended the mock auction. Reportedly, this unique event was broadcast as part of the national news coverage of Senator Kennedy's North Carolina campaign. Coliseums, airports, and even college stadiums were common, but outside of eastern North Carolina, a tobacco warehouse was a rare sight. (Courtesy of the *Daily Reflector* and J.Y. Joyner Library, East Carolina University.)

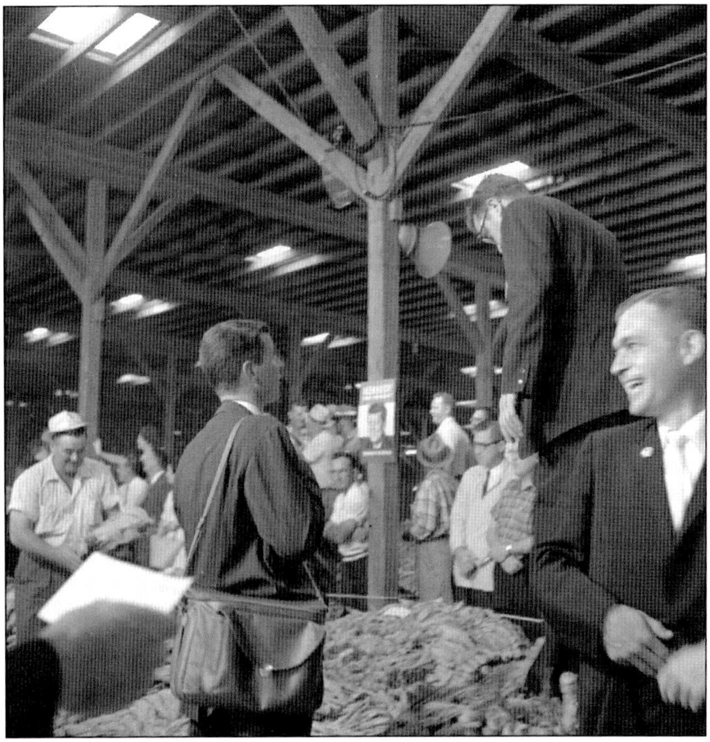

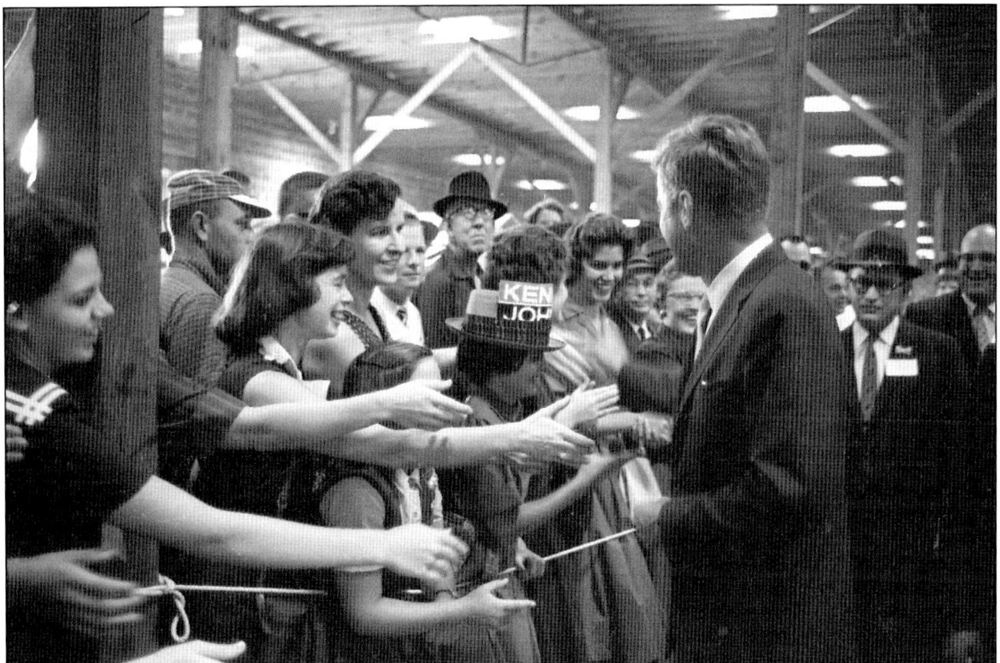

Inside Farmers Warehouse, all welcomed Senator Kennedy enthusiastically, and his exceptional ability to relate to people without condescension went over well with the down-home sensibilities of much of eastern North Carolina. (Courtesy of the *News and Observer* and the North Carolina State Archives.)

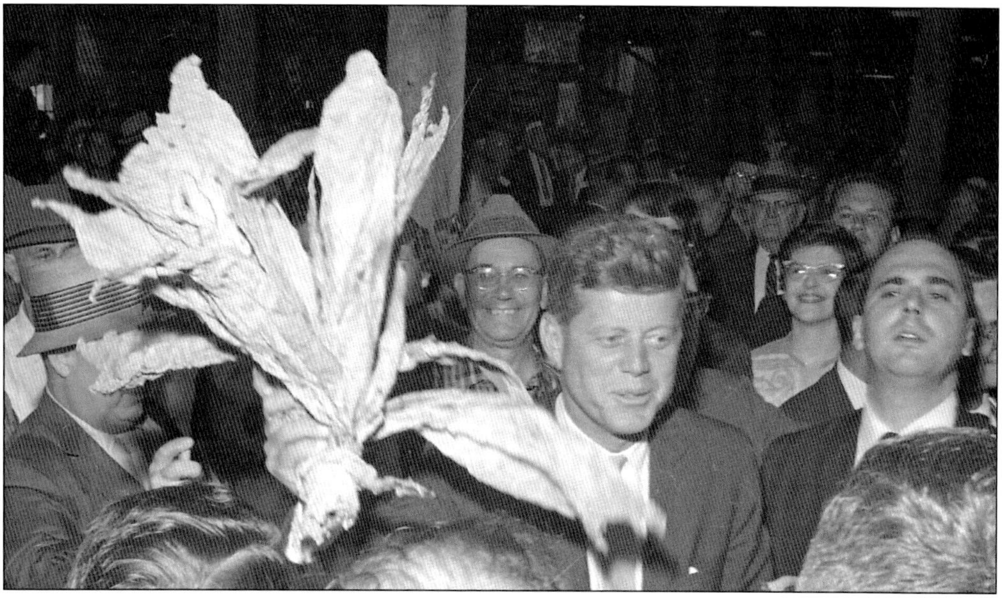

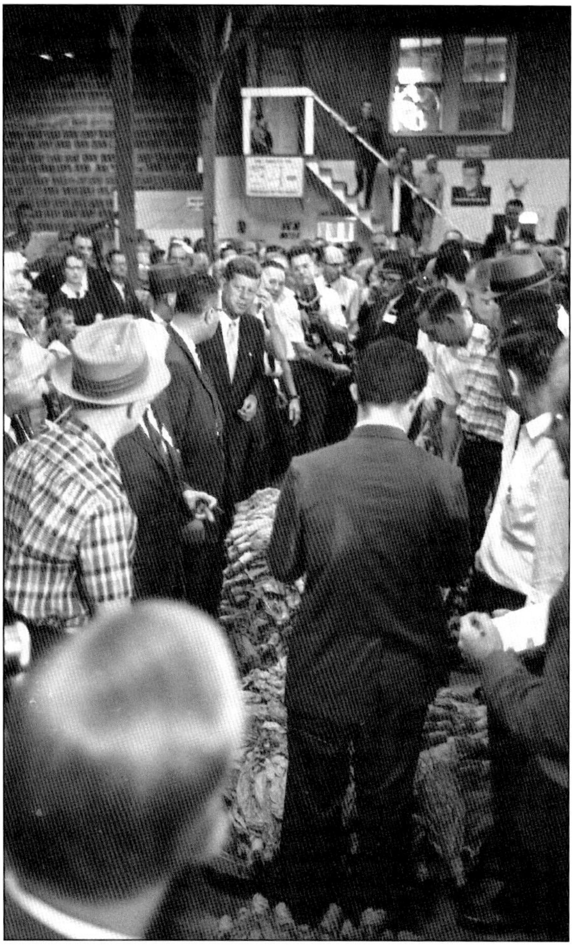

Senator Kennedy bought a pile of tobacco at 81¢ per pound, considerably above the average at that time. Allegedly, "Nixon tobacco" brought only 5¢ per pound. Kennedy's fascination with tobacco culture, evident as he held up a bunch of tobacco, connected him directly to the local scene. (Courtesy of the *News and Observer* and the North Carolina State Archives.)

Warehouses had their tobacco lined up in 100-plus pound piles in long rows ready for auction. Auctioneers would lead a procession of buyers down the row, singing out prices for each pile. Buyers could bid on the piles, determining the final sale price. Walking down a row listening to Ray Oglesby's rapid chant, Senator Kennedy gained direct insight into the region. (Courtesy of the *News and Observer* and the North Carolina State Archives.)

To Senator Kennedy's left is Arthur Tripp, co-owner of Farmers Warehouse. On Kennedy's right is Ray Oglesby, renowned auctioneer. Next to Oglesby is Rep. Herbert Bonner. Holding his bunch of tobacco, Kennedy tries to listen to all three at once as a farmer gestures decisively about the tobacco, the premier cash crop of eastern North Carolina and serious business for everyone. (Courtesy of the *News and Observer* and the North Carolina State Archives.)

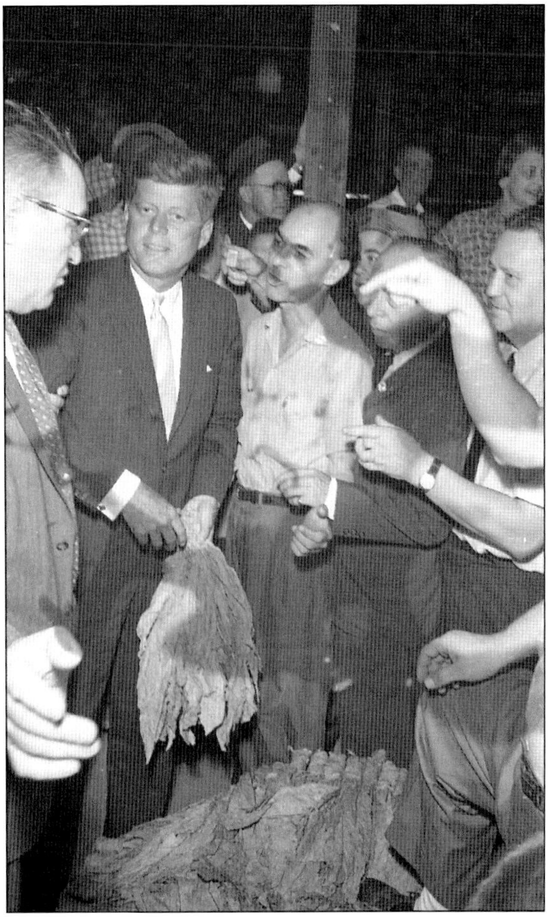

Arthur Tripp turns to the crowd behind the auctioneer's line as Senator Kennedy looks across the warehouse in the opposite direction. The man wearing the hat between Tripp and Kennedy is one of Kennedy's bodyguards. Just behind Kennedy is Ray Oglesby. Behind Oglesby is Rep. Herbert Bonner. (Courtesy of the *News and Observer* and the North Carolina State Archives.)

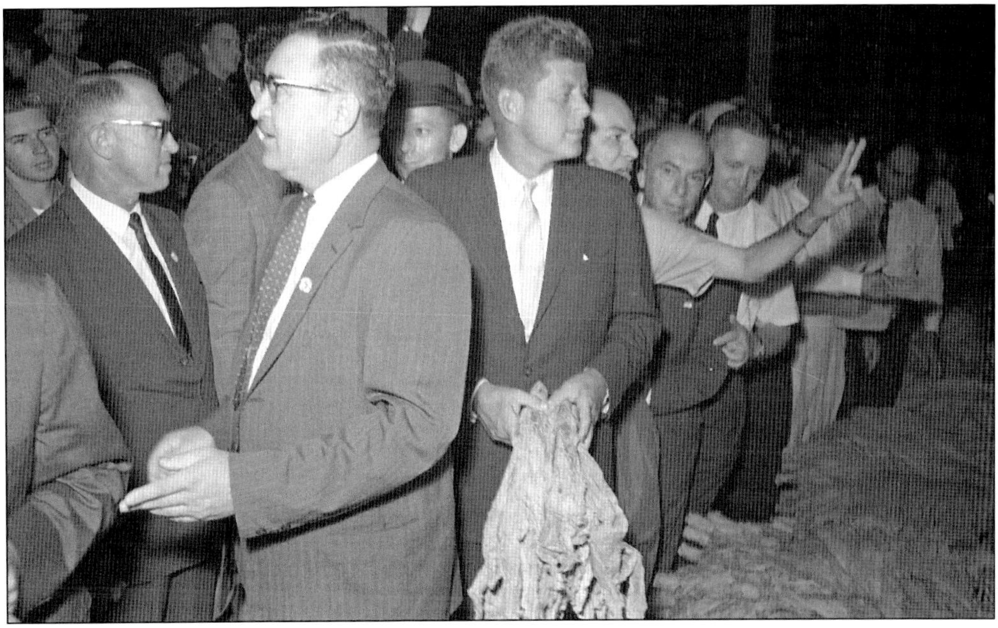

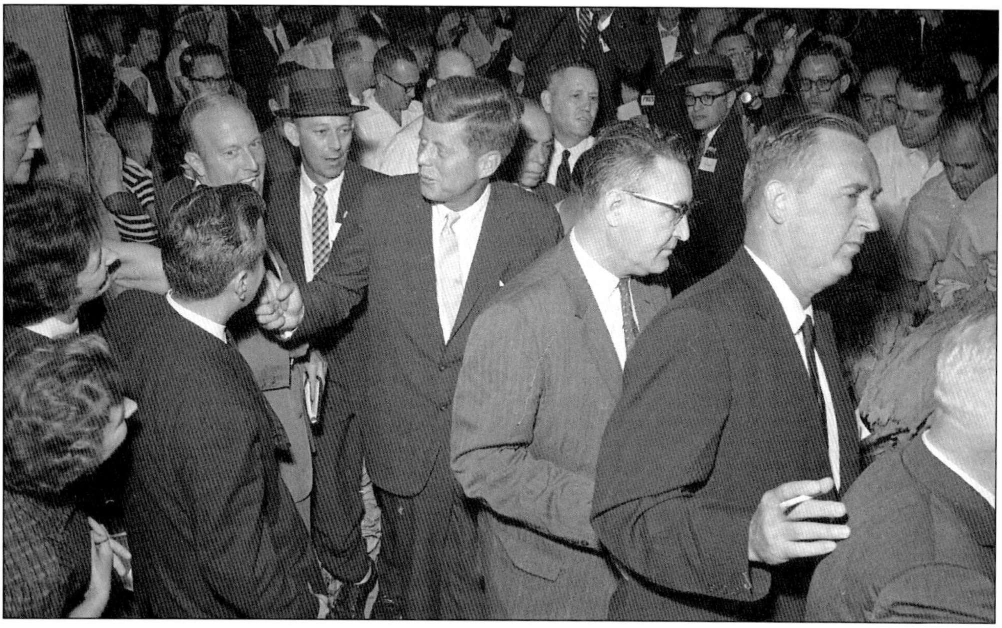

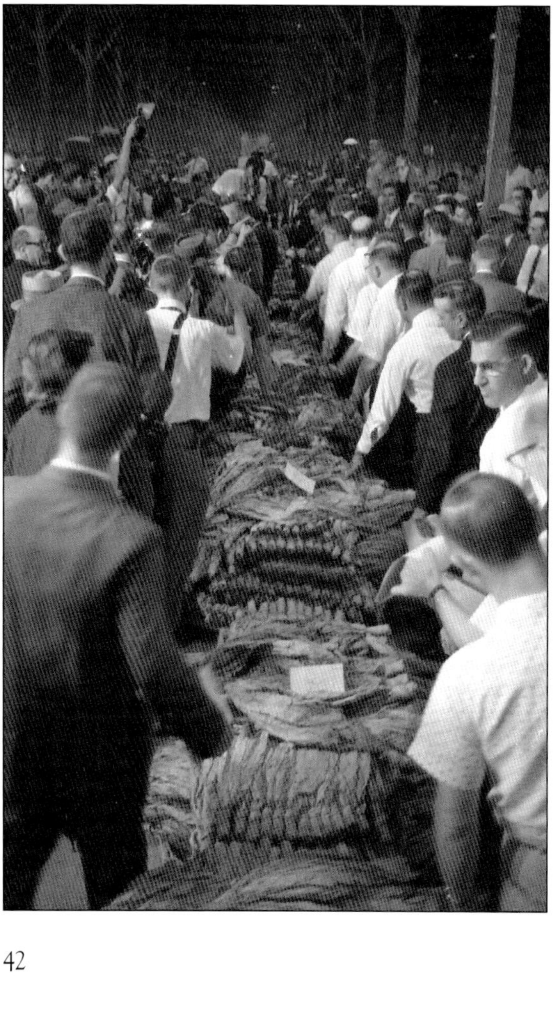

As Senator Kennedy shakes hands with a local woman in the crowd, Arthur Tripp and Greenville mayor Eugene West, with a cigarette, proceed down the row of tobacco. Just behind Kennedy's right shoulder wearing a hat is a Kennedy bodyguard. (Courtesy of the *News and Observer* and the North Carolina State Archives.)

The crowd following Senator Kennedy and the dignitaries at the front of the line was considerable. At this time, tobacco was prepared for auction by farmhands who first graded the tobacco, sorting it according to color, texture, and aroma, and then wrapped it into bunches that could be easily picked up and inspected. (Courtesy of the *News and Observer* and the North Carolina State Archives.)

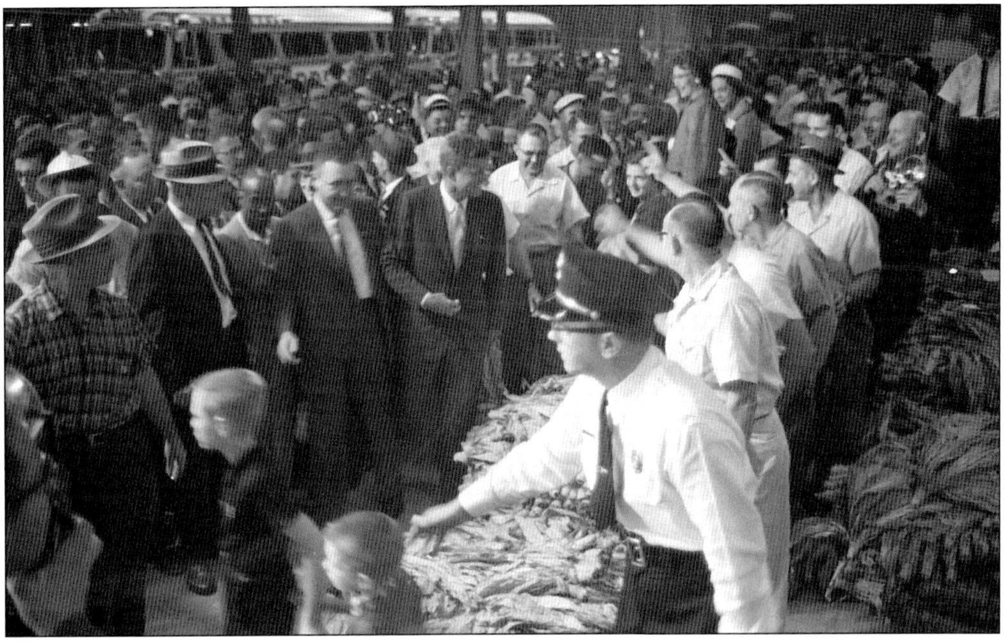

As the auctioneer's procession continued down the row, Greenville police chief Sullivan Gibbs shooed two boys away from the mock sale. Although nothing was made of this, Gibbs was also a Catholic. In the background, several women stood on piles of tobacco to get a better look at Senator Kennedy. (Courtesy of the *News and Observer* and the North Carolina State Archives.)

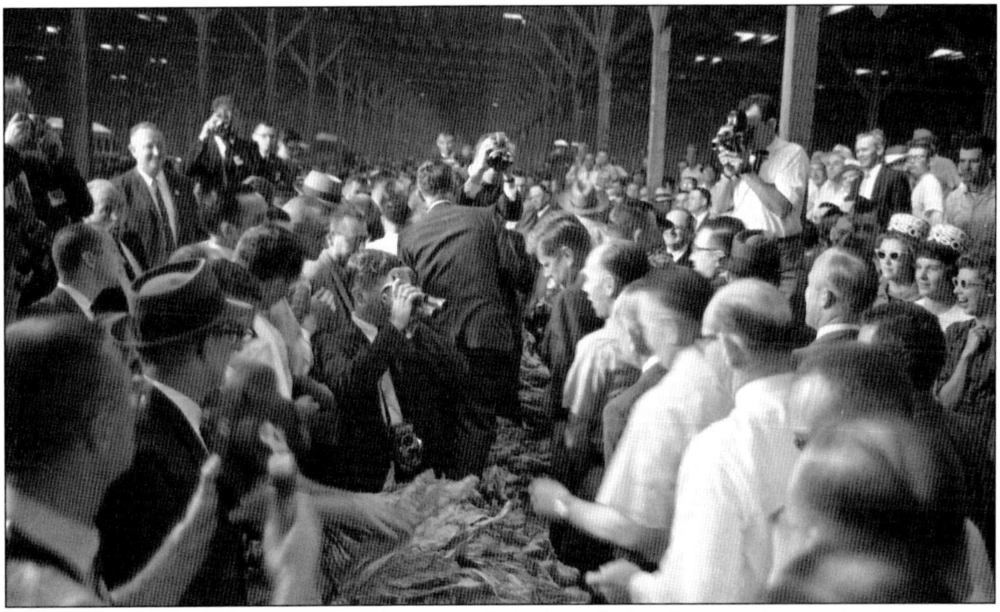

Throughout the day, Senator Kennedy graciously dealt with the photographers and videographers recording the rallies for newspapers and television networks. Events in Greenville were covered extensively because it was the first stop. (Courtesy of the *News and Observer* and the North Carolina State Archives.)

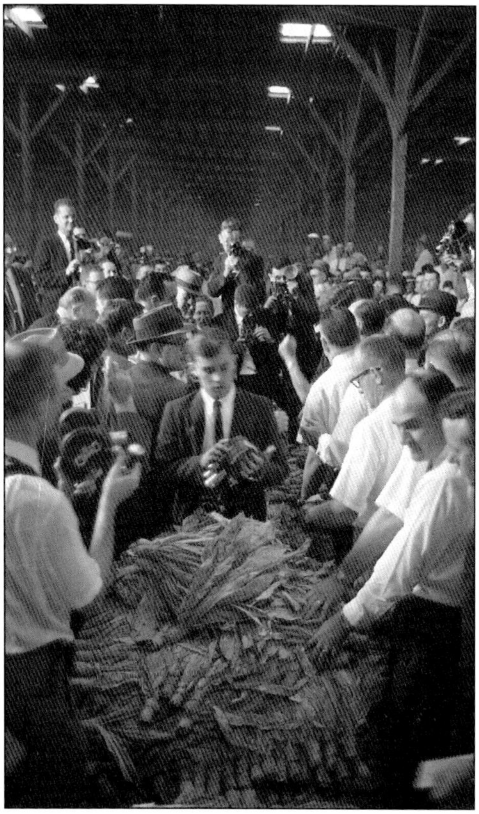

Few, if any, events inside a tobacco warehouse had ever attracted the media attention that Senator Kennedy's stop at Farmers Warehouse did. It was arguably the most distinctively "North Carolina" moment of the day, and one that many who attended would recall even half a century later. (Courtesy of the *News and Observer* and the North Carolina State Archives.)

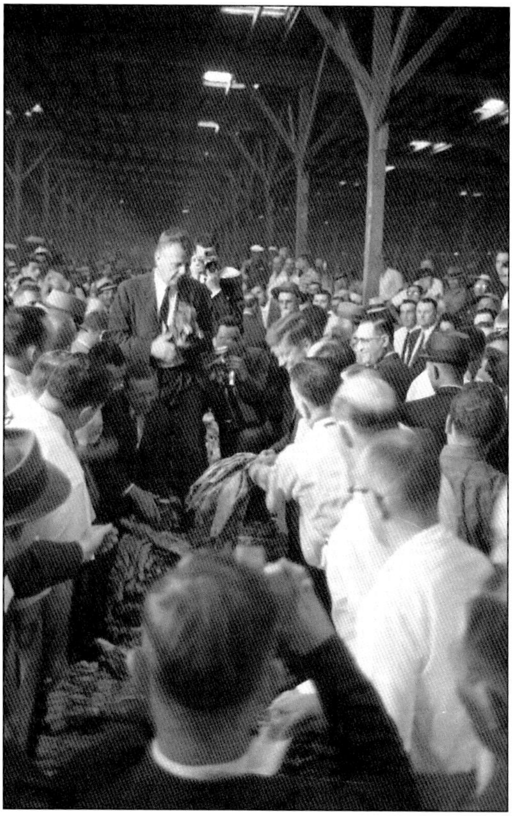

Surrounded by farmers participating in the mock sale, Senator Kennedy enjoys a light moment even as the cameras bear down on him. Although tobacco warehouses are not known as places of exceptional civility, on September 17, 1960, Kennedy's reception was apparently entirely positive. (Courtesy of the *News and Observer* and the North Carolina State Archives.)

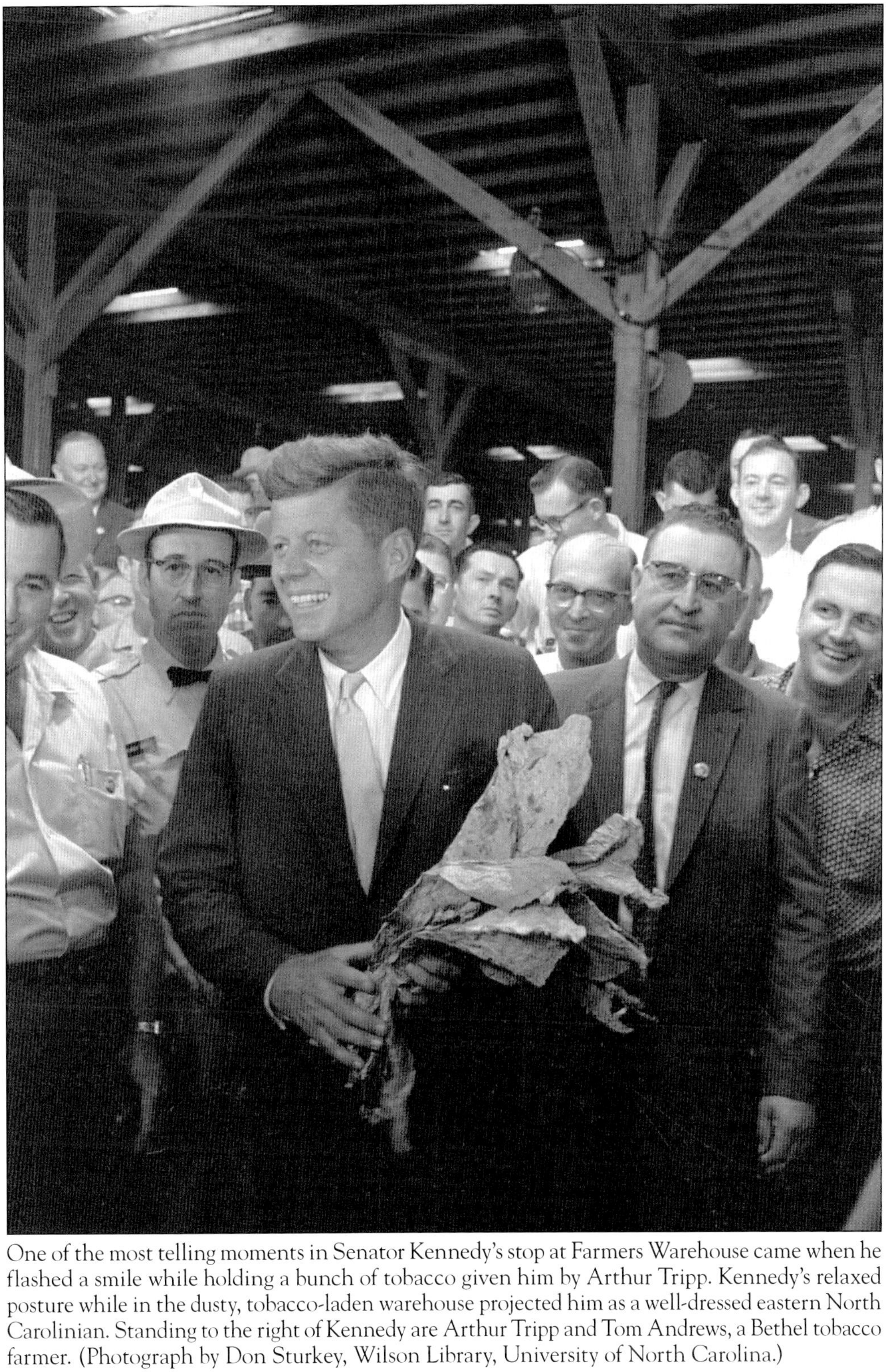

One of the most telling moments in Senator Kennedy's stop at Farmers Warehouse came when he flashed a smile while holding a bunch of tobacco given him by Arthur Tripp. Kennedy's relaxed posture while in the dusty, tobacco-laden warehouse projected him as a well-dressed eastern North Carolinian. Standing to the right of Kennedy are Arthur Tripp and Tom Andrews, a Bethel tobacco farmer. (Photograph by Don Sturkey, Wilson Library, University of North Carolina.)

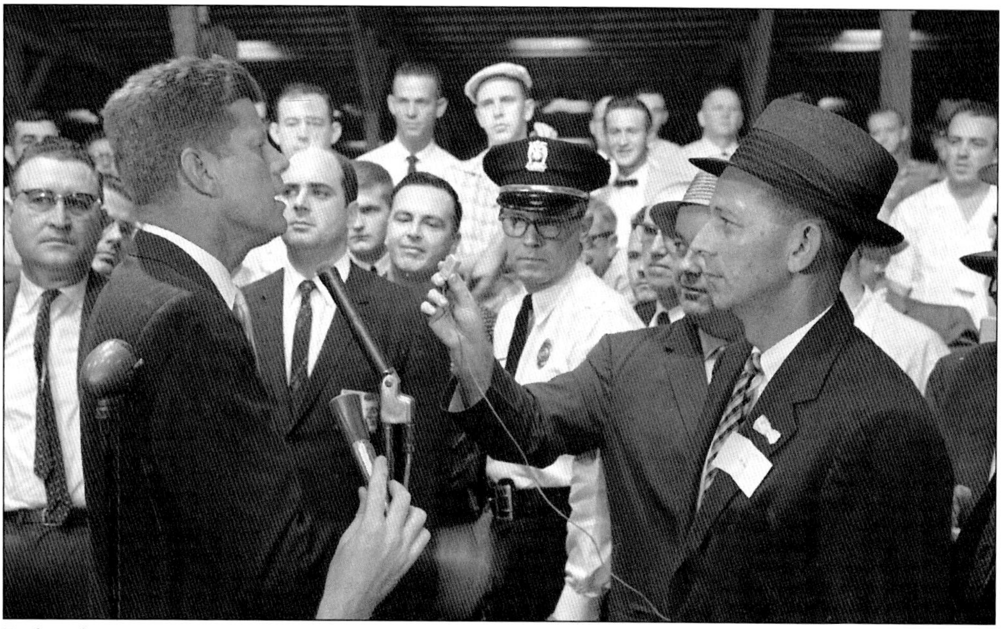

Before leaving Farmers Warehouse, Senator Kennedy issued a brief statement declaring his commitment to the Democratic Party's "affirmative" farm program, especially that related to tobacco. To Kennedy's left is Arthur Tripp. Greenville police chief Sullivan Gibbs stands at center. The man wearing the hat to the right of Kennedy is one of his bodyguards. (Courtesy of the *News and Observer* and the North Carolina State Archives.)

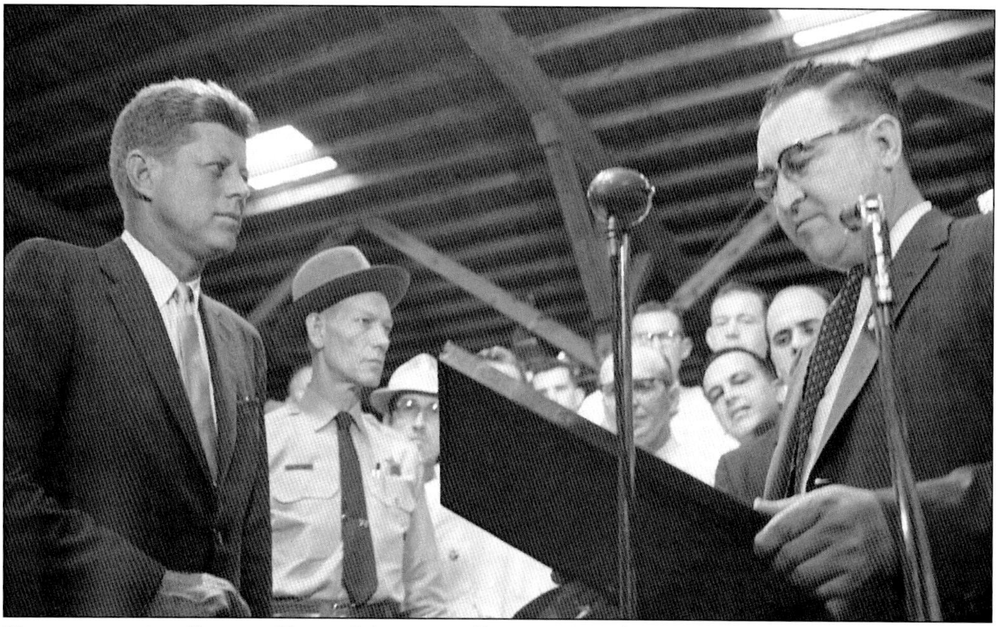

Commemorating Senator Kennedy's visit to Farmers Warehouse, Arthur Tripp presented the senator with a plaque. After Kennedy's assassination in 1963, the warehouse was one of many venues in Greenville where memorial services were held. The bond Kennedy forged that day with farmers and eastern North Carolinians made his tragic death all the more heartfelt. (Courtesy of the *News and Observer* and the North Carolina State Archives.)

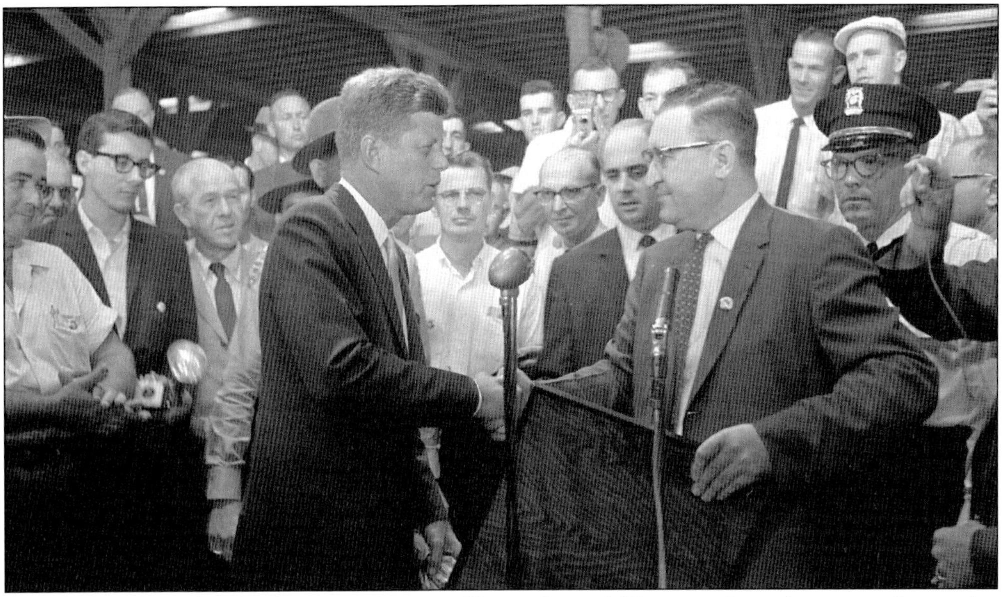

The parting handshake between Senator Kennedy and Tripp spoke volumes to those who witnessed it. That Kennedy had not stumbled over a pile of tobacco, wheezed, or coughed, even while immersed in aromatic leaf, or responded negatively to the Spartan warehouse facilities helped him to win the hearts and minds of all who were there. Just a week before, Kennedy had persuasively addressed hundreds of Protestant clergy in Houston. Now, with ease and sincerity, he mixed with the eastern North Carolina tobacco scene, establishing his credibility as a man of the people. (Photograph by Don Sturkey, Wilson Library, University of North Carolina.)

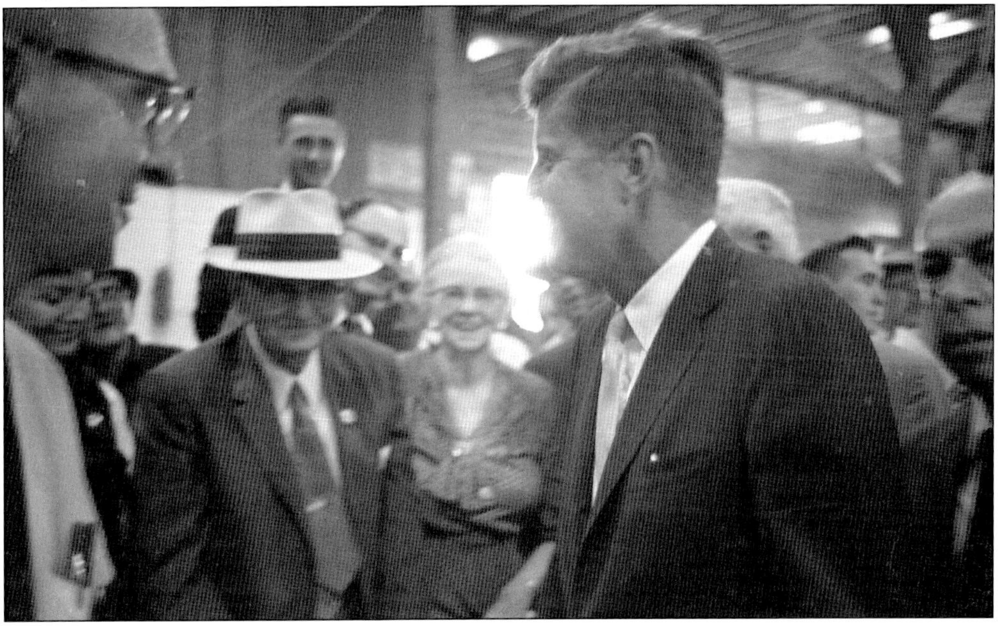

Senator Kennedy's appeal to young people is well known, but that his charisma worked with farmers both young and old is less so. This photograph shows the senator exchanging greetings with a section of elderly farmers who had made the effort to see him. Their pleasure with the experience is evident. (Courtesy of the *News and Observer* and the North Carolina State Archives.)

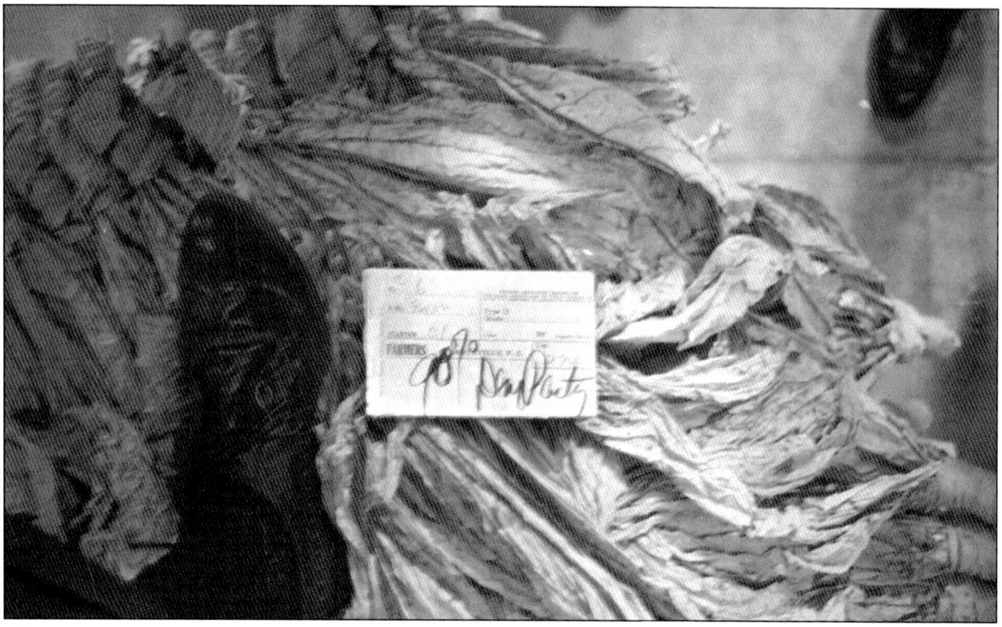

The tag on this pile of tobacco, declaring "90% Dem. Party," communicated the exceptionally solid support that rural eastern North Carolina gave Democratic candidates. Some even joked that eastern North Carolinians were "yellow dog Democrats," meaning that they would vote for any Democratic candidate, even a yellow dog, if one ran for office. (Courtesy of the *News and Observer* and the North Carolina State Archives.)

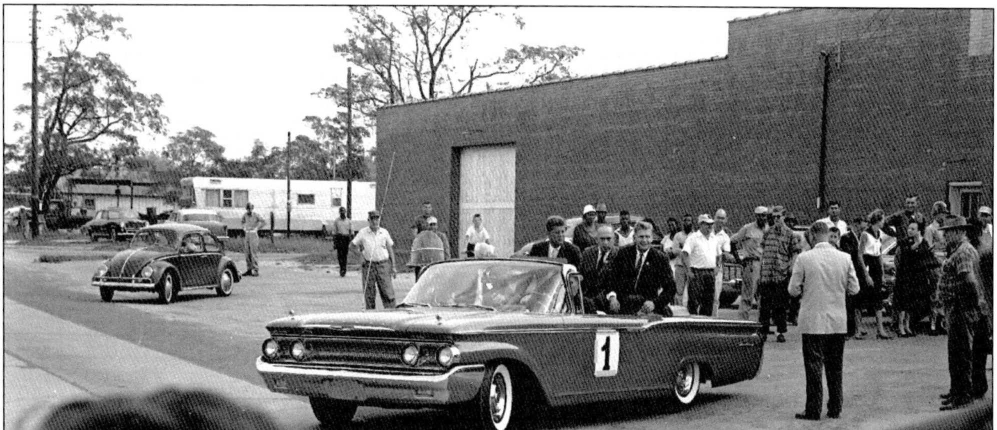

Leaving Farmers Warehouse, the Kennedy motorcade turned left on to Greene Street and headed south across the Tar River into uptown Greenville. In the back are, from left to right, Senator Kennedy, Representative Bonner, and Terry Sanford. (Courtesy of the *News and Observer* and the North Carolina State Archives.)

Four

The Greenville Motorcade

From Farmers Warehouse, the eight-car motorcade led by eight policemen on motorcycles brought Senator Kennedy and two dozen Tar Heel Democratic luminaries across the Tar River, up Greene Street to Fifth Street, and then eastward on Fifth to College Stadium on the East Carolina campus. Along the way, Kennedy passed six marching bands representing eastern North Carolina high schools. One of the more memorable was the C.M. Eppes High School Band directed by Johnny Wooten. Greenville's schools had yet to desegregate, and Eppes was the town's African American high school. The Eppes band stood just west of the historic Sycamore Hill Missionary Baptist Church, the first African American church in Greenville, chartered just after the Civil War. Wooten well understood the event's significance and so saved the uniform he wore that day. It is now part of the Eppes Cultural Heritage Center.

The people lining the streets of Greenville reflected the farm town ethic of eastern North Carolina, one that precluded segregation in its worst forms. Schools were still separate, as were many other dimensions of life, but on September 17, the sidewalk crowds thought little about the color of those around them. Kennedy might have noticed, just before the turn onto Fifth Street, one of the relatively few Catholics in Greenville at the time: Fr. Maurice Tew, who stood with a group of African American children, most likely parishioners at St. Gabriel's, a predominantly African American Catholic church in west Greenville. Father Tew, the senior clergy at St. Gabriel's, was surely proud of Kennedy and the town for hosting him.

As the motorcade moved up Fifth Street, Kennedy saw East Carolina College and its Spanish mission-style architecture. This was a feature requested by one of the founding fathers of the school, a former governor and ambassador to Brazil, Thomas Jarvis, a resident of Greenville. The college provided a counterpoint to the overgrown airport and tobacco warehouse across the river. Kennedy saw, as all of Greenville did, the power that an institution of higher education could exert in an otherwise economically disadvantaged and backwards, rural region.

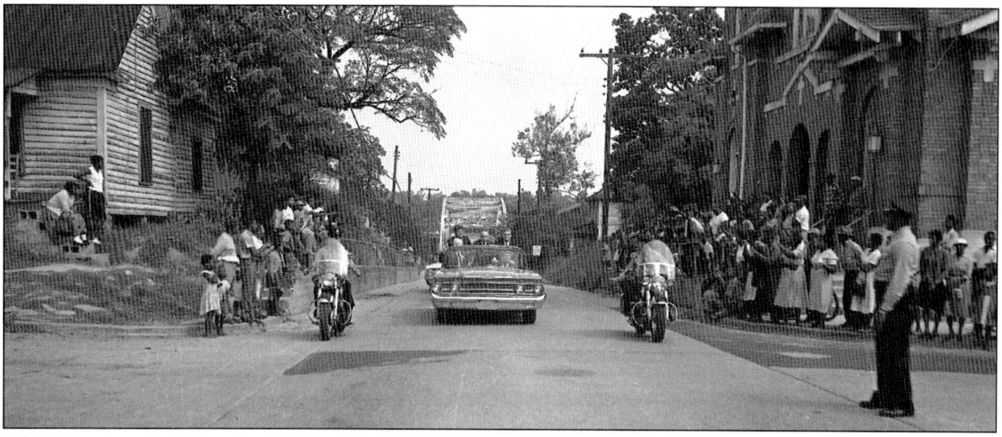

The motorcade proceeded on Greene Street, which, like the town, was named after Nathanael Greene, commander of the Southern Continental forces during the Revolutionary War. The first neighborhood south of the Tar River had as its nucleus the historic Sycamore Hill Missionary Baptist Church, chartered in 1865 as the African Baptist Church. The officer standing on the right is Ceasar Corbett Jr., Greenville's first African American policeman. (Courtesy of the *News and Observer* and the North Carolina State Archives.)

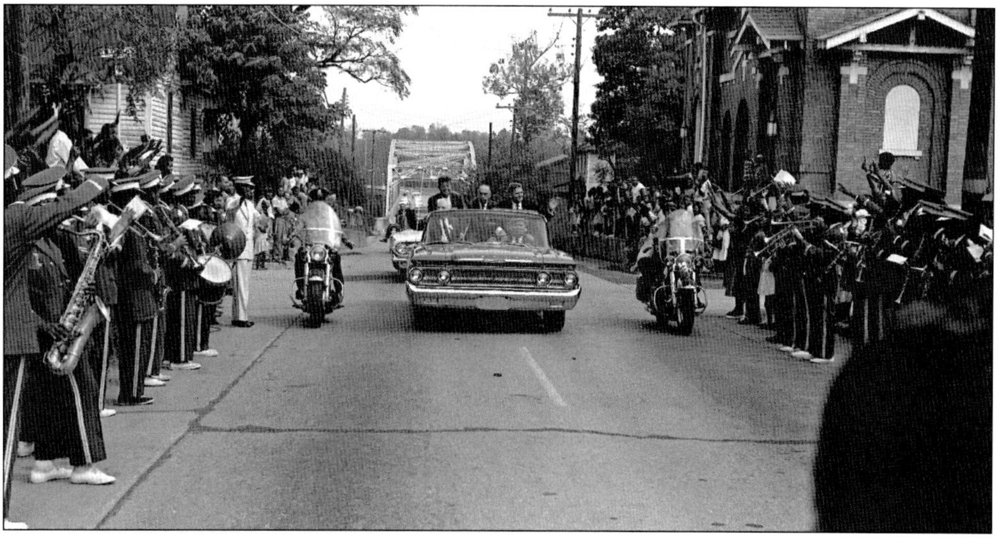

The C.M. Eppes band lined both sides of Greene Street near the church. Led by director Johnny Wooten, the Eppes band had rehearsed "Carolina in the Morning" in preparation for Senator Kennedy's visit only to see the motorcade, on a very tight schedule, pass without pausing to enjoy the music. (Photograph by Don Sturkey, Wilson Library, University of North Carolina.)

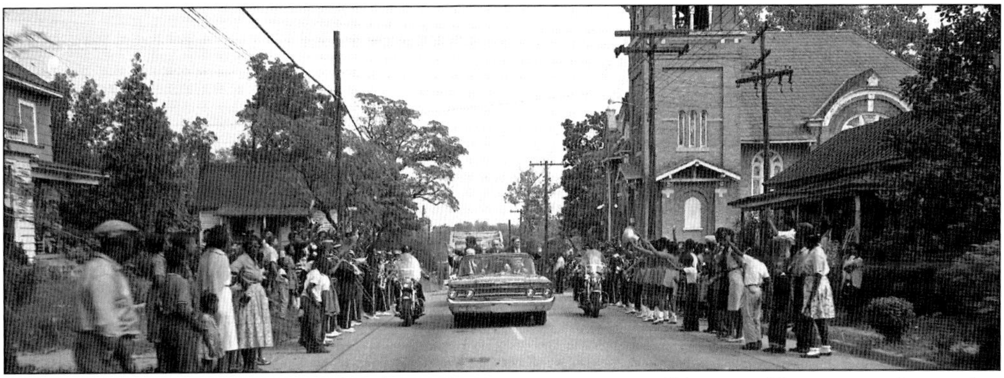

Senator Kennedy's popularity with African American voters is well known. However, in September 1960, that was not the case. Dr. Martin Luther King's father, a prominent clergy, supported Nixon. Only after Kennedy later facilitated Dr. King's release from a Georgia prison did things change. While in North Carolina, Kennedy did not highlight civil rights, even though the Greensboro sit-ins had brought those issues to the fore. (Courtesy of the *News and Observer* and the North Carolina State Archives.)

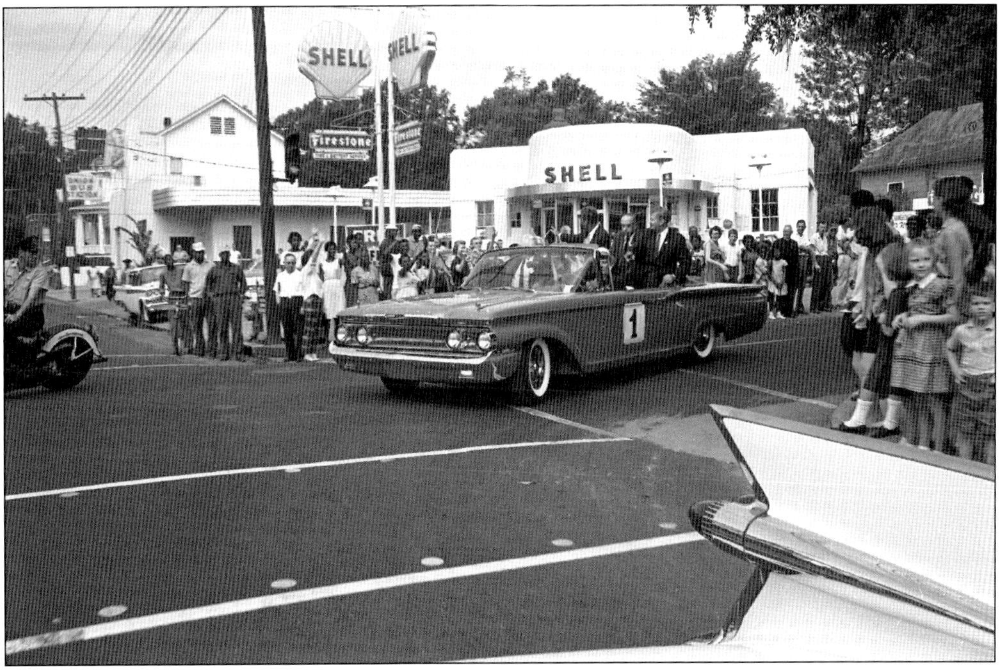

From Greene Street, the Kennedy motorcade turned onto Fifth Street. Standing in the crowd with a group of African American children (off the right end of the Kennedy car) is Fr. Maurice Tew, pastor of St. Gabriel's Catholic Church in the traditional African American community of Greenville. (Courtesy of the *News and Observer* and the North Carolina State Archives.)

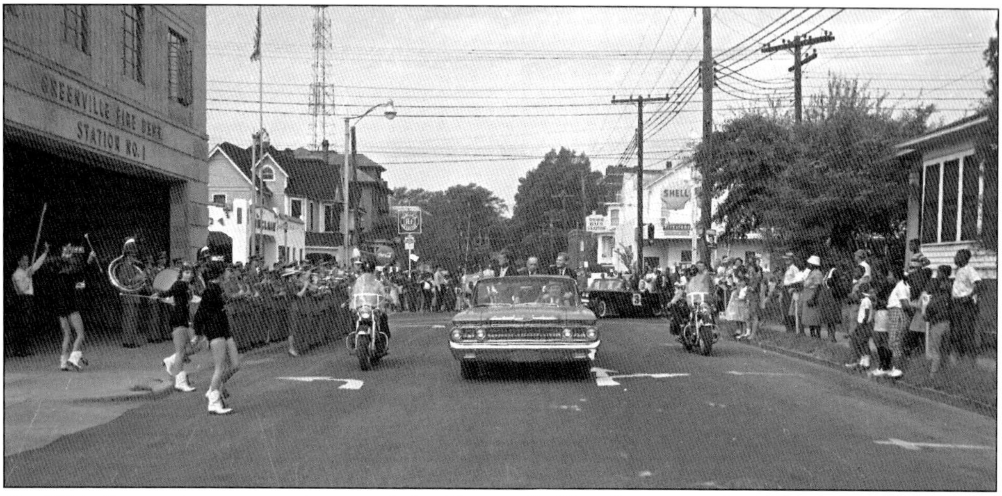

On Fifth Street, the motorcade passed the Greenville Fire Station and another of the half-dozen bands lining the route. To the left of the fire station was Jarvis Memorial Methodist Church, the oldest Methodist Church in Greenville. Its senior clergy, Rev. Howard McLamb, was one of the most outspoken anti-Catholics in the area. Though a prominent clergy, McLamb's remarks swayed very few voters in the election. (Courtesy of the *News and Observer* and the North Carolina State Archives.)

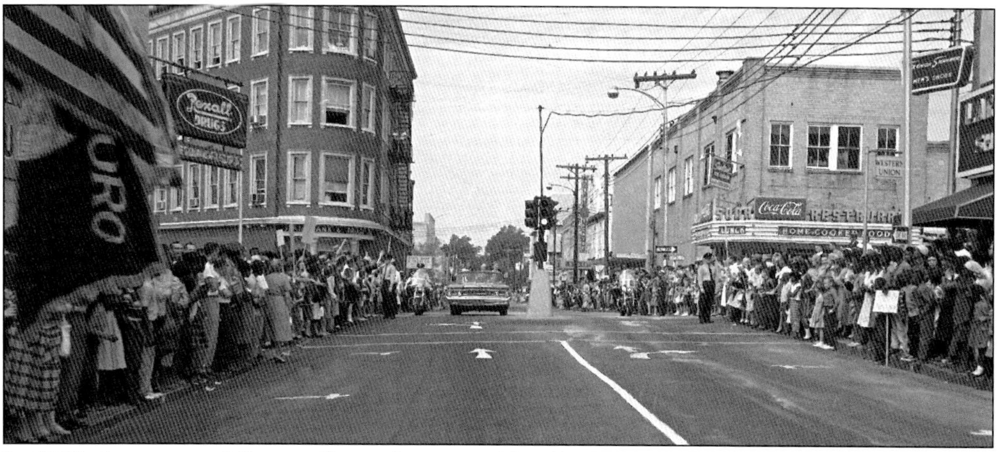

In 1960, the center of Greenville was known as Five Points. Here, Fifth Street, running east to west, intersected Evans Street, running north to south. Bisecting the southwest quadrant of the intersection was Dickinson Avenue, forming the fifth point. Half of the bisected quadrant was occupied by the flatiron-style State Bank Building. (Courtesy of the *News and Observer* and the North Carolina State Archives.)

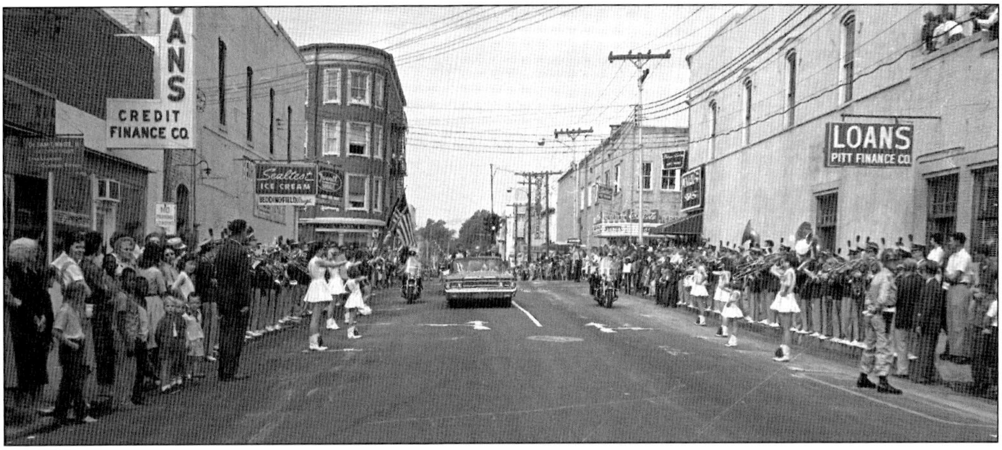

Crossing Evans Street going east, the motorcade passed another band that lined the north and south side of Fifth Street. Majorettes in white uniforms and boots stood at the front. (Courtesy of the *News and Observer* and the North Carolina State Archives.)

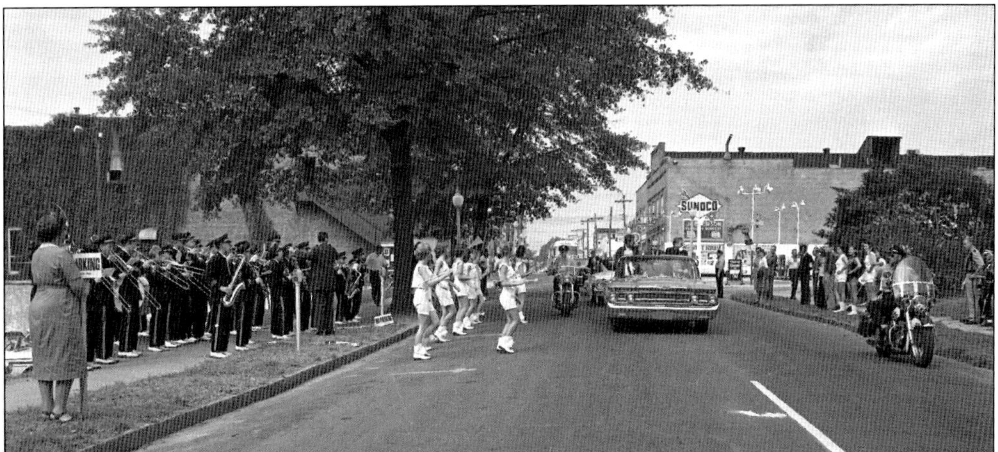

Above, the Kennedy motorcade approaches Harrington Hill and the campus of East Carolina College on the south side of Fifth Street. Off to the right, but not apparent, was the Greenville Junior High School. (Courtesy of the *News and Observer* and the North Carolina State Archives.)

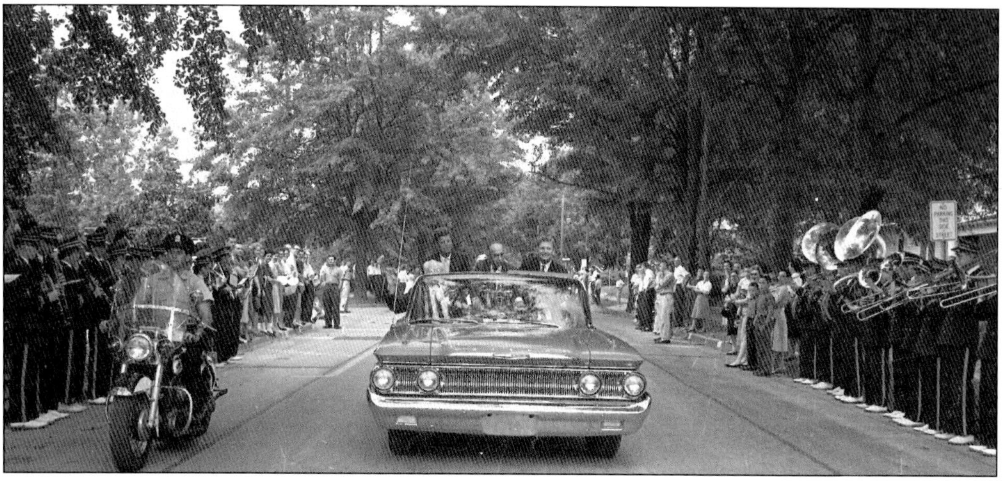

Traveling down Fifth Street under a canopy of large, curbside oak trees, the Kennedy motorcade passes yet another marching band. (Courtesy of the *News and Observer* and the North Carolina State Archives.)

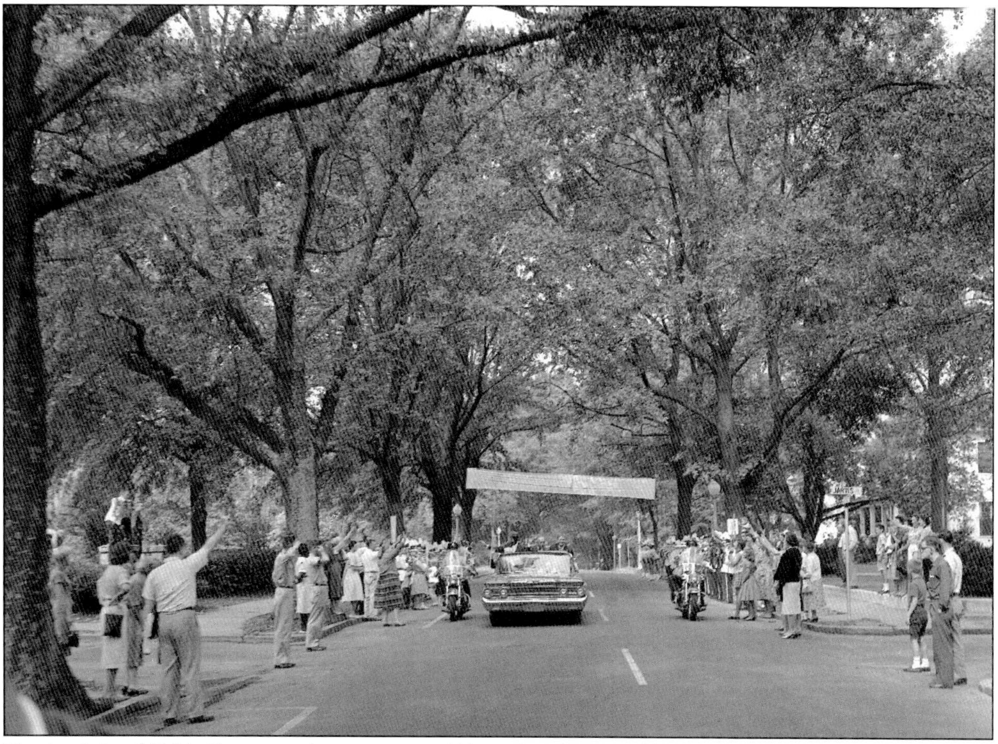

To the left of Fifth Street is the campus of East Carolina College. To the right, Fifth Street is lined with residences that in 1960 belonged to many prominent citizens of Greenville. Of all the homes, the most recognizable was the official residence of the president of East Carolina College. In 1960, Dr. Leo Jenkins's family, which included six children, lived there. Here, the motorcade passes the intersection of Fifth and Jarvis Streets at the southeast corner of the president's home. (Courtesy of the *Daily Reflector*, J.Y. Joyner Library, East Carolina University.)

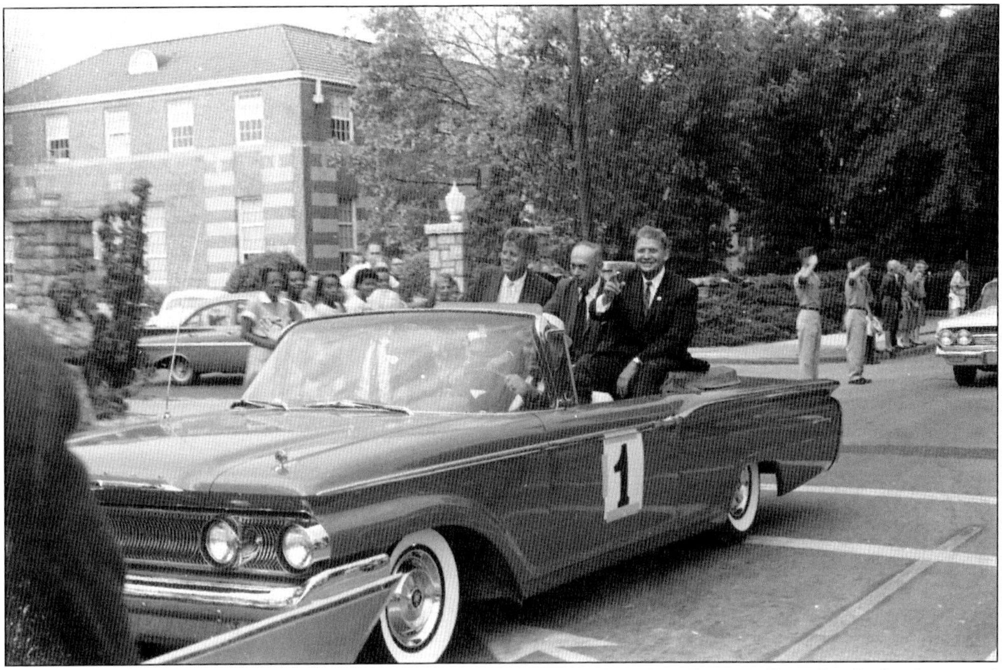

The Kennedy motorcade passes one of the main entrances to East Carolina College. In the background is the Spillman Building. Some of the housekeeping staff lined the sidewalk behind the vehicle. (Photograph by Hugh Morton; courtesy of Wilson Library, University of North Carolina.)

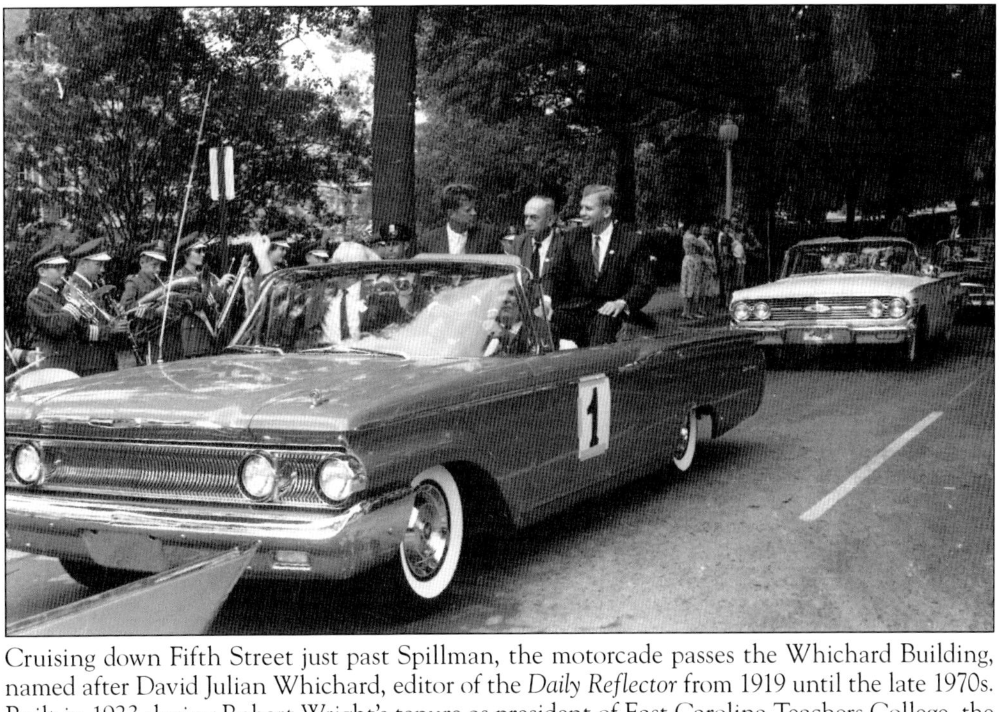

Cruising down Fifth Street just past Spillman, the motorcade passes the Whichard Building, named after David Julian Whichard, editor of the *Daily Reflector* from 1919 until the late 1970s. Built in 1923 during Robert Wright's tenure as president of East Carolina Teachers College, the building was named after Whichard in late 1959. (Photograph by Hugh Morton; courtesy of Wilson Library, University of North Carolina.)

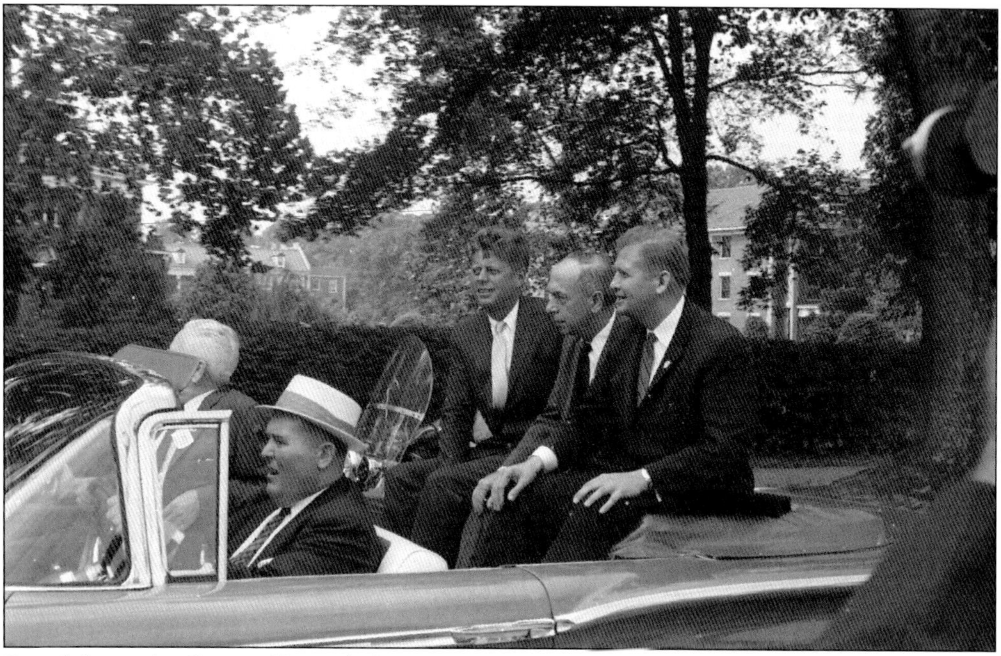

From left to right, Senator Kennedy, Representative Bonner, and Terry Sanford approach the turn to College Stadium. Detective Henry F. Lawson drives while John G. Clark looks toward campus from the front passenger seat. In the distance, the dormers of the Flanagan Building are visible. (Photograph by Hugh Morton; courtesy of Wilson Library, University of North Carolina.)

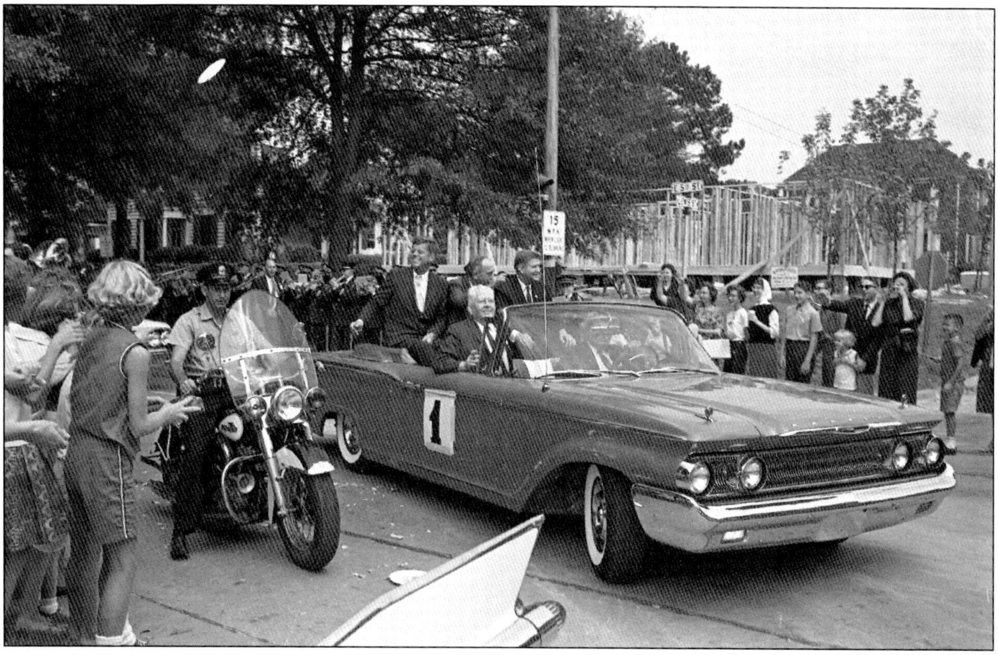

The motorcade turned off Fifth Street at the corner of Fifth and Lewis Streets. Many youngsters who attended Wahl-Coates Elementary School, then located on the campus of East Carolina College, attended the Kennedy rally that day. (Courtesy of the *News and Observer* and the North Carolina State Archives.)

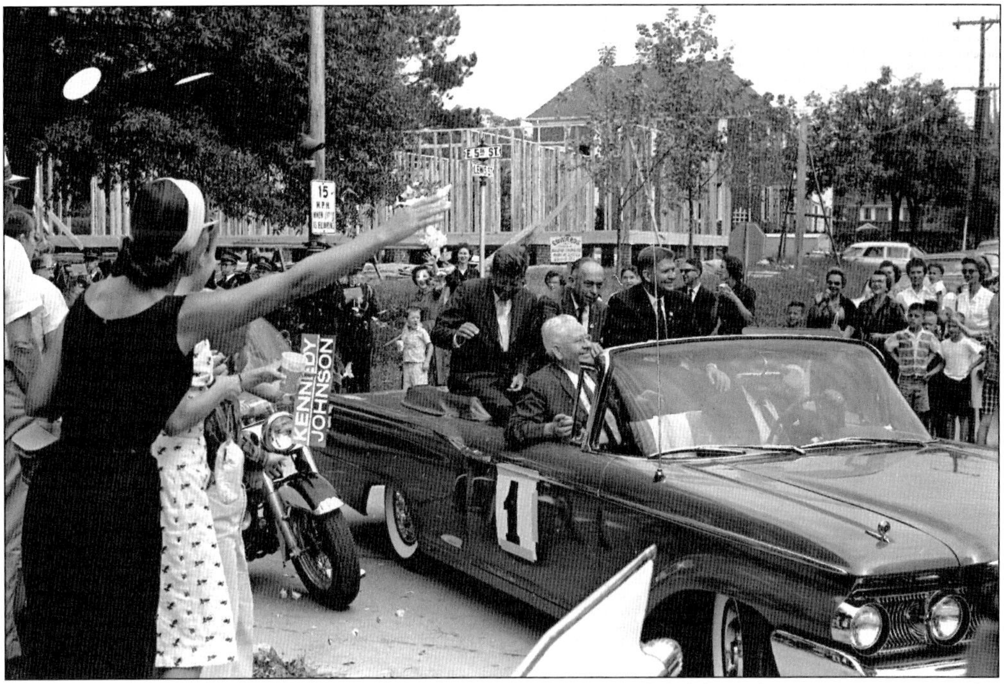

September 17, 1960, a Saturday morning, provided parents and children the opportunity to make the Kennedy rally at College Stadium a family outing. Along with confetti, the cheering crowds lining the turn onto the campus sent paper plates flying through the air. (Courtesy of the *News and Observer* and the North Carolina State Archives.)

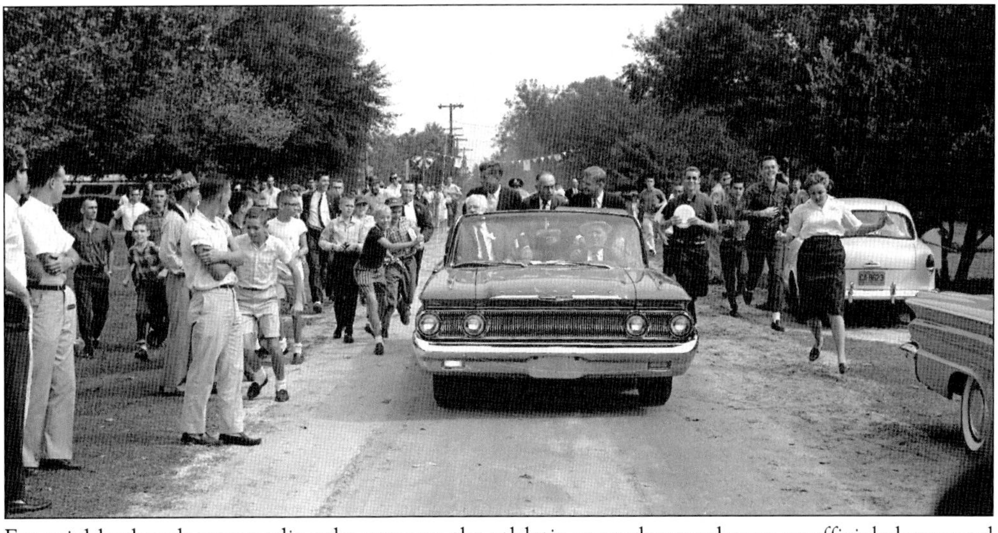

For neighborhoods surrounding the campus, the athletic grounds served as an unofficial playground area. Running beside the Kennedy motorcade were children, college students, and adults from the community who added to the excitement of the morning. (Photograph by Don Sturkey, Wilson Library, University of North Carolina.)

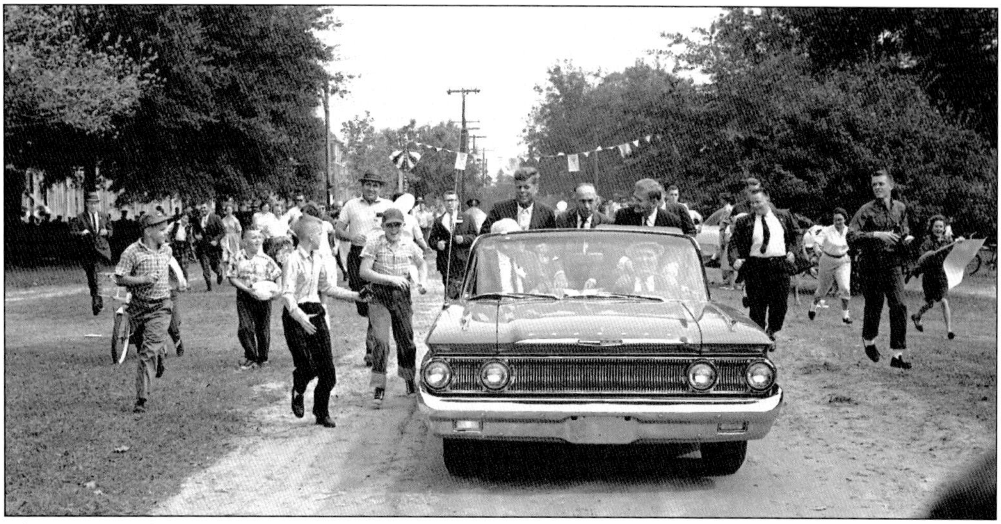

The motorcade turned onto campus via a dirt road providing access to the athletic grounds. College Stadium was little more than a football field with wooden bleachers and a press box. East Carolina had yet to begin construction of Ficklen Stadium (later Dowdy-Ficklen Stadium). Within three years, however, that stadium was completed. (Photograph by Don Sturkey, Wilson Library, University of North Carolina.)

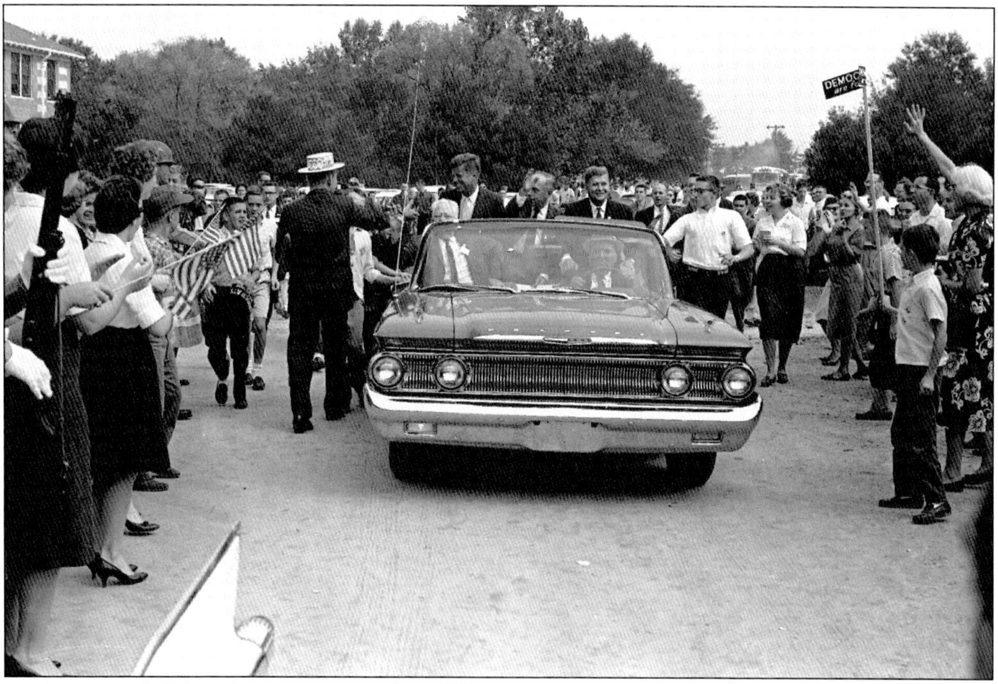

In the upper-left-hand corner, part of Wahl-Coates Elementary School on the East Carolina College campus is visible. East Carolina was founded in 1907 as East Carolina Teachers Training School with the mission of educating public school teachers. It later developed into a four-year liberal arts college and then into a research university. Wahl-Coates served as the "laboratory school" for teachers-in-training. (Photograph by Don Sturkey, Wilson Library, University of North Carolina.)

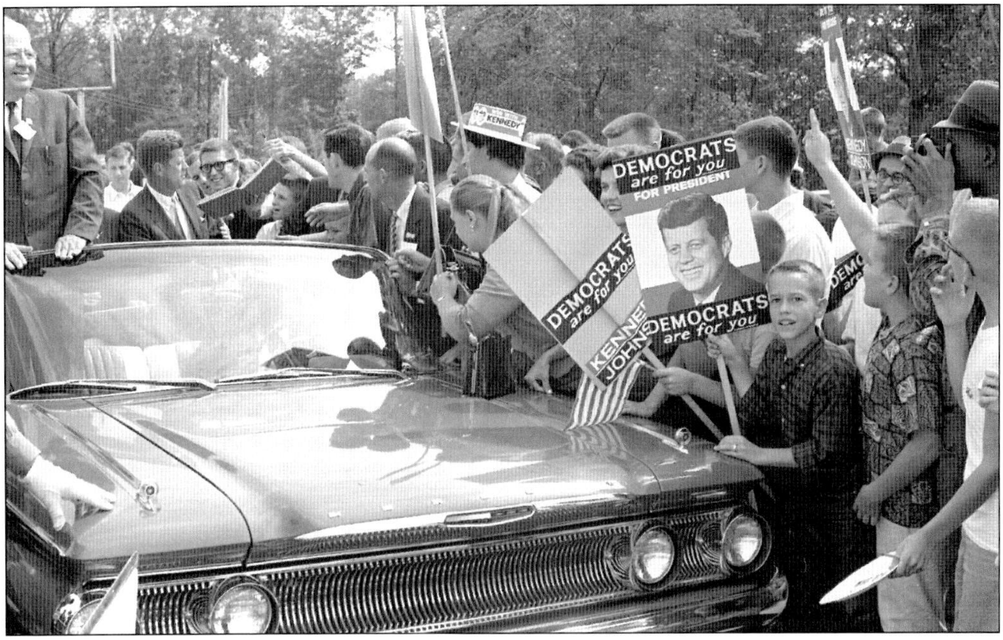

The Kennedy car came to a stop just past the goal posts of College Stadium, near what is today the A.J. Fletcher Music Building. Standing in the front passenger side of the Mercury is John G. Clark. The woman leaning over the hood to take a picture is Janice Faulkner, organizer of Coeds for Kennedy and an instructor of English at East Carolina. (Photograph by Don Sturkey, Wilson Library, University of North Carolina.)

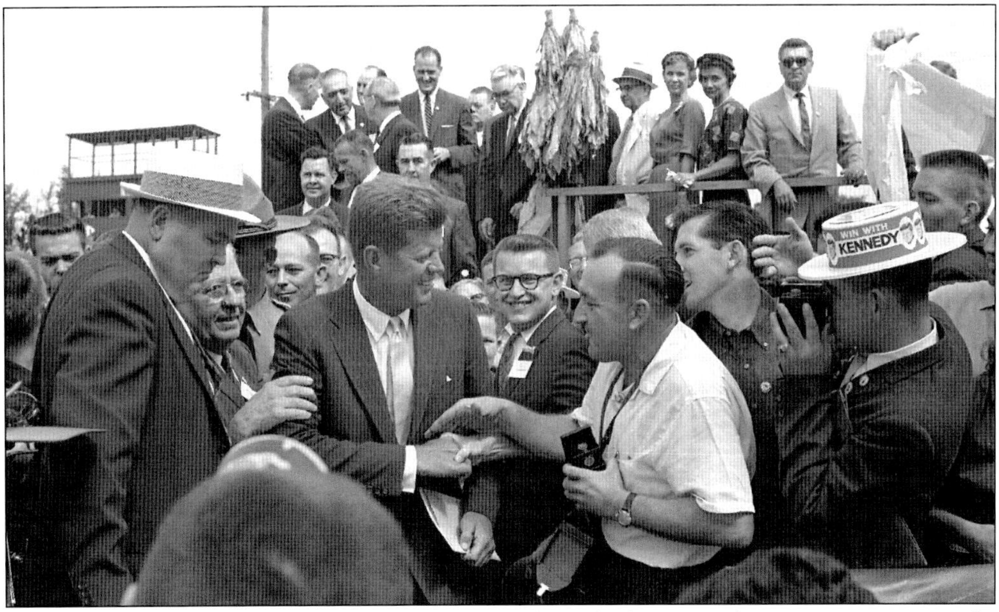

Senator Kennedy shakes a final hand as John Clark guides him into the Mercury Monterey for departure. Henry Lawson, preacher and police officer, holds the door open. In the background, attorney and tobacco industry representative J. Con Lanier, wearing a white suit, stands next to several bunches of tobacco that had been prominently displayed during the rally. (Photograph by Don Sturkey, Wilson Library, University of North Carolina.)

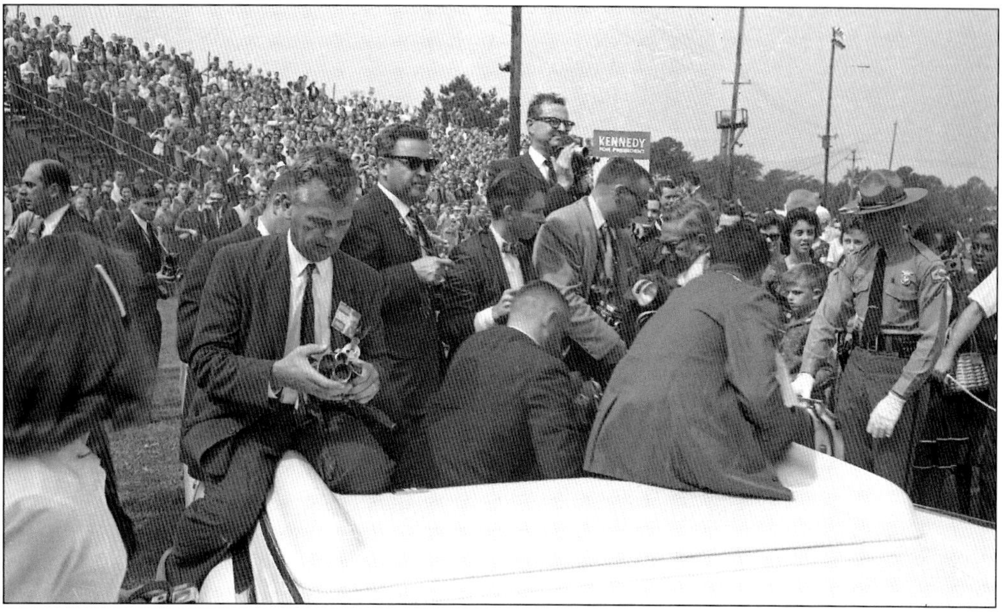

Photographers from the major newspapers in the state as well as members of the national press had squeezed into a Cadillac convertible. In the midst of them, wearing a bow tie, is Don Sturkey, senior photographer for the *Charlotte Observer.* (Courtesy of the *News and Observer* and the North Carolina State Archives.)

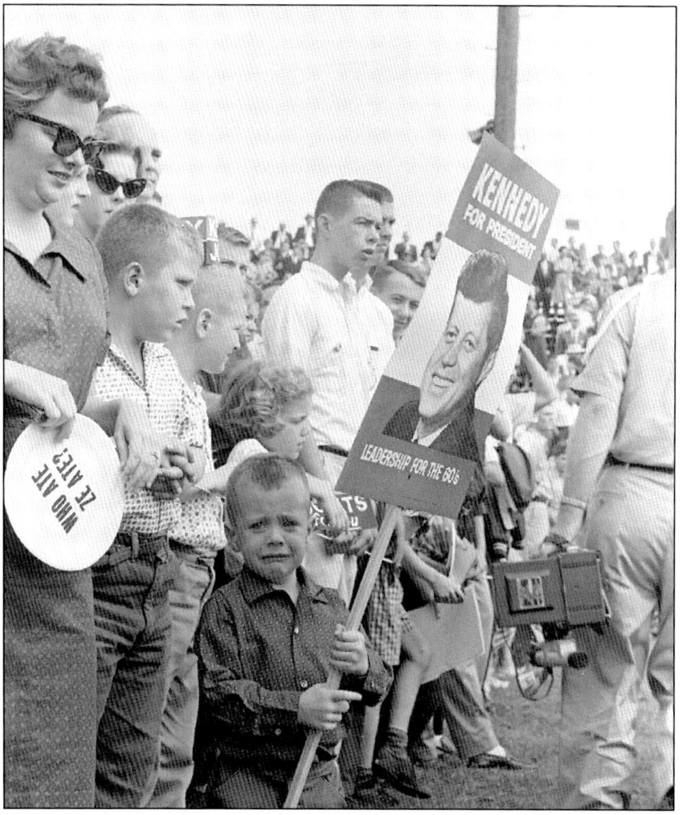

Louis Clark, grandson of John G. Clark, chair of the Pitt County Democratic Party, burst into tears upon seeing his grandfather exiting College Stadium without him. Louis apparently wanted to jump in the automobile with his granddad and Senator Kennedy. His mother, standing next to him in sunglasses, decided otherwise. (Photograph by Don Sturkey, Wilson Library, University of North Carolina.)

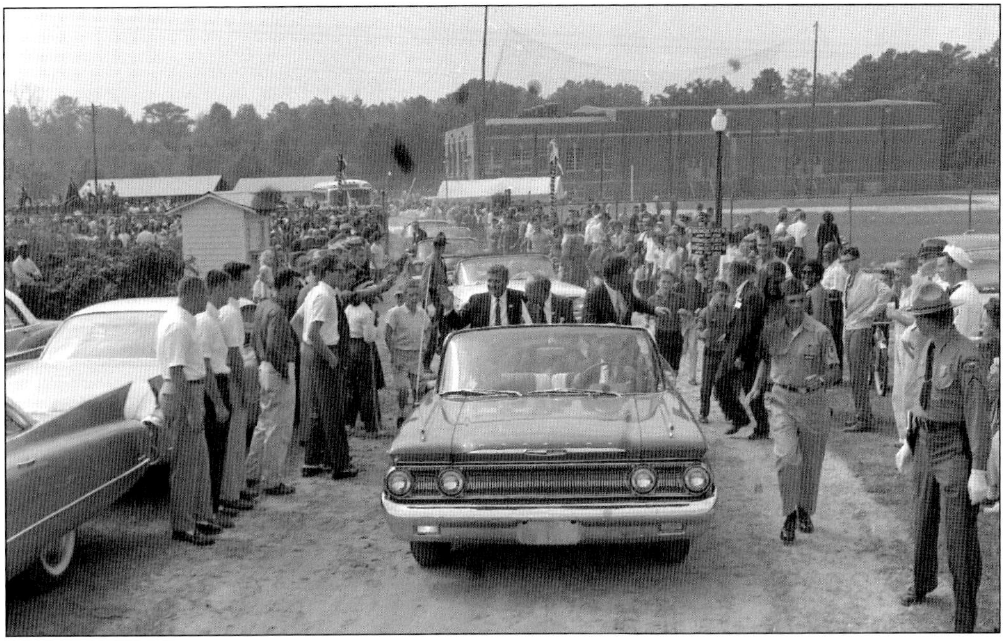

The Kennedy car leaves College Stadium heading for Fifth Street. In the background on the right is John B. Christenbury Memorial Gymnasium, built in 1952 and dedicated to Christenbury and all East Carolina alumni who died in World War II. (Courtesy of the *Daily Reflector* and J.Y. Joyner Library, East Carolina University.)

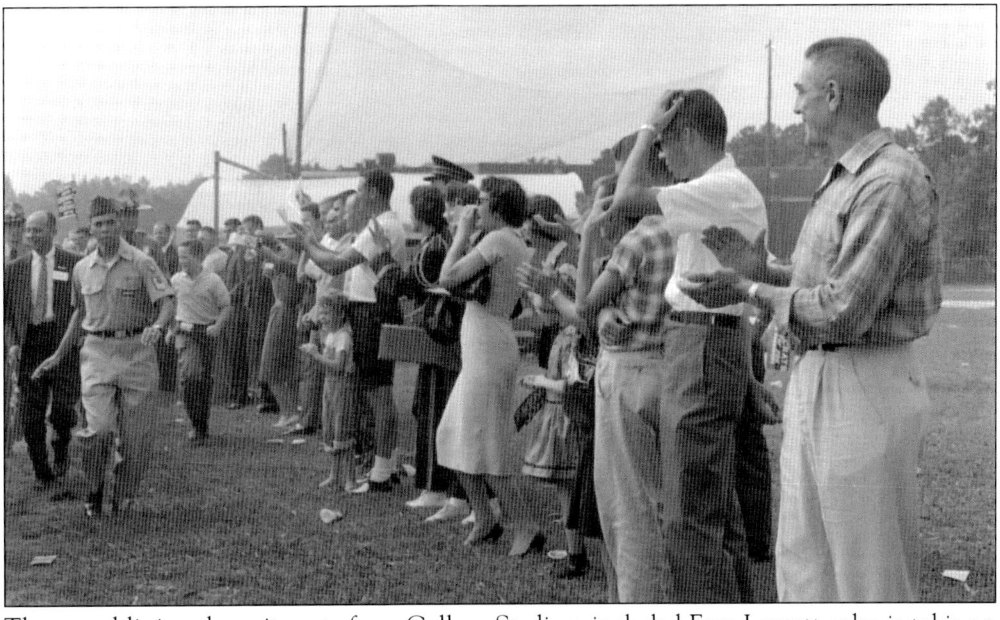

The crowd lining the exit route from College Stadium included Faye Leggett, who is taking a movie of the motorcade. Later, East Carolina alumnus Amy Leggett Brake identified her mother, her father Amos, her sisters, and herself in the photograph. Brake's sister Susan Leggett Hancock donated the Brownie movie camera and the video of Kennedy at College Stadium to the East Carolina University Archives. (Courtesy of the *Daily Reflector* and J.Y. Joyner Library, East Carolina University.)

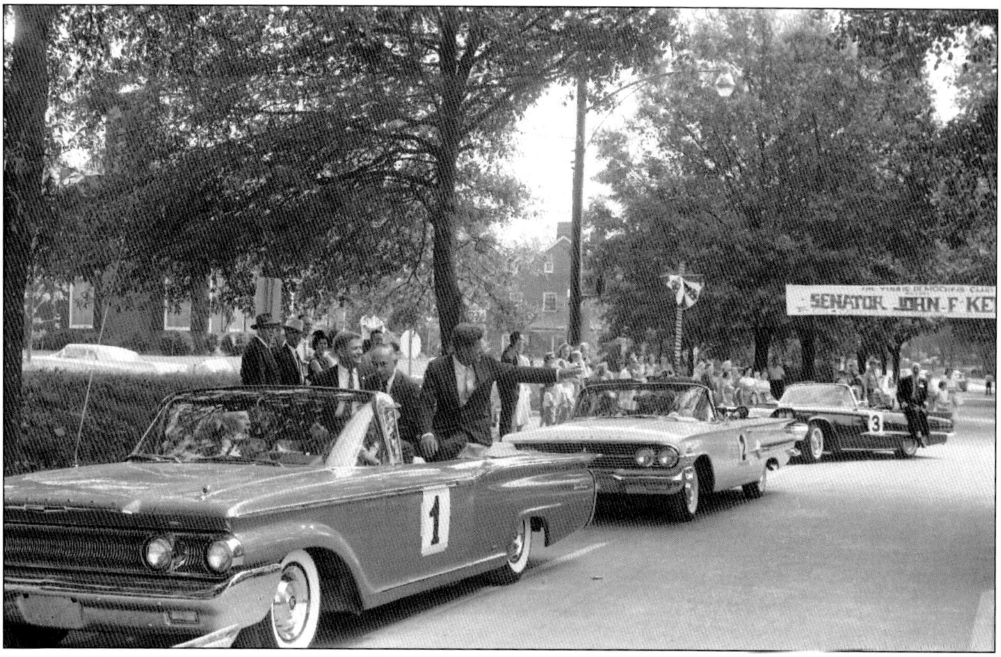

Senator Kennedy turns to wave goodbye as his car proceeds down Fifth Street toward the airport. The banner across Fifth Street reads, "The Young Democrats Club Welcomes Senator John F. Kennedy to East Carolina College." (Photograph by Hugh Morton; courtesy of Wilson Library, University of North Carolina.)

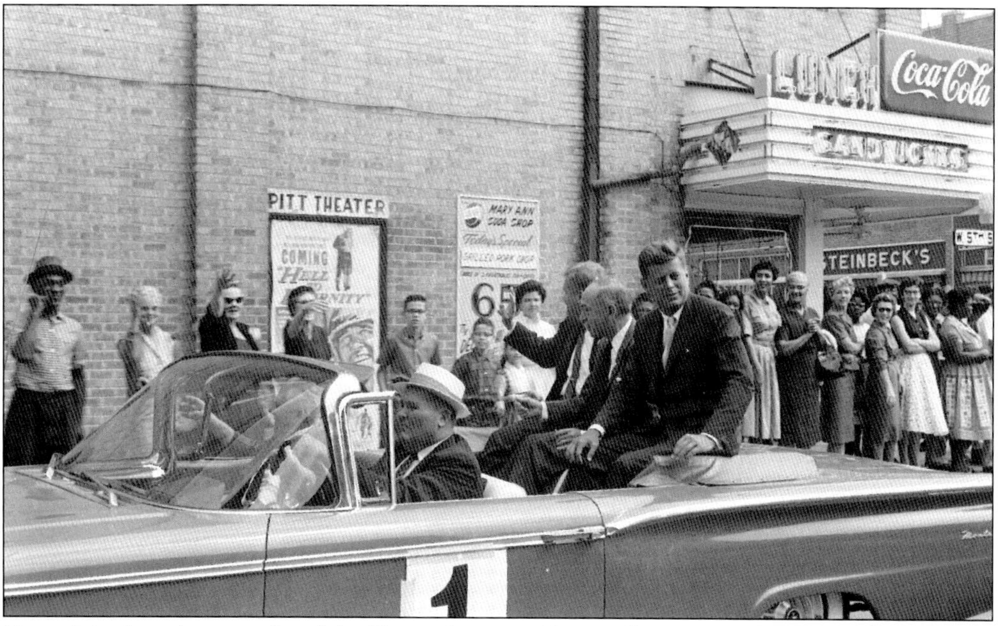

One of the last photographs of the Kennedy car in Greenville captures it passing through Five Points. Thereafter, the motorcade sped to the airport. The lady with clasped hands standing to the right of Senator Kennedy is Gladys Hagen Clark, one of the first African Americans to join St. Gabriel's Catholic Church in Greenville. Clark's daughter is to her right. (Photograph by Hugh Morton; courtesy of Wilson Library, University of North Carolina.)

Five

East Carolina College Stadium

Senator Kennedy's Greenville stop climaxed with the College Stadium rally. That Greenville and East Carolina were on the itinerary was in no small part due to the efforts of Dr. Leo W. Jenkins, president of East Carolina. Jenkins, a New Jersey native, wrote Kennedy in January 1960 inviting him to speak on campus. Kennedy declined, citing his decision to run for the presidency. Ironically, that decision was what later brought Kennedy to East Carolina.

More broadly, the Greenville stop resulted from a partnership between Terry Sanford and Jenkins in matters political and educational. The two became friends in 1950, when Jenkins helped Sanford stage a Young Democrats Club banquet in Wright Auditorium on the East Carolina campus. The keynote speaker was Vice Pres. Alben Barkley. Then US senator Frank Graham, Sanford's mentor at Chapel Hill, also attended. Barkley tacitly endorsed Graham's candidacy before the packed house of local Democrats. Appointed to the Senate by Gov. Kerr Scott, Graham ran in 1950 against conservative Willis Smith. Smith's campaign smeared Graham, suggesting that Graham was a communist and an advocate of the mixing of the races at a time when most North Carolinians were culturally and psychologically unprepared for this. Despite the efforts of Jenkins and Sanford on behalf of Graham, Smith won the primary.

A positive by-product of the banquet was the partnership between the New Jersey Democrat-turned-college president Dr. Leo Jenkins and the Fayetteville attorney with political aspirations, Terry Sanford. The two worked together during the 1950s with Jenkins often providing Sanford an on-campus forum for Democratic causes.

None were nearly so grand as the Kennedy rally at College Stadium. Sanford's prospects for election as governor were at stake. His speech seconding Kennedy's nomination at the Democratic National Convention made it imperative that he convince voters that Kennedy was their choice as well. Jenkins's prospects as president of East Carolina were also at stake. He knew that political connections could help him to grow East Carolina College into what it was becoming—a university serving eastern North Carolina. By successfully staging a rally on campus, Jenkins earned capital statewide as virtually every major Democratic office holder was present. This event was a coup for East Carolina and a signature statement of the Jenkins presidency.

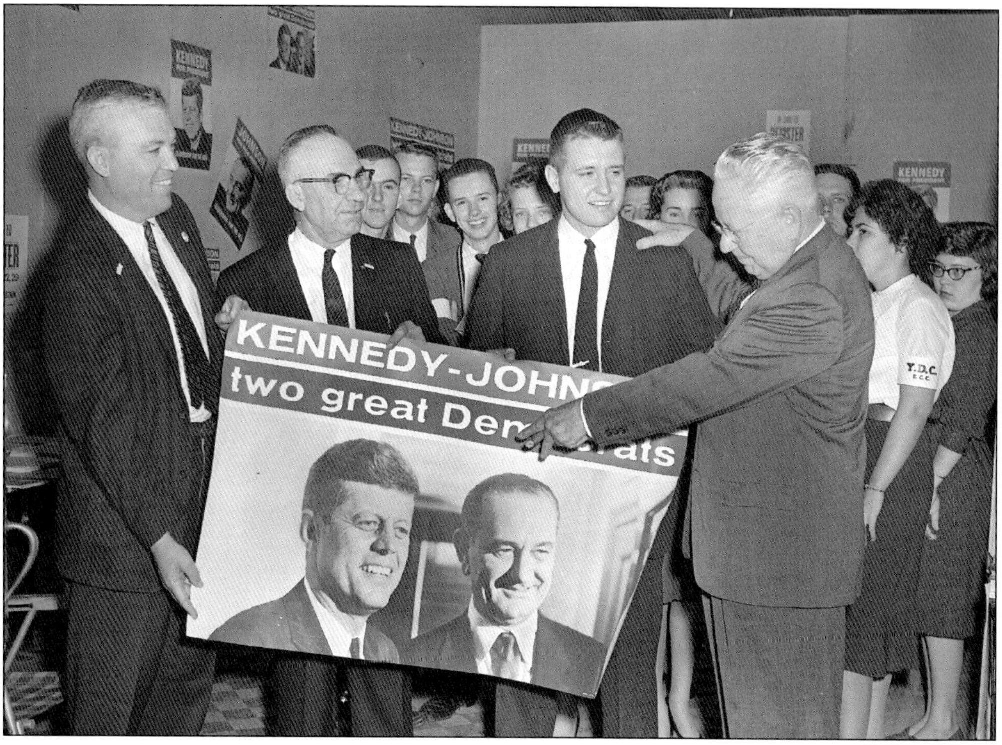

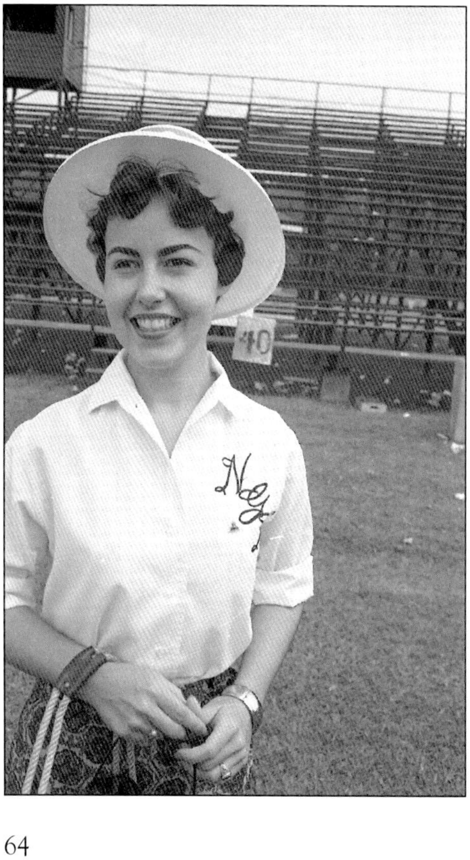

The Young Democrats Club at East Carolina College worked closely with John G. Clark, chair of the Pitt County Democratic Party and cochair, with Charles Horne, of the Eastern Carolina Kennedy Rally Planning Committee. Clark, with his trademark cigar, points to the Kennedy-Johnson banner that J.B. Spillman, his assistant, and Glenn Jernigan, vice president of the ECCYDC, are holding. (Courtesy of the *Daily Reflector*, J.Y. Joyner Library, East Carolina College.)

East Carolina College offered classes on Saturday mornings, making the Kennedy rally inconvenient for many students. Dr. Leo Jenkins made it clear to faculty and students that their time would be well spent at the rally, and many students decided to secure a good seat by arriving early. (Courtesy of the *News and Observer* and the North Carolina State Archives.)

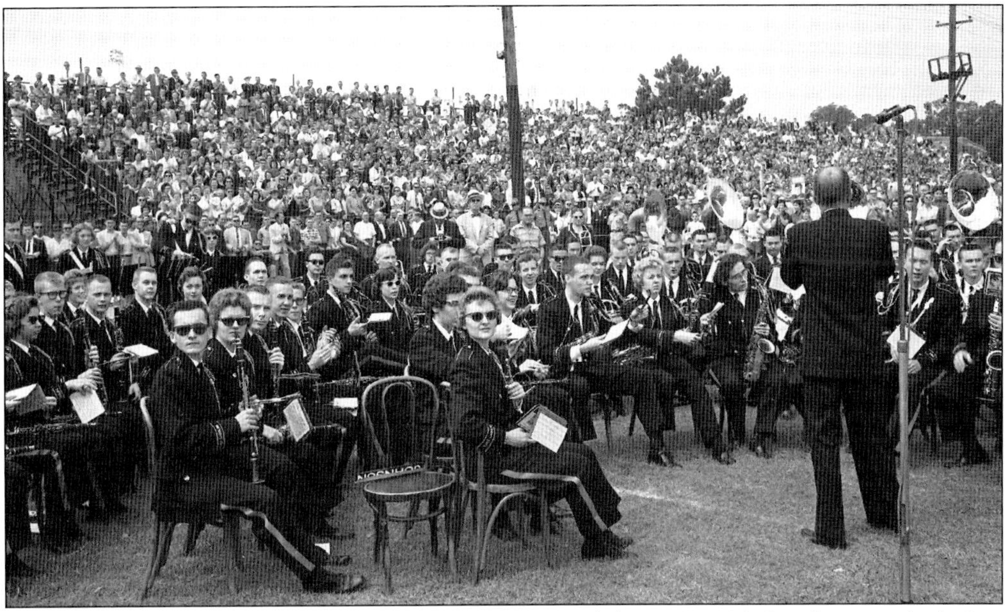

East Carolina band director Herbert L. Carter organized the 1960–1961 band just weeks before the Kennedy rally and began rehearsals for the band's first major event. As was common at the time, among the rousing tunes played before and after the rally was "Dixie." (Courtesy of the *News and Observer* and the North Carolina State Archives.)

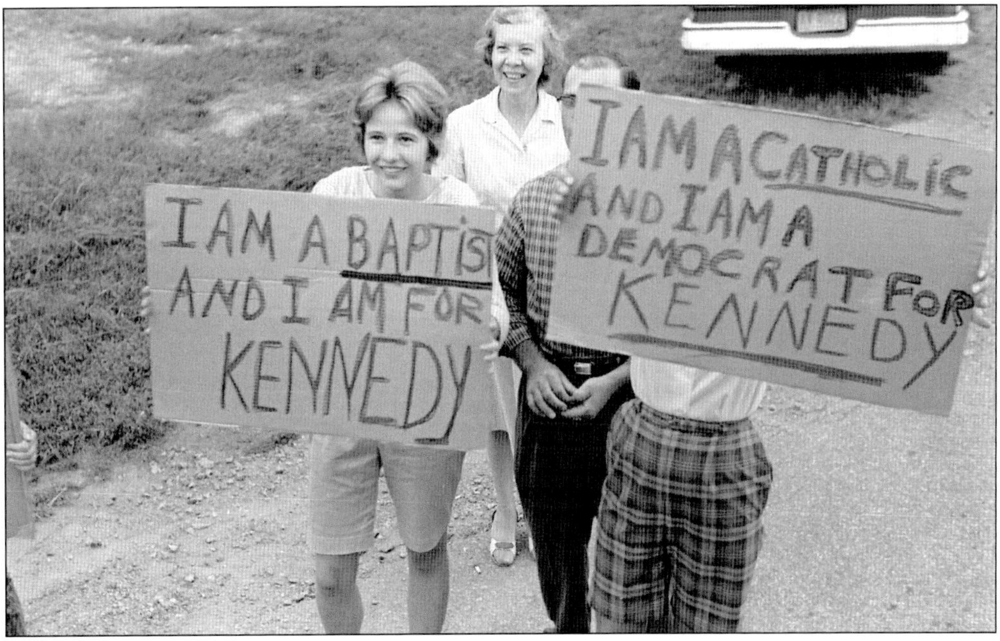

Before Kennedy, a Catholic had never been elected president of the United States. On September 13, just before his North Carolina campaign, Kennedy addressed the Greater Houston Ministerial Association. He made it clear to the Protestant clergy assembled that as president, his priorities would be America and the Constitution. The young people pictured show that regardless of the anti-Catholic rhetoric circulating, many transcended it. (Photograph by Don Sturkey, Wilson Library, University of North Carolina.)

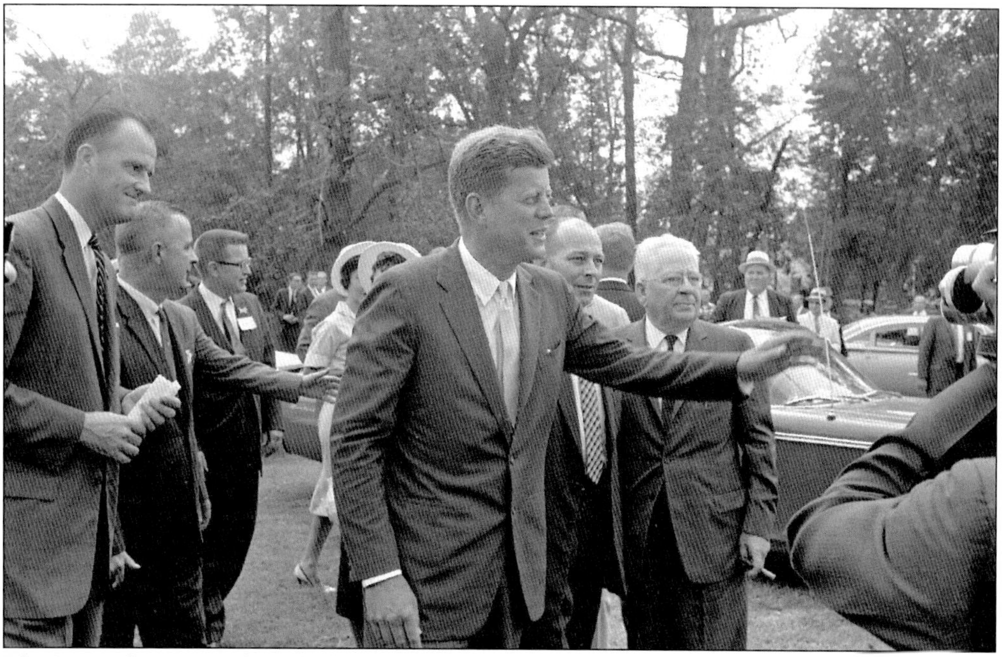

The Kennedy motorcade parked near Shady Lane on the east end of campus. Senator Kennedy was greeted by Dr. Leo Jenkins, president of East Carolina College. Here, Jenkins trails behind Kennedy with his arm extended out toward him. The tall man on the left is Louis Gaylord, a local attorney who served as the master of ceremonies at the rally. John G. Clark, with his trademark cigar in hand, looks toward the crowd. (Photograph by Don Sturkey, Wilson Library, University of North Carolina.)

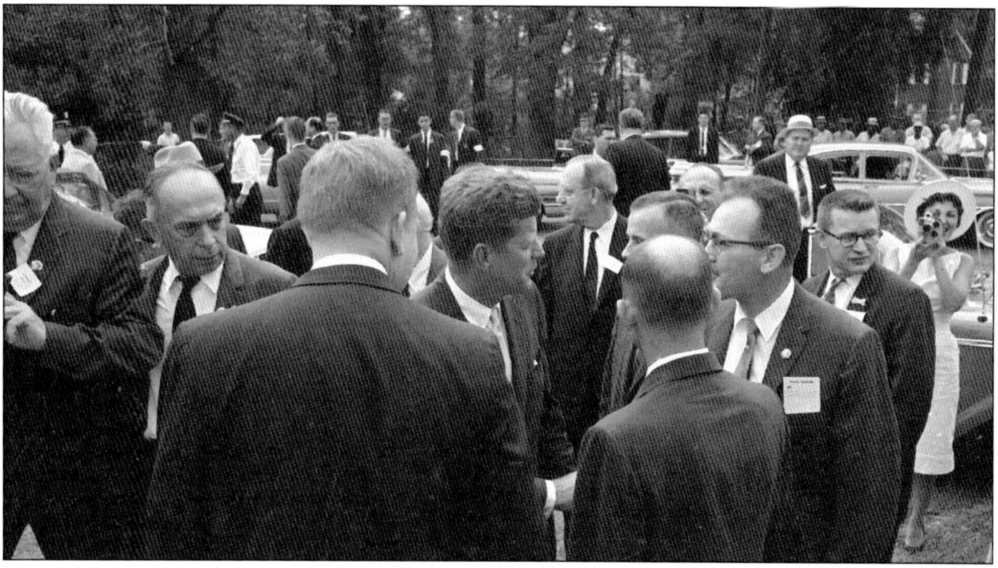

Here, Senator Kennedy meets some of his campus supporters before ascending the stage. From left to right are John G. Clark, Rep. Herbert Bonner, Terry Sanford, and Kennedy. The top of Jenkins's head is visible just behind the bald man standing in front of him. The bald man with his back to the camera is one of Kennedy's bodyguards. Earlier, he had been wearing a hat. (Courtesy of the *News and Observer* and the North Carolina State Archives.)

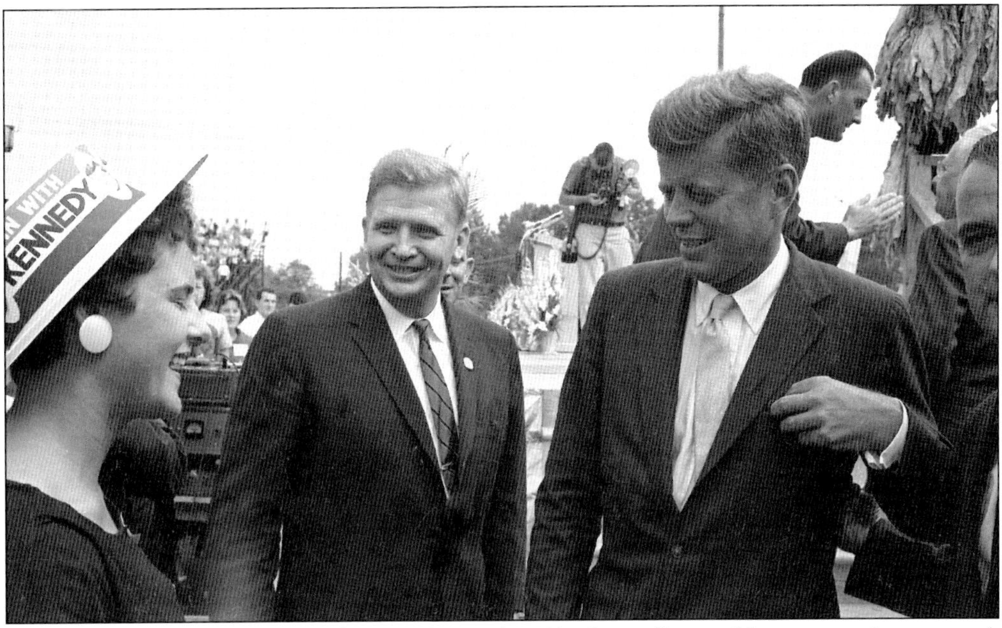

Terry Sanford wrote Dr. Leo Jenkins on September 14 asking if he could arrange to have a coed, Barbara Smith, meet Senator Kennedy before the rally. Smith's mother had helped Sanford with transportation arrangements and he wanted to return those favors with this one. Jenkins is partially pictured on the right. (Courtesy of the *News and Observer* and the North Carolina State Archives.)

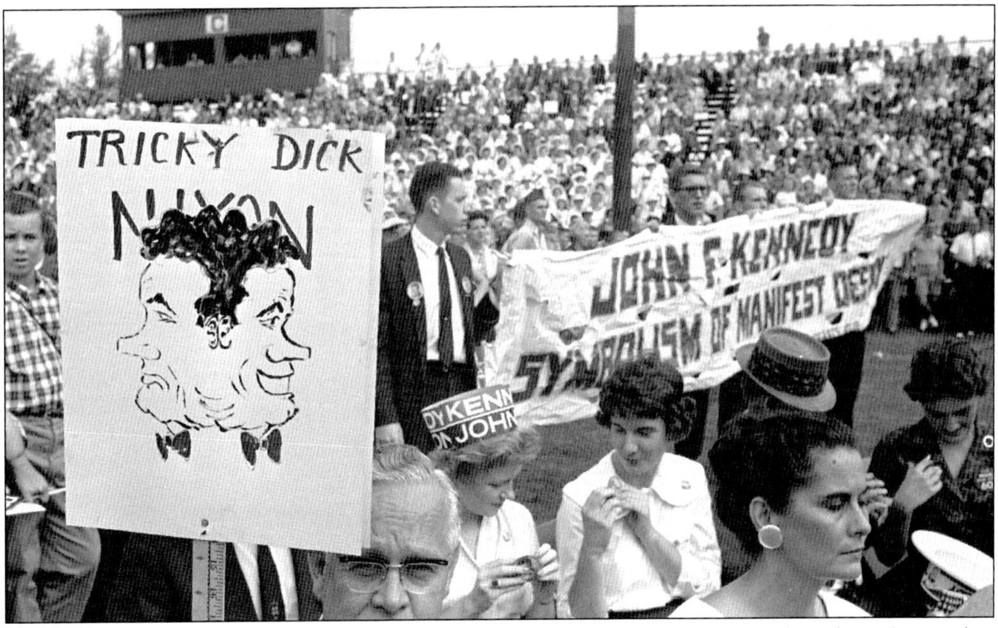

Apart from this man's sign reading, on one side, "Tricky Dick Nixon," and on the other, "Remember Hoover," anti-Republican politicking was not conspicuous. The Young Democrats Club banner read, "John F. Kennedy Symbolism of Manifest Destiny." The YDC also made a banner stretching across Fifth Street welcoming Senator Kennedy to East Carolina. (Photograph by Don Sturkey, Wilson Library, University of North Carolina.)

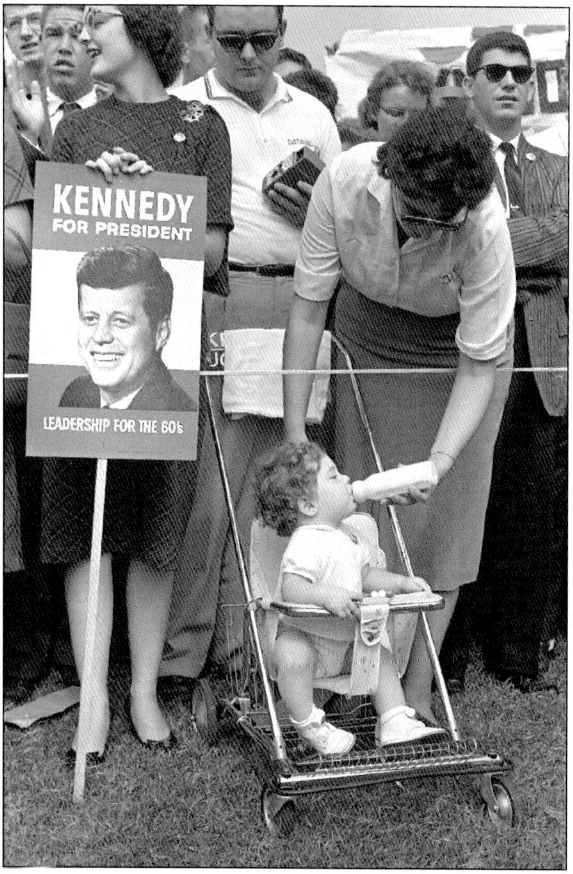

Supporters of all ages attended. In addition to the baby in the carriage, a professor of business at East Carolina College, Dr. James Bearden, stands with arms folded, wearing sunglasses. Dr. Bearden, like many East Carolina faculty, met briefly with his Saturday class, but then adjourned to attend the rally. (Photograph by Don Sturkey, Wilson Library, University of North Carolina.)

On the platform, Senator Kennedy greeted a young boy. To Kennedy's left is Terry Sanford. Right of Kennedy are Sen. Sam Ervin and Sen. B. Everett Jordan, Kennedy's colleagues from North Carolina in the Senate. Their presence helped make evident North Carolina's Democratic solidarity in support of Kennedy. (Courtesy of the *Daily Reflector*, J.Y. Joyner Library, East Carolina University.)

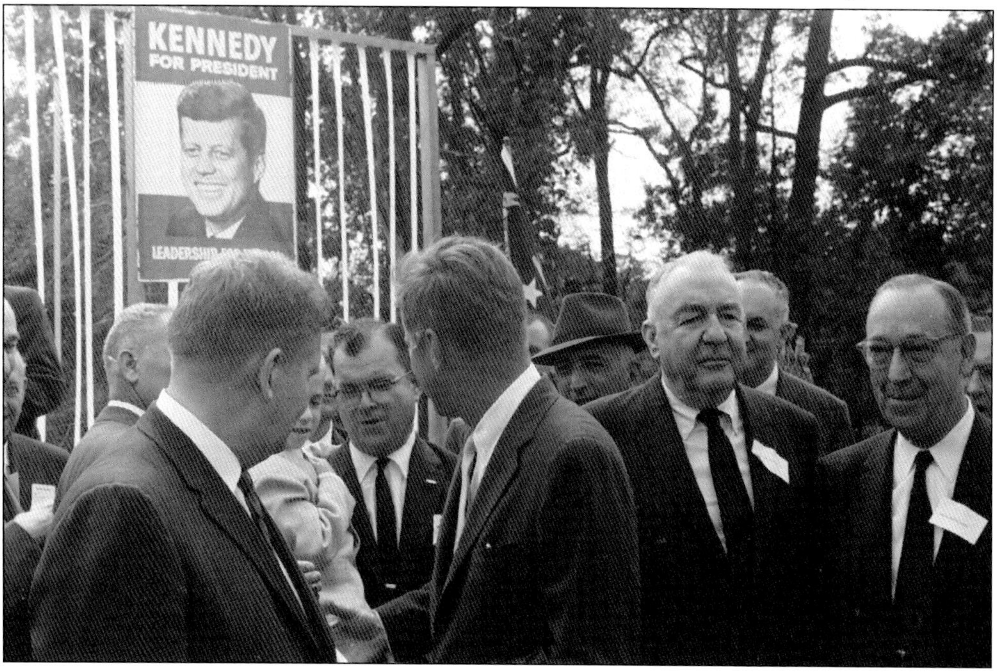

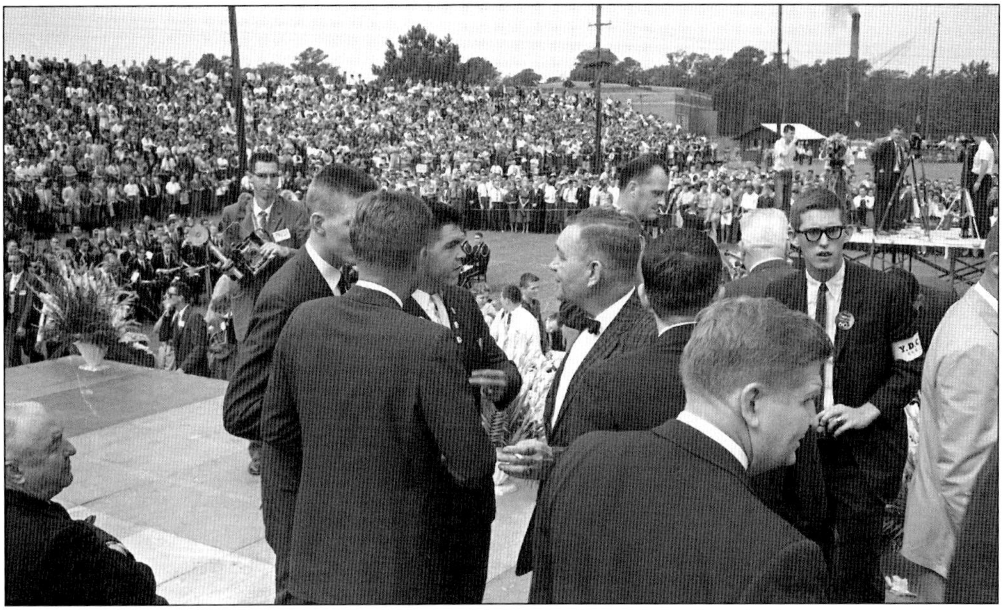

Select members of the Young Democrats Club were allowed on the platform to meet Senator Kennedy briefly before the rally began. Kennedy has his back turned to the camera in the lower central part of the photograph. In the lower left-hand corner is Sen. Sam J. Ervin. In the right corner, Sanford speaks with a YDC member. (Courtesy of the *News and Observer* and the North Carolina State Archives.)

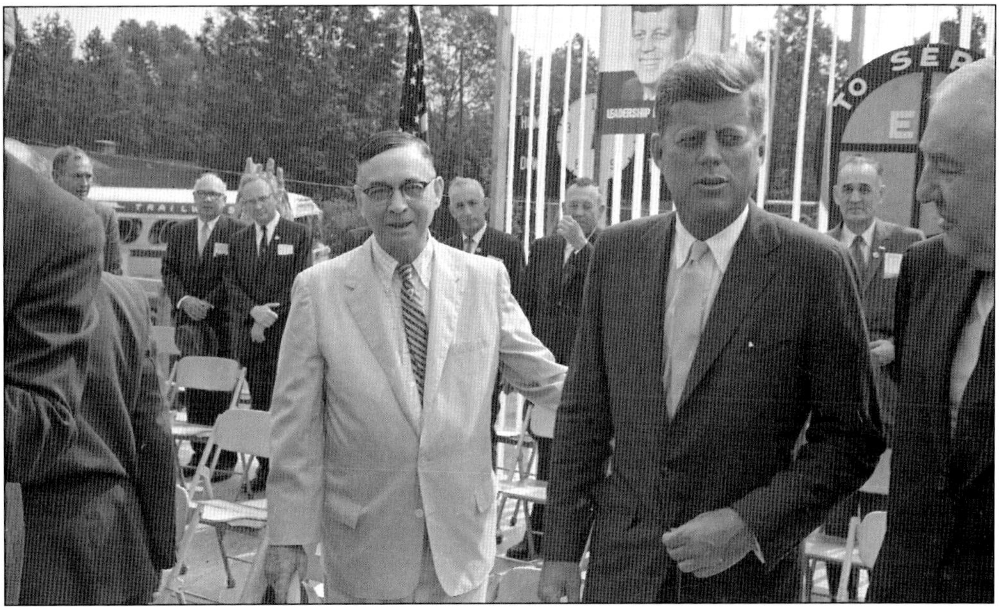

The importance of the tobacco industry for eastern North Carolina and the Democratic Party was very evident at the rally. J. Con Lanier, in the white suit, helped the Roosevelt administration develop the national tobacco program to ensure price stability and controlled production of the crop. Lanier later served as counsel for the Tobacco Association of the United States, executive secretary of the Leaf Tobacco Exporters Association, and counsel for the Leaf Tobacco Exporters Association. (Courtesy of the *Daily Reflector*, J.Y. Joyner Library, East Carolina University.)

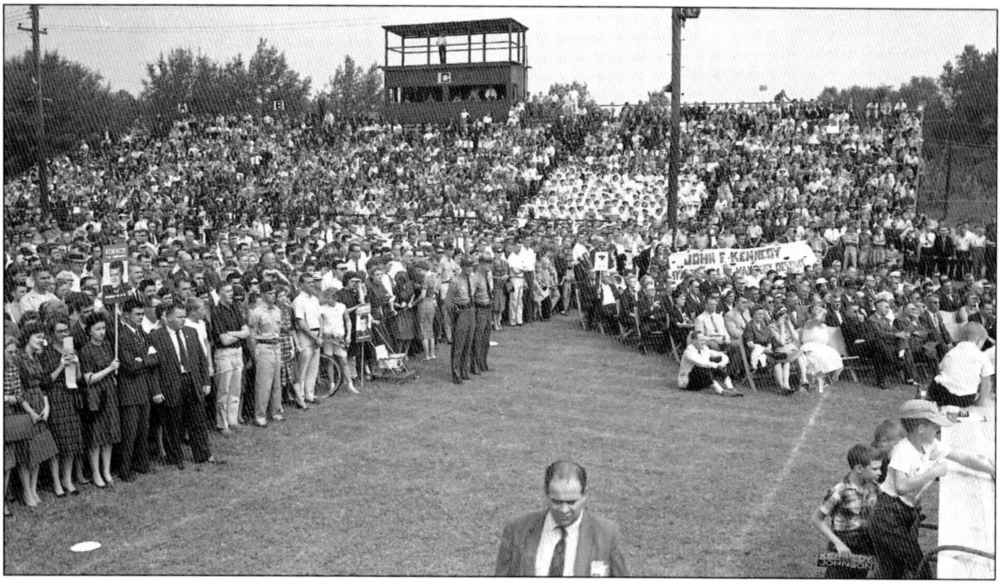

East Carolina College Stadium in 1960 was a modest facility. In an oral interview for the Kennedy Presidential Library, the Kennedy advance man for the Greenville rally, Edward A. Dragon, recalled his work in Greenville. In the interview, Dragon mistakenly said the Greenville rally was at a "high school stadium." (Courtesy of the *News and Observer* and the North Carolina State Archives.)

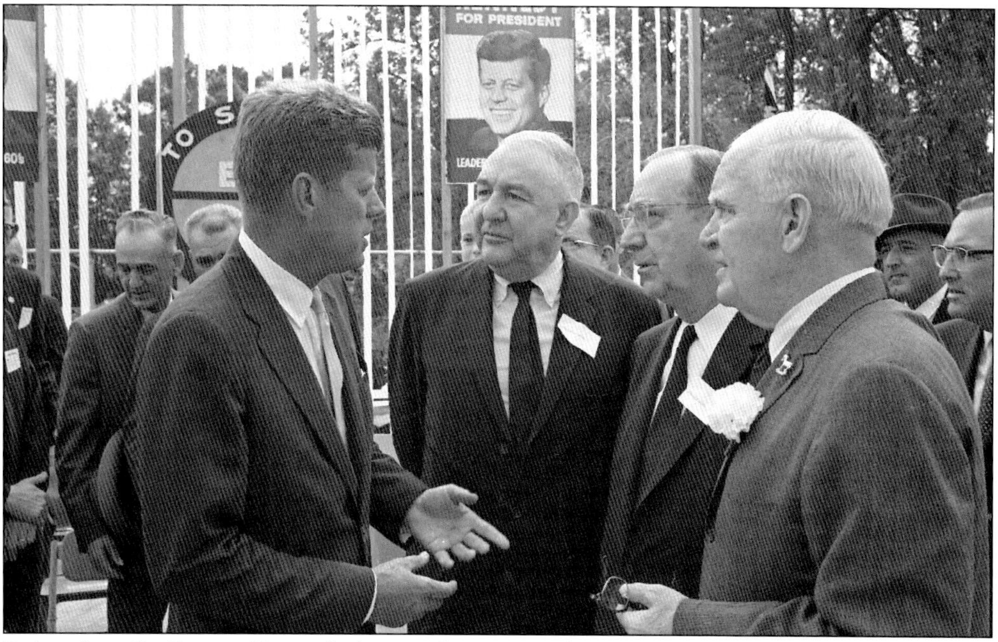

Before the rally, Senator Kennedy discussed matters with Sen. Sam Ervin, Sen. B. Everett Jordan, and Gov. Luther H. Hodges, North Carolina's most powerful politicians. Eastern North Carolina was hardly accustomed to having them gather simultaneously. To the right of Hodges and wearing glasses is Rev. Floyd B. Cherry, senior clergyman at Black Jack Free Will Baptist Church. Cherry opened the rally with an invocation. (Courtesy of the *News and Observer* and the North Carolina State Archives.)

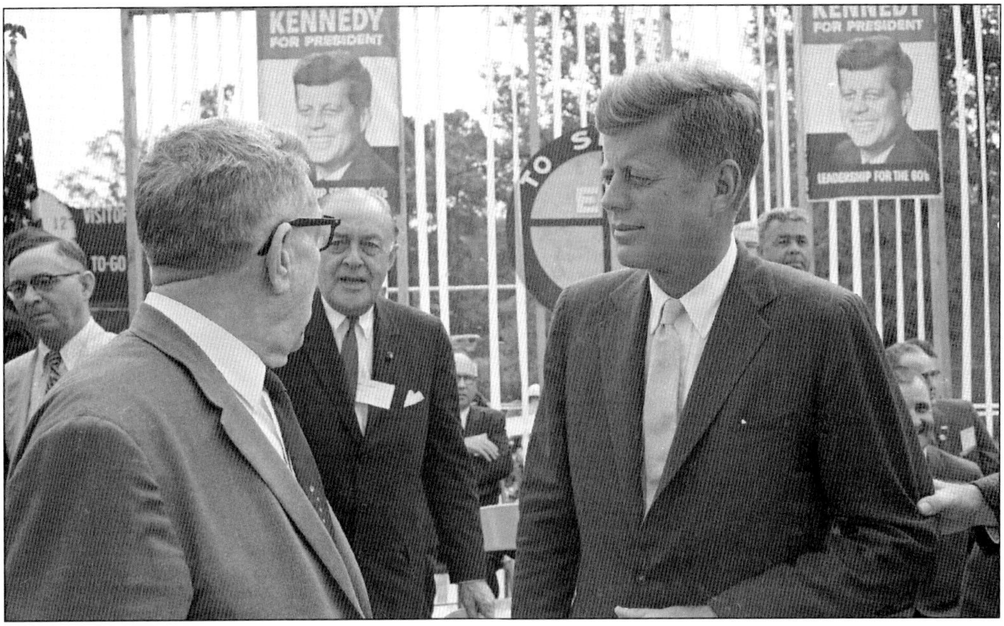

As Senator Kennedy spoke with a representative of the tobacco industry, Rep. Harold D. Cooley, chair of the House Agriculture Committee, approached. Cooley, a native of Nashville, North Carolina, had served as a congressman since 1934 and was instrumental in defining the national farm program. In the white suit is J. Con Lanier, a leading representative of the tobacco industry. (Courtesy of the *News and Observer* and the North Carolina State Archives.)

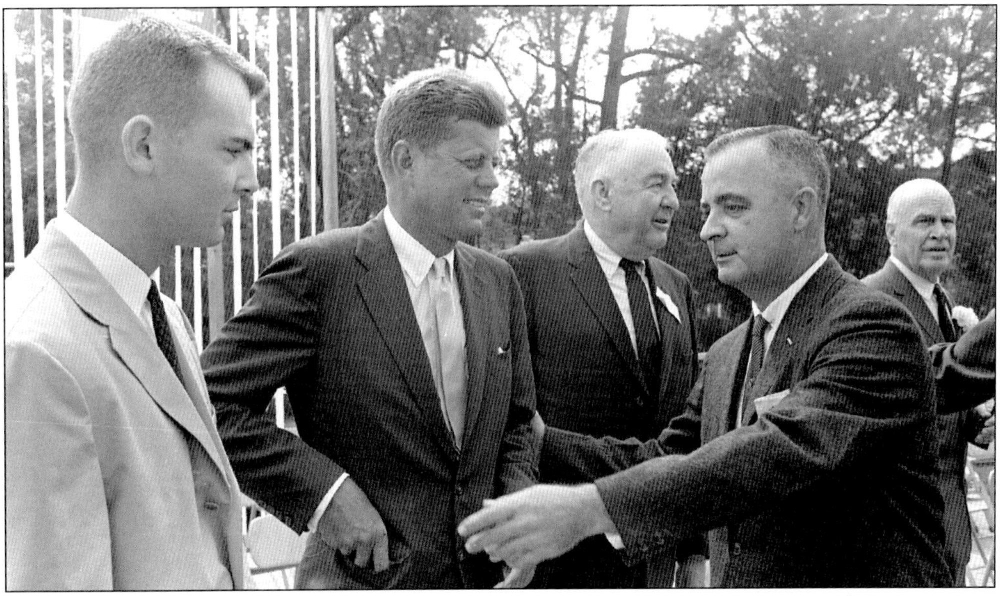

Dr. Leo W. Jenkins, president of East Carolina College, first invited Senator Kennedy to campus in January 1960, shortly after Kennedy had given a talk at Duke University. Here, Jenkins introduces Kennedy to James Speight, president of the East Carolina Student Government Association. Between Kennedy and Jenkins is Sen. Sam Ervin. Right of Jenkins is Gov. Luther H. Hodges. Jenkins's energetic nature is evident in this photograph. (Photograph by Don Sturkey, Wilson Library, University of North Carolina.)

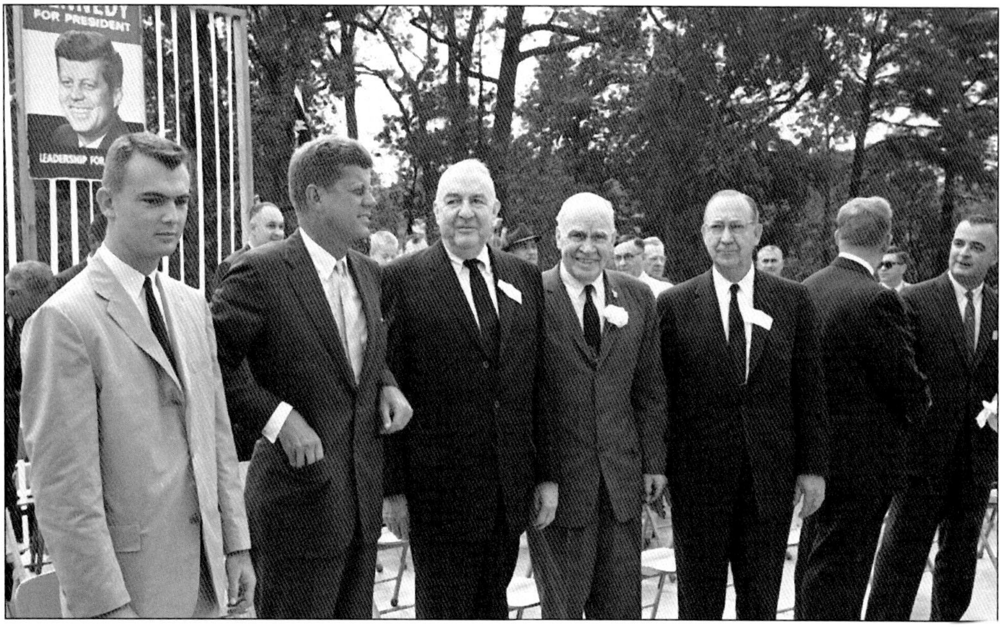

Before the rally began, the major political figures posed for a photograph. From left to right are James Speight (East Carolina Student Government Association president), Kennedy, Sen. Sam Ervin, Gov. Luther H. Hodges, and Sen. B. Everett Jordan. Terry Sanford and Dr. Leo W. Jenkins chat together at right, renewing a long friendship grounded in Democratic Party politics. (Courtesy of the *News and Observer* and the North Carolina State Archives.)

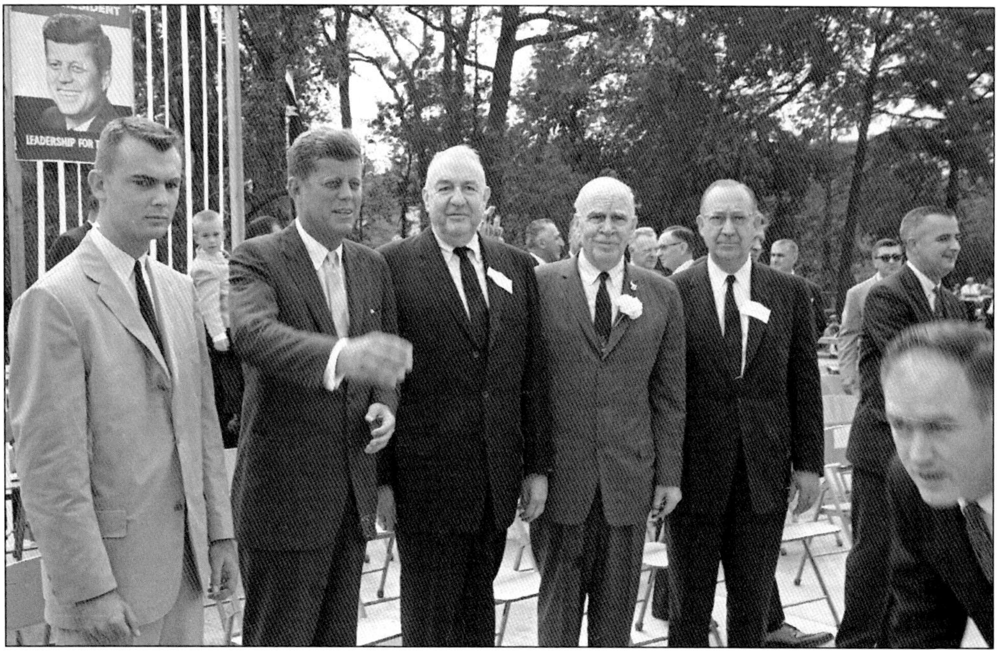

In a light moment, Senator Kennedy motions to Farmville attorney and Democratic Party supporter Robert Rouse to join the picture. Rouse served on the Eastern Carolina Kennedy Rally Planning Committee as director of arrangements for dignitaries. (Courtesy of the *News and Observer* and the North Carolina State Archives.)

This photograph by Roy Hardee was donated to East Carolina University in 2010 along with Hardees's papers and negatives, which covered his half-century career in journalism in eastern North Carolina. Most likely the hand on Kennedy's elbow belonged to Dr. Leo Jenkins, who was about to introduce Kennedy to another representative of East Carolina. (Courtesy of the *Daily Reflector* and J.Y. Joyner Library, East Carolina University.)

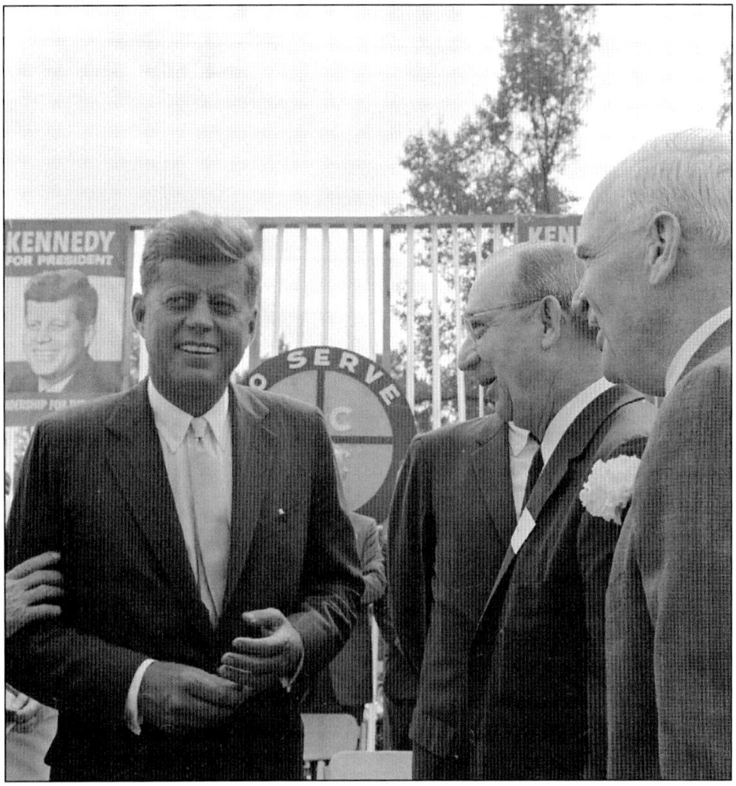

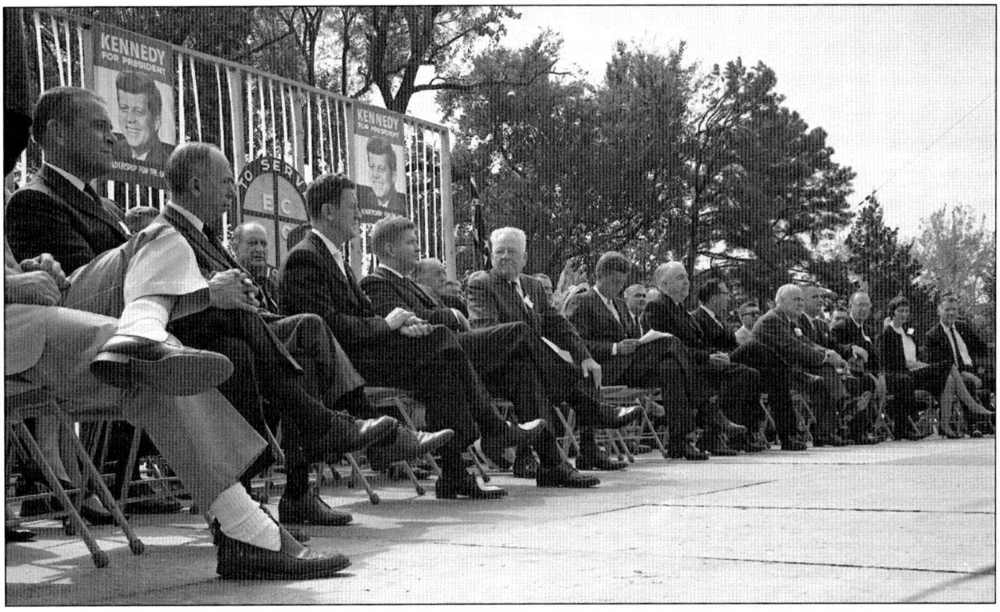

With dignitaries seated on the platform, the rally was ready to begin. From the left are Cloyd Philpott (Democratic nominee for lieutenant governor), Rep. Herbert C. Bonner, Rep. L.H. Fountain, Terry Sanford, John G. Clark, Senator Kennedy, Sen. Sam Ervin, Rev. Floyd B. Cherry, Gov. Luther H. Hodges, Dr. Leo W. Jenkins, Sen. B. Everett Jordan, Martha C. McKay (a leading Democratic feminist), and unidentified. (Courtesy of the *News and Observer* and the North Carolina State Archives.)

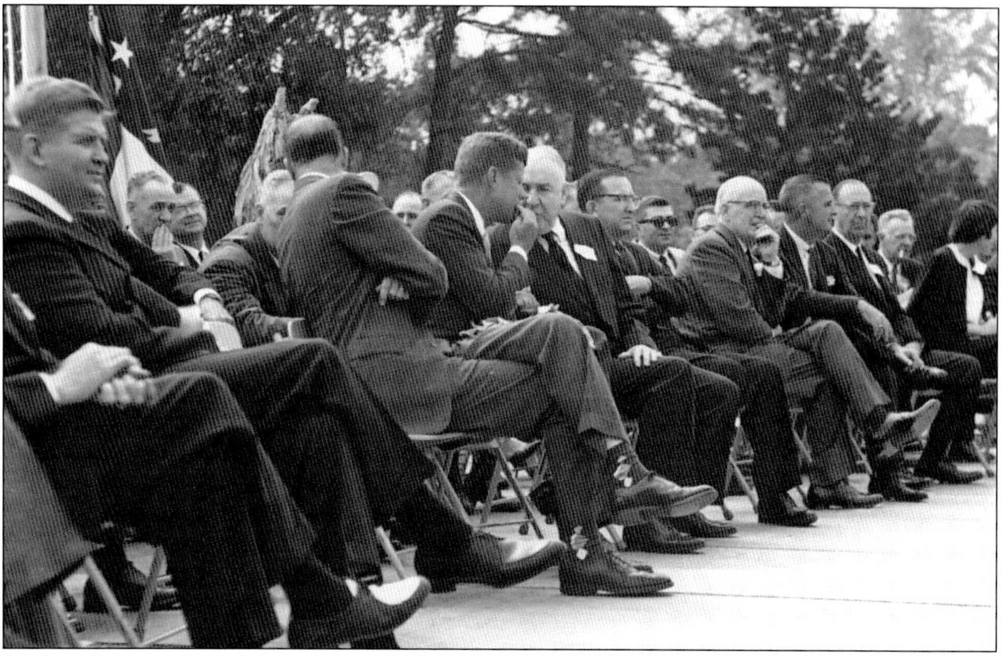

In this close-up, from left to right, Terry Sanford gazes thoughtfully at the crowd; Greenville attorney Louis Gaylord, master of ceremonies for the rally, has turned to speak to someone; Senator Kennedy chats with Sen. Sam Ervin; and Rev. Floyd B. Cherry looks out on the crowd, as does Gov. Luther H. Hodges beside him. Dr. Leo W. Jenkins and Sen. B. Everett Jordan are conversing briefly. (Courtesy of the *News and Observer* and the North Carolina State Archives.)

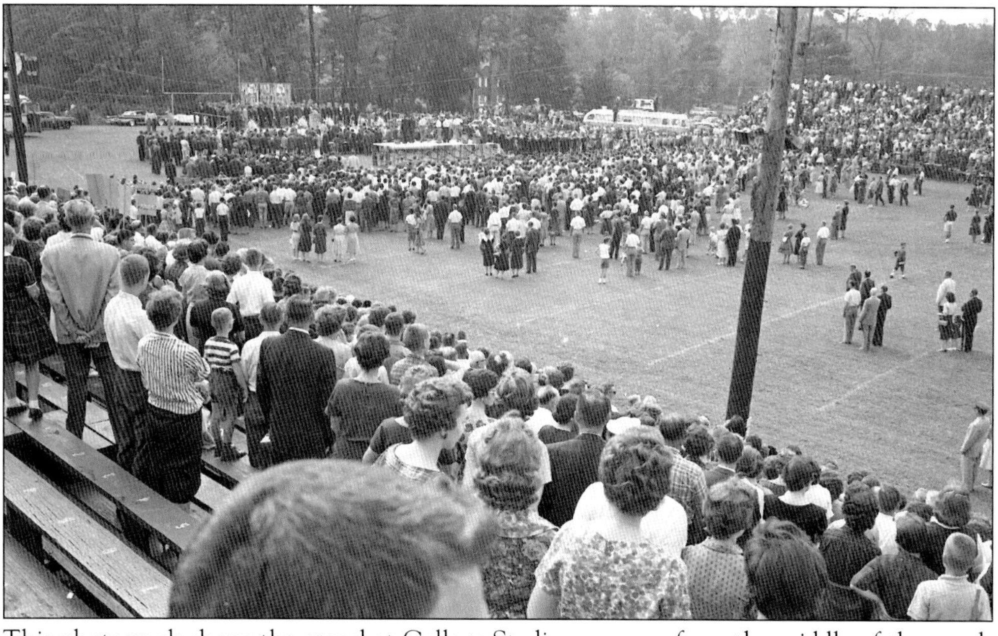

This photograph shows the crowd at College Stadium as seen from the middle of the north bleachers. Estimates vary, but the turnout fell short of the 25,000 predicted earlier in the week. Hurricane Donna's impact just a few days before the rally surely dampened some of the enthusiasm. (Courtesy of the *News and Observer* and the North Carolina State Archives.)

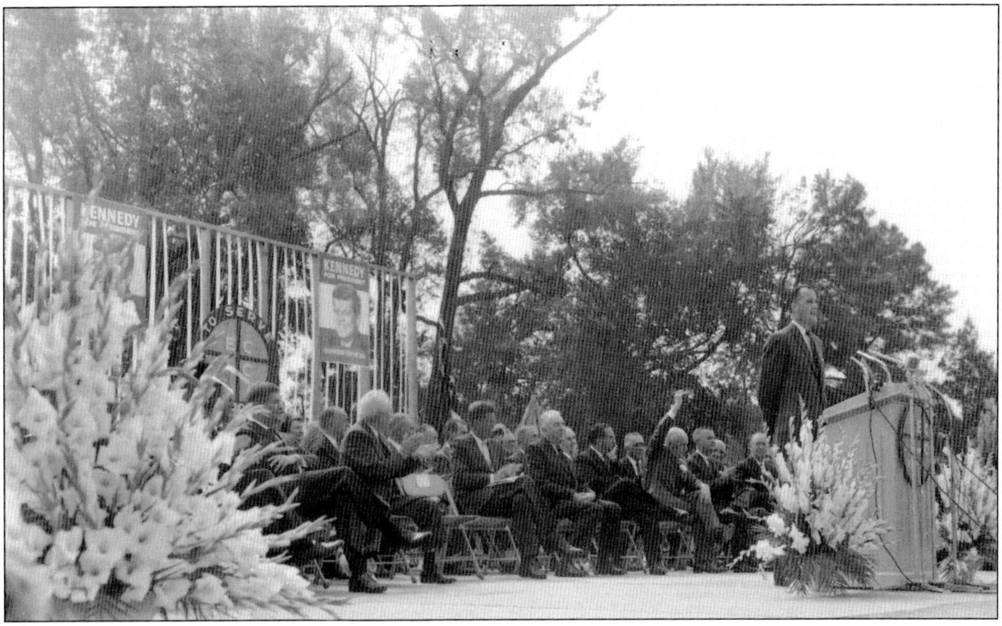

Louis W. Gaylord Jr., one of Greenville's most respected attorneys, addresses the College Stadium audience as master of ceremonies. Gaylord, as an old friend of Terry Sanford, agreed to chair Sanford's campaign in Pitt County. The close ties between Sanford and Senator Kennedy prompted Gaylord's selection for the honors that day. (Courtesy of the *Daily Reflector* and J.Y. Joyner Library, East Carolina University.)

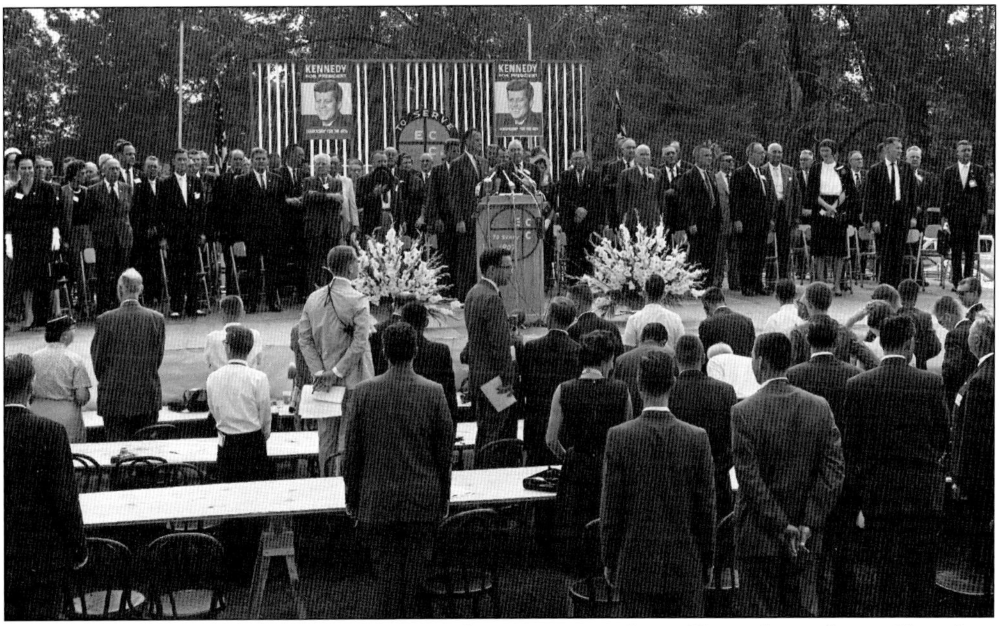

Sen. Sam J. Ervin introduced Senator Kennedy, reiterating a theme Kennedy emphasized less than a week before to the Houston Ministerial Association on September 12: as president, Kennedy would continue to demonstrate "true faith and allegiance" to his country and "to all Americans of all creeds and all races." (Courtesy of the *Daily Reflector* and J.Y. Joyner Library, East Carolina University.)

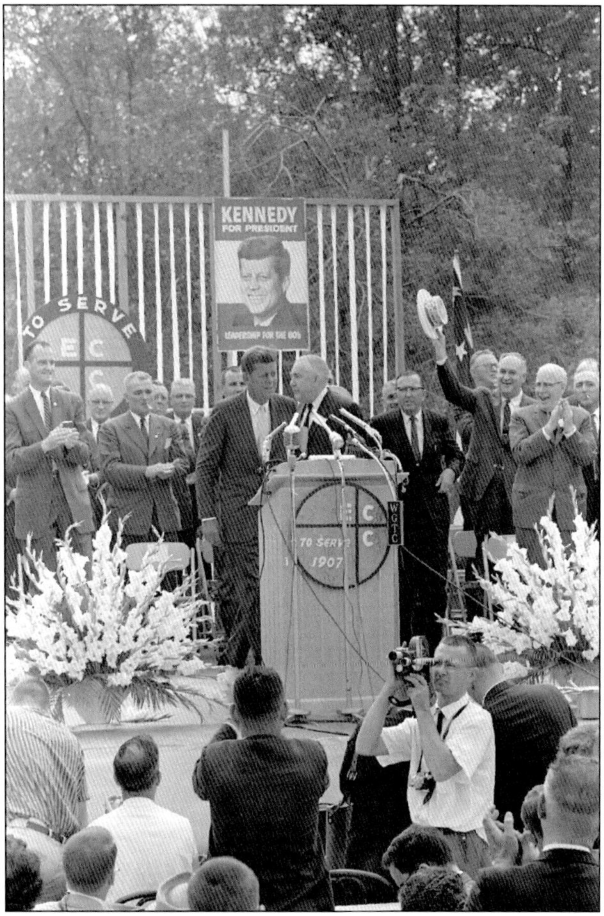

Senator Kennedy's remarks at College Stadium were brief. In just over 1,000 words, he highlighted the region's historic character, wished the college well on its bid to enter the Southern Conference, touted the strengths of the Democratic Party and its distinguished legacy, lambasted Republicans and their disregard for farmers, and extolled the blessings of freedom provided in the US Constitution. (Photograph by Don Sturkey, Wilson Library, University of North Carolina.)

At the podium, Senator Kennedy quickly won the crowd with his flattering line, "I come here today from a section of the United States which claims to be the oldest section of the United States, to North Carolina, which is the oldest section of the United States." Applause followed. (Courtesy of the *News and Observer* and the North Carolina State Archives.)

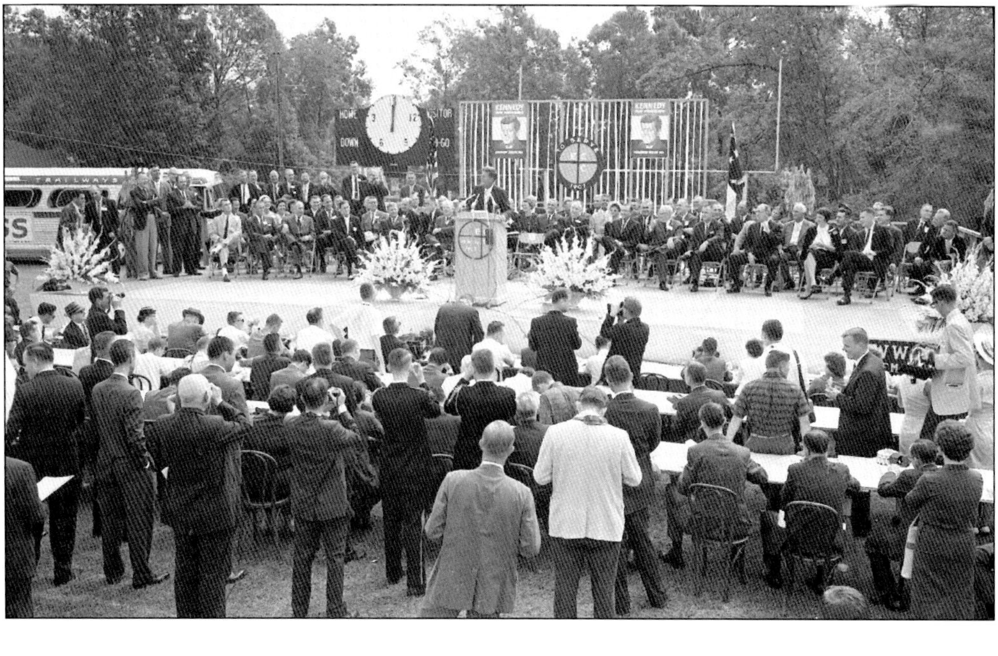

Senator Kennedy also thanked East Carolina for hosting the rally, but mistakenly called it "Eastern Carolina College." He next praised the college for its rapid growth and aspirations of joining the Southern Conference. Kennedy added that he, too, was "scheduled in the Southern Conference." He wished the college well and expressed his hope that he would have similar good fortune. (Photograph by Don Sturkey, Wilson Library, University of North Carolina.)

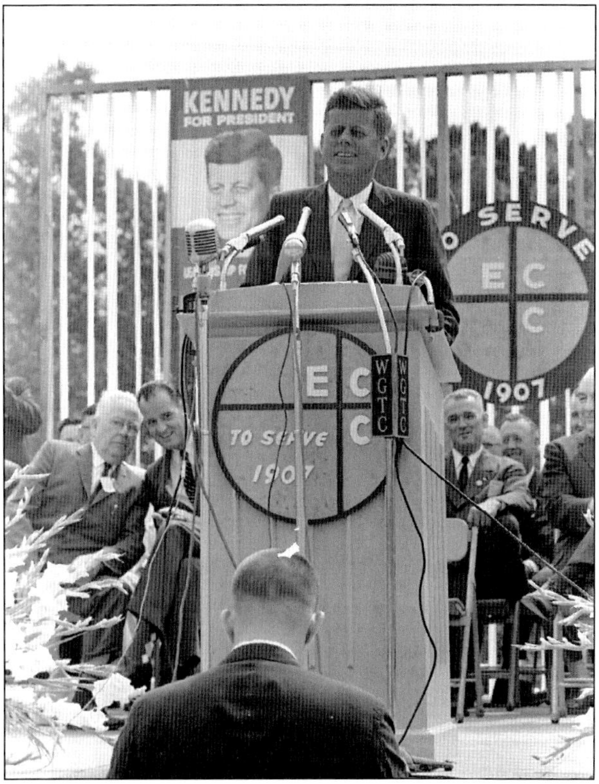

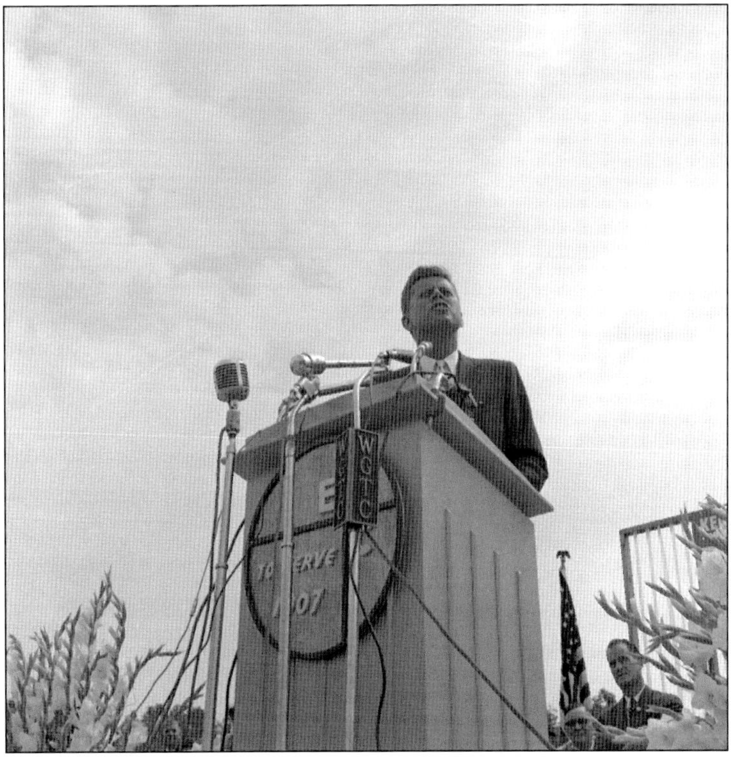

Even before Senator Kennedy left Greenville, clouds were gathering in the sky, remnants of Hurricane Donna. (Courtesy of the *Daily Reflector* and J.Y. Joyner Library, East Carolina University.)

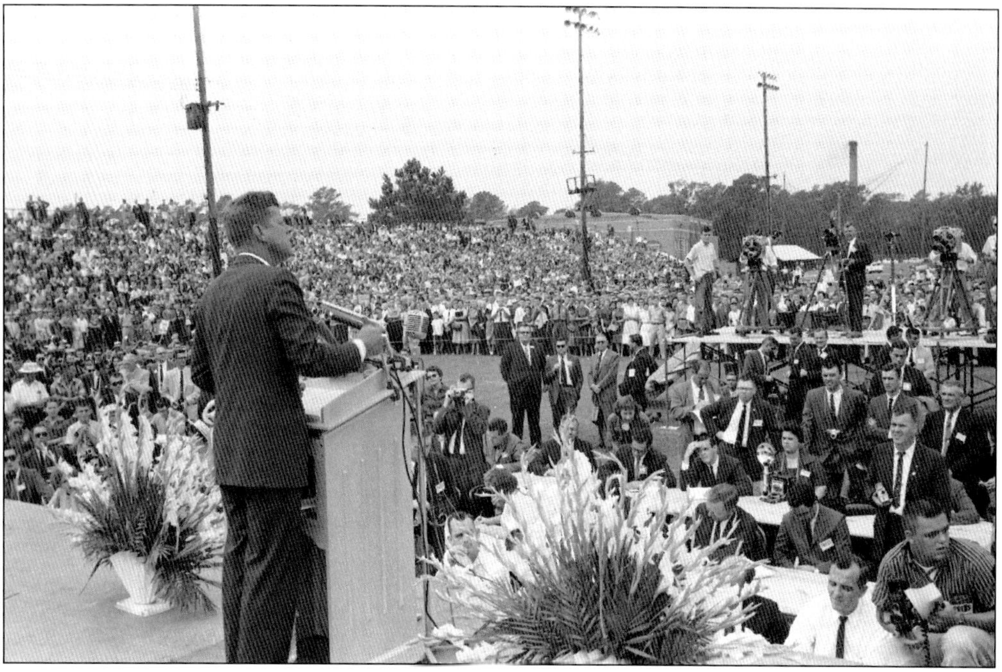

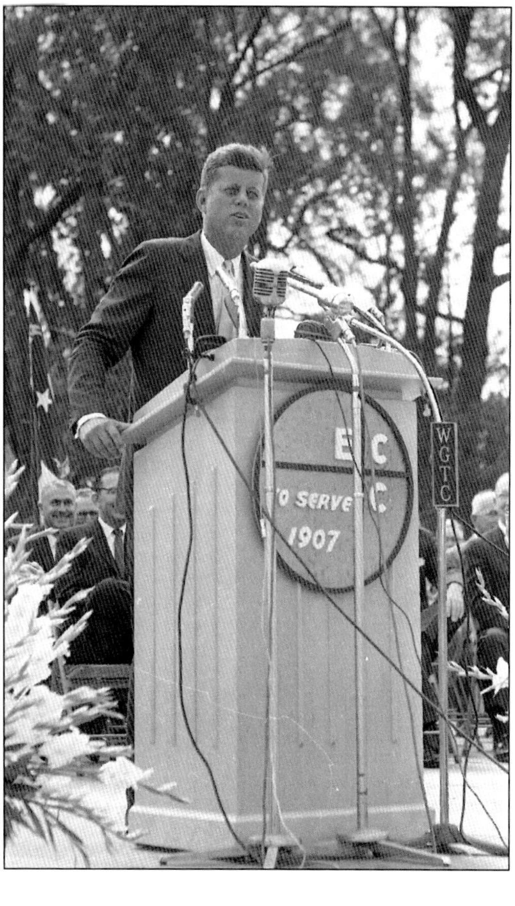

Assembled in front of Senator Kennedy were over 100 journalists, including videographers from various national, state, and local television stations and networks; news reporters typing out their stories; and dozens of newspaper and press photographers. (Photograph by Hugh Morton, Courtesy of Wilson Library, University of North Carolina.)

Senator Kennedy noted North Carolina's distinguished contributions to the Democratic Party which, though founded by Virginia, had been given "its modern form as the party of the people by a great citizen of this state, Andrew Jackson." (Courtesy of the *News and Observer* and the North Carolina State Archives.)

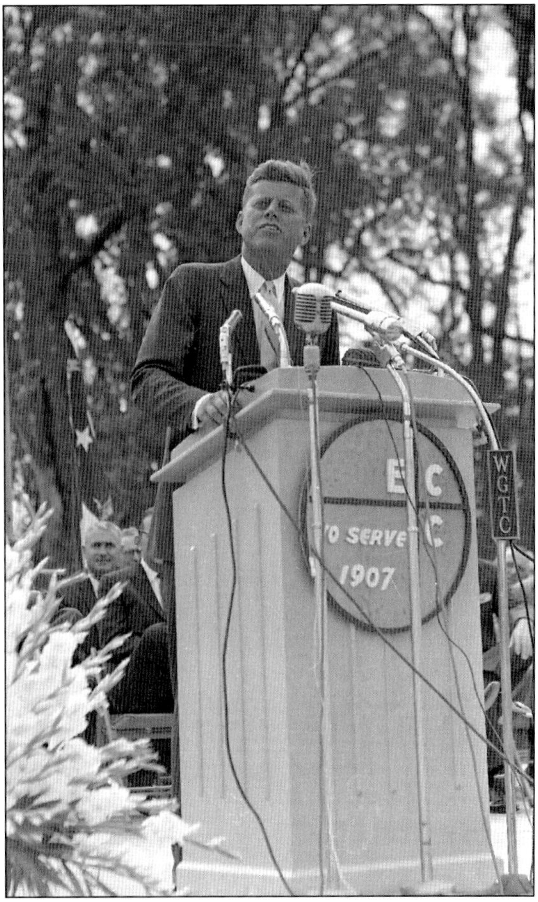

Senator Kennedy's North Carolina campaign coincided with Constitution Day, a national holiday celebrating the date on which George Washington sent the Constitution to be ratified by the states. By reiterating his respect for the Constitution, Kennedy reminded North Carolinians of his sworn and loyal dedication to its principles. (Courtesy of the *News and Observer* and the North Carolina State Archives.)

Senator Kennedy's call for greater American power and prestige internationally was tied to his vision of a strong farm program for the future. Specifically, through federal programs promoting international peace, Kennedy wanted more American food provided to the world. (Courtesy of the *News and Observer* and the North Carolina State Archives.)

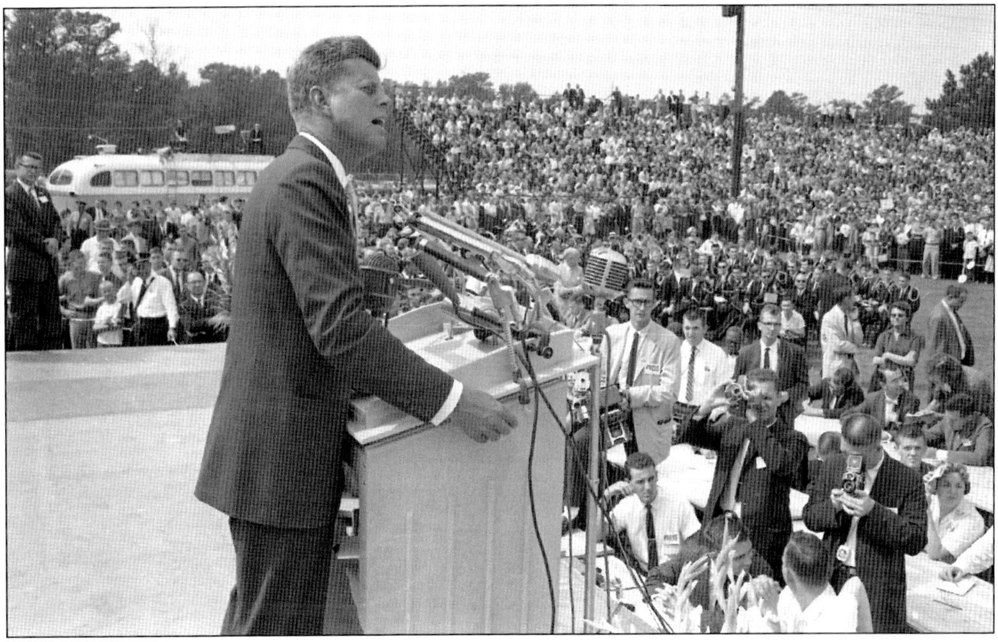

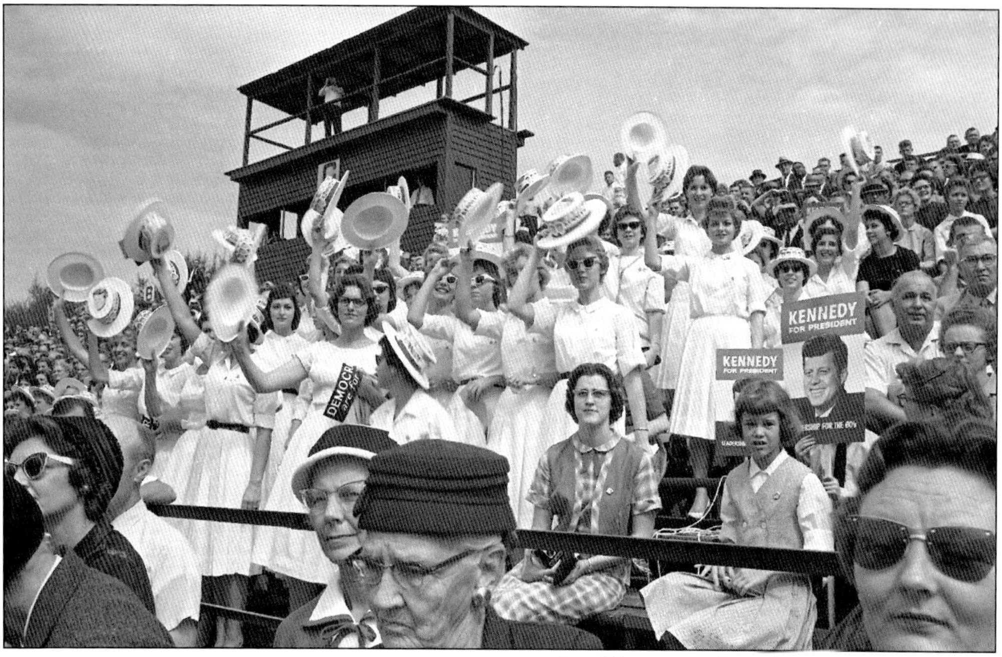

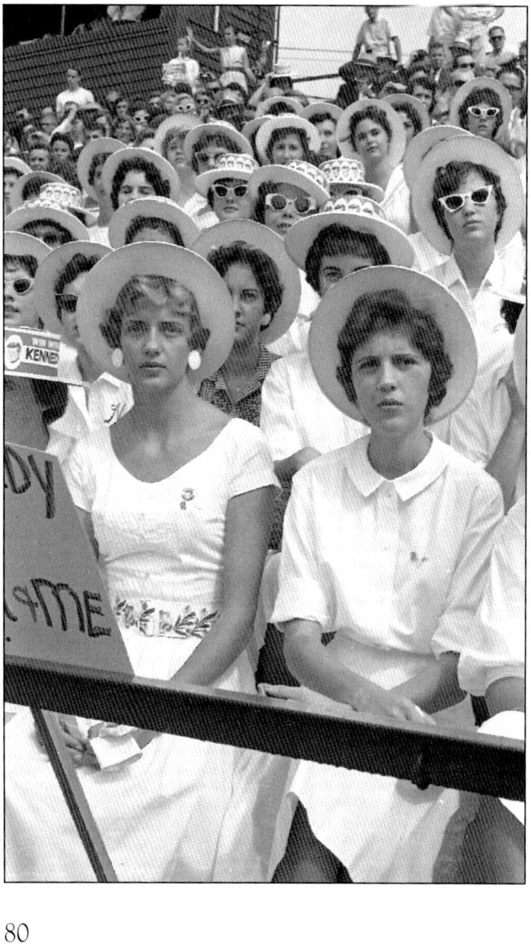

In addition to the Alpha Delta Pi sisters who greeted Senator Kennedy at the Pitt-Greenville Airport, College Stadium had 200 of the Coeds for Kennedy cheering Kennedy on. Janice Faulkner, an instructor of English composition, organized this group. (Both, courtesy of the *News and Observer* and the North Carolina State Archives.)

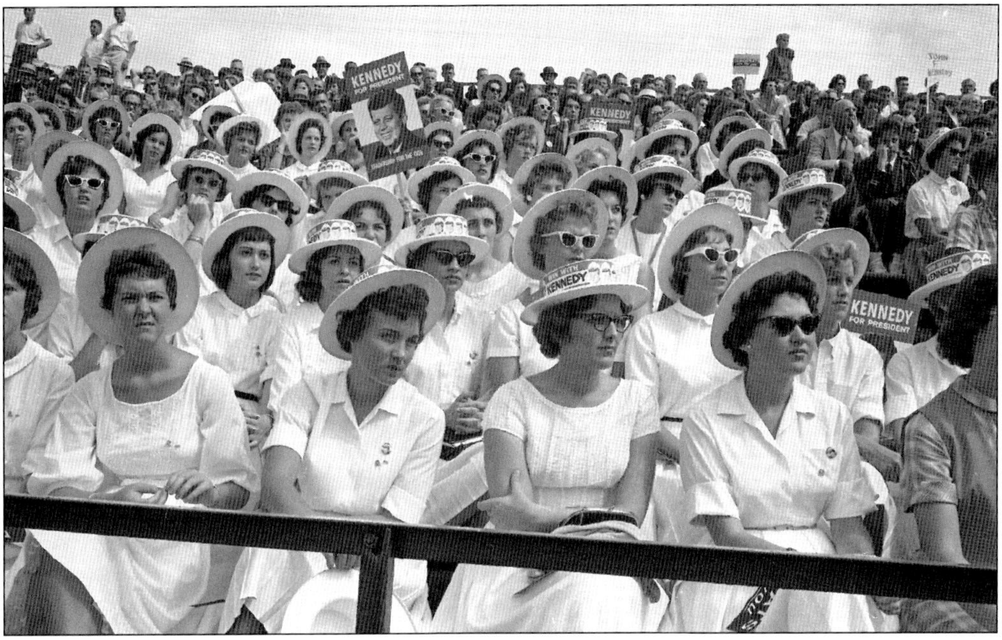

The Coeds for Kennedy contingent was one of the more visible and enthusiastic in the crowd of approximately 12,000. (Both, courtesy of the *News and Observer* and the North Carolina State Archives.)

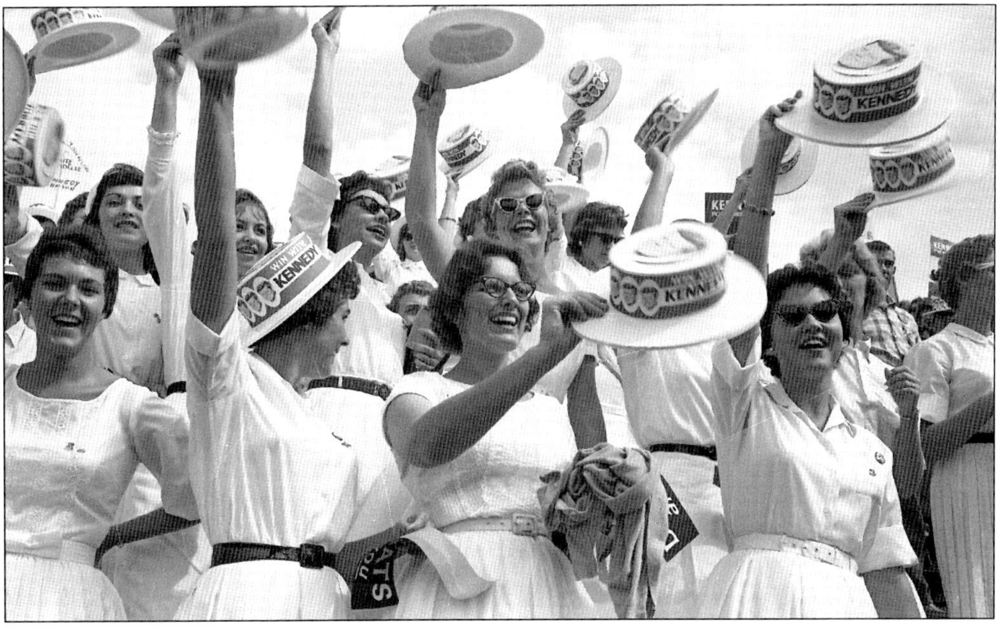

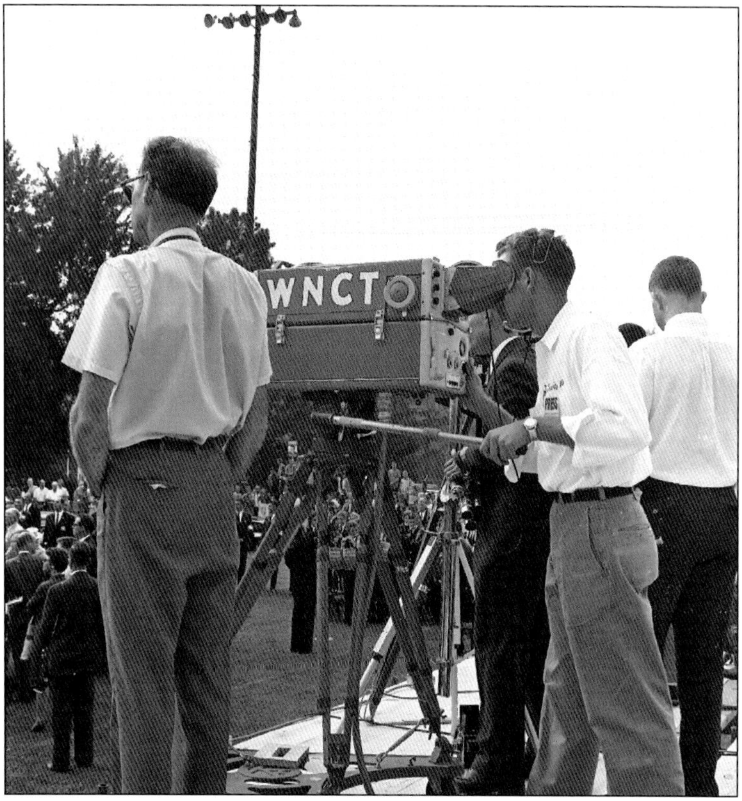

Among the local television networks filming the rally was Greenville's WNCT, a CBS affiliate established in 1953 as the first television station in the eastern part of the state. Segments of the Greenville rally were featured in newscasts later that day. (Photograph by Roy Hardee, courtesy of J.Y. Joyner Library, East Carolina University.)

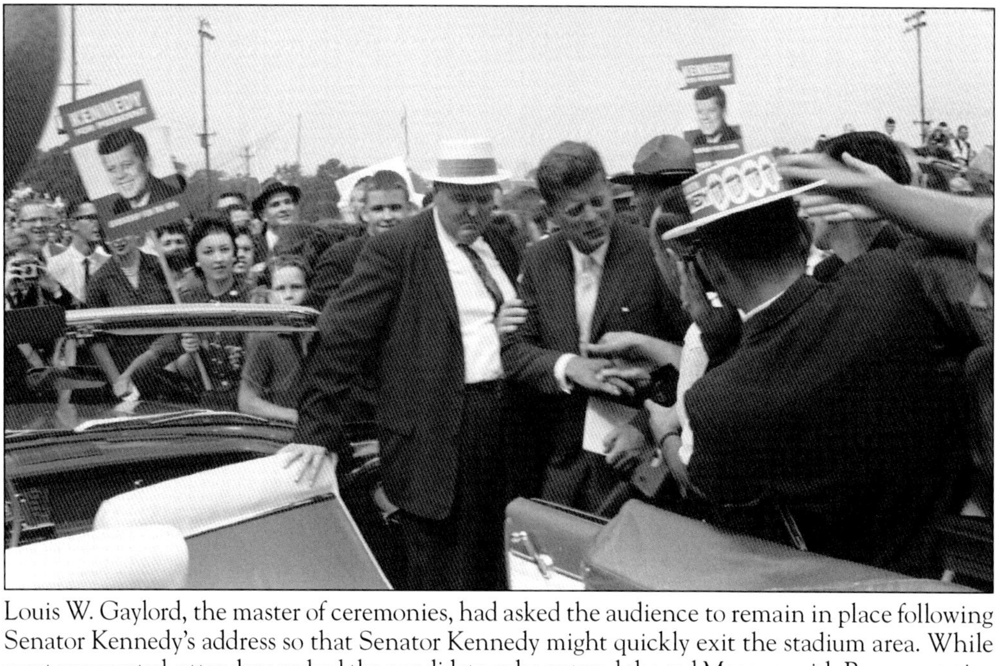

Louis W. Gaylord, the master of ceremonies, had asked the audience to remain in place following Senator Kennedy's address so that Senator Kennedy might quickly exit the stadium area. While most cooperated, attendees rushed the candidate as he entered the red Mercury with Representative Bonner and Terry Sanford. Henry Lawson, a police detective, was the driver. (Courtesy of the *News and Observer* and the North Carolina State Archives.)

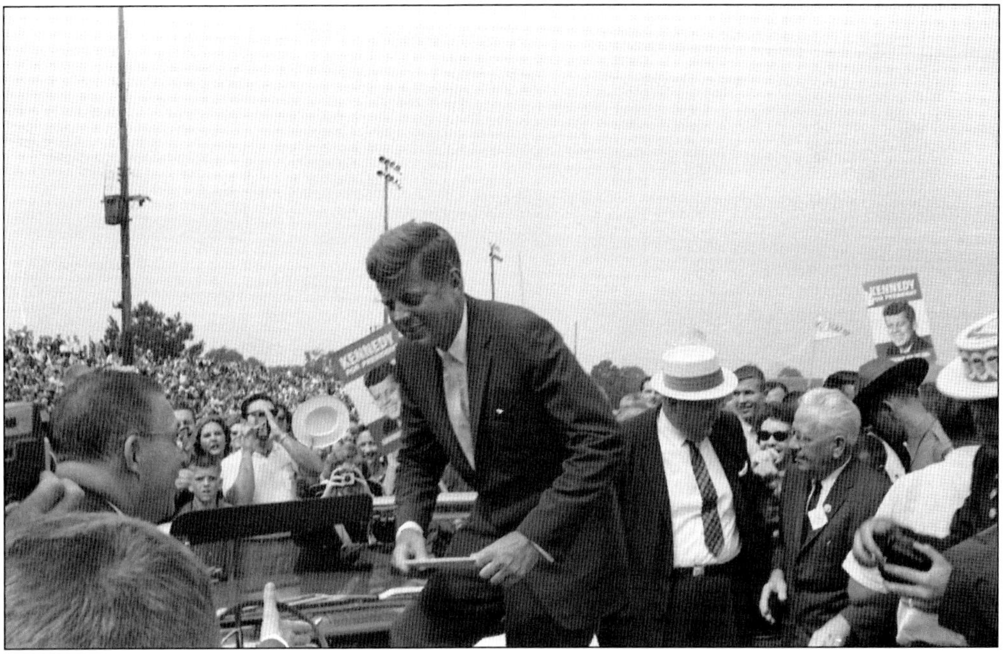

Following Senator Kennedy, John G. Clark got into the front seat of the red Mercury convertible. Clark accompanied Kennedy throughout his morning in Greenville. (Photograph by Hugh Morton; courtesy of Wilson Library, University of North Carolina.)

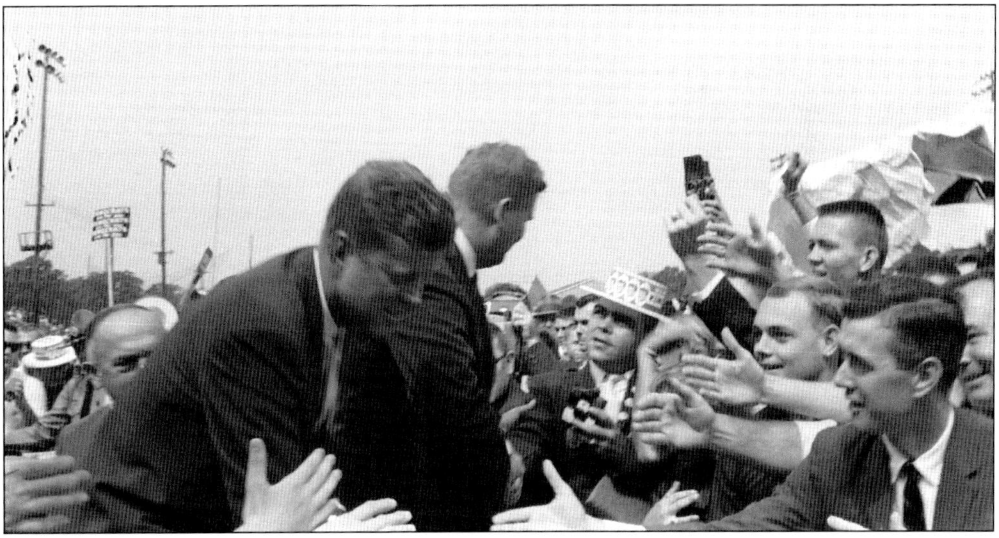

As the Kennedy car was about to leave, members of the East Carolina College Young Democrats Club swarmed around the vehicle hoping to shake hands with Kennedy and Sanford. Representative Bonner, between the two young office-seekers, remained seated during this last contact before departure. (Courtesy of the *News and Observer* and the North Carolina State Archives.)

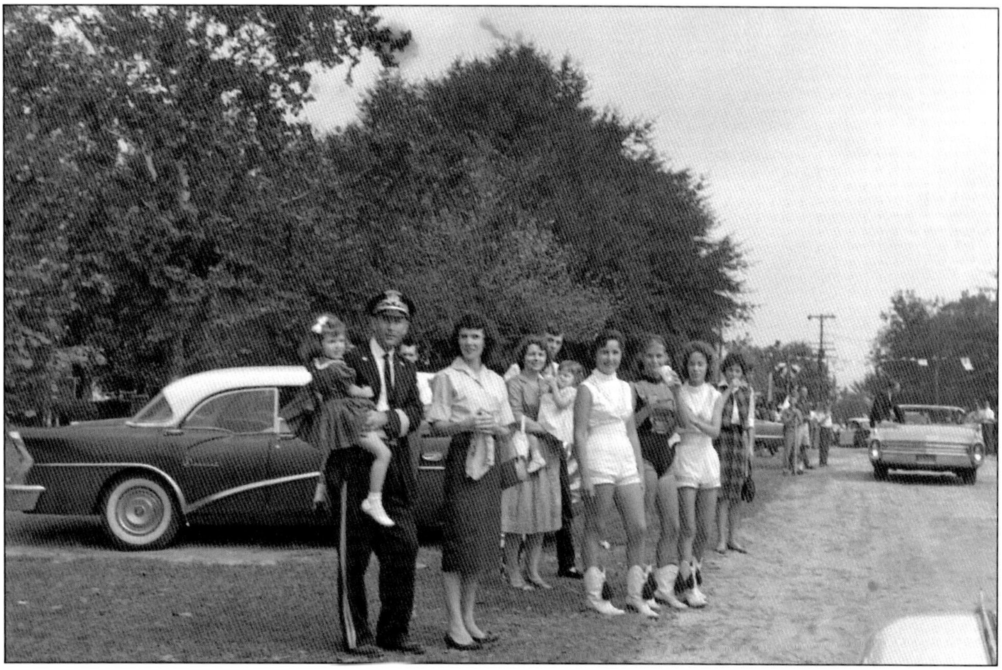

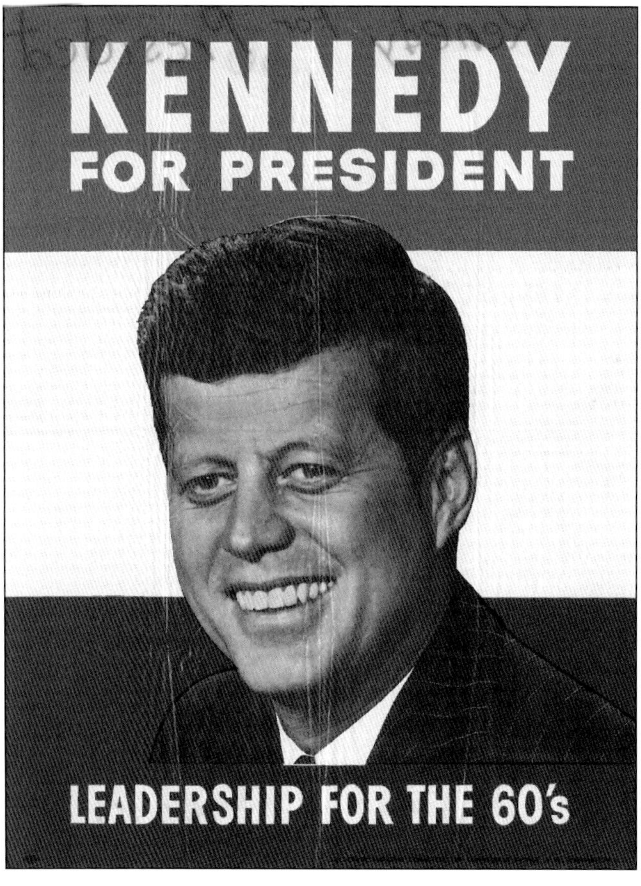

Exiting the athletic grounds of East Carolina College via the same dirt road the motorcade had used to approach the stadium, the Kennedy car passed scattered well-wishers, such as this group of majorettes from one of the half-dozen bands lining Greene and Fifth Streets. (Courtesy of the *Daily Reflector* and J.Y. Joyner Library, East Carolina University.)

The campaign poster most visible in Greenville at the College Stadium rally was a red, white, and blue one featuring a close-up portrait of Senator Kennedy with a friendly, engaging smile. The writing on the back of this poster unfortunately misspelled the candidate's name as "Kenedy." (Courtesy of J.Y. Joyner Library, East Carolina University.)

Six

Greensboro Airport Rally

Senator Kennedy's whirlwind campaign moved next to Greensboro, the most politically charged city in the state at that time. In February 1960, four African American students from North Carolina Agricultural and Technical College staged a sit-in at a Woolworth's, protesting the store's policy of denying lunch-counter service to African Americans. Day after day, the protesters returned, their ranks swelling. Soon, the sit-in spread statewide, then to 54 cities in nine states. Woolworth's acquiesced in July, allowing African Americans lunch-counter service. Nevertheless, in the minds of many, civil rights remained at the forefront of Southern issues.

At high noon, Kennedy arrived in Greensboro but went no further than the airport tarmac and stayed no longer than 20 minutes. Approximately 6,000 people came to greet him. Kennedy had decided not to compete with Nixon at Greensboro Coliseum. Greensboro was not a Democratic stronghold—Eisenhower carried much of the Greater Greensboro area in 1956, and Charles R. Jonas, then North Carolina's only Republican congressman, represented the 10th District adjoining Greensboro. Kennedy realized that Southern Democrats remained supportive of the status quo socially, meaning they were unsympathetic to the sit-in movement. Overall, Kennedy avoided the issue. Preempting another controversy, the religion issue, Kennedy shared the stage with two Baptists, one a layman and the other C.B. Deane, president of the Baptist State Convention. The layman, H. Cloyd Philpott Jr., was Democratic nominee for lieutenant governor. Philpott declared that he was "a lifelong Baptist" and proud to introduce Kennedy. In his remarks, Kennedy downplayed his Massachusetts origins, instead emphasizing his pride in the Democratic Party, "the oldest political party in the world," and the hope it offered Americans for a better future.

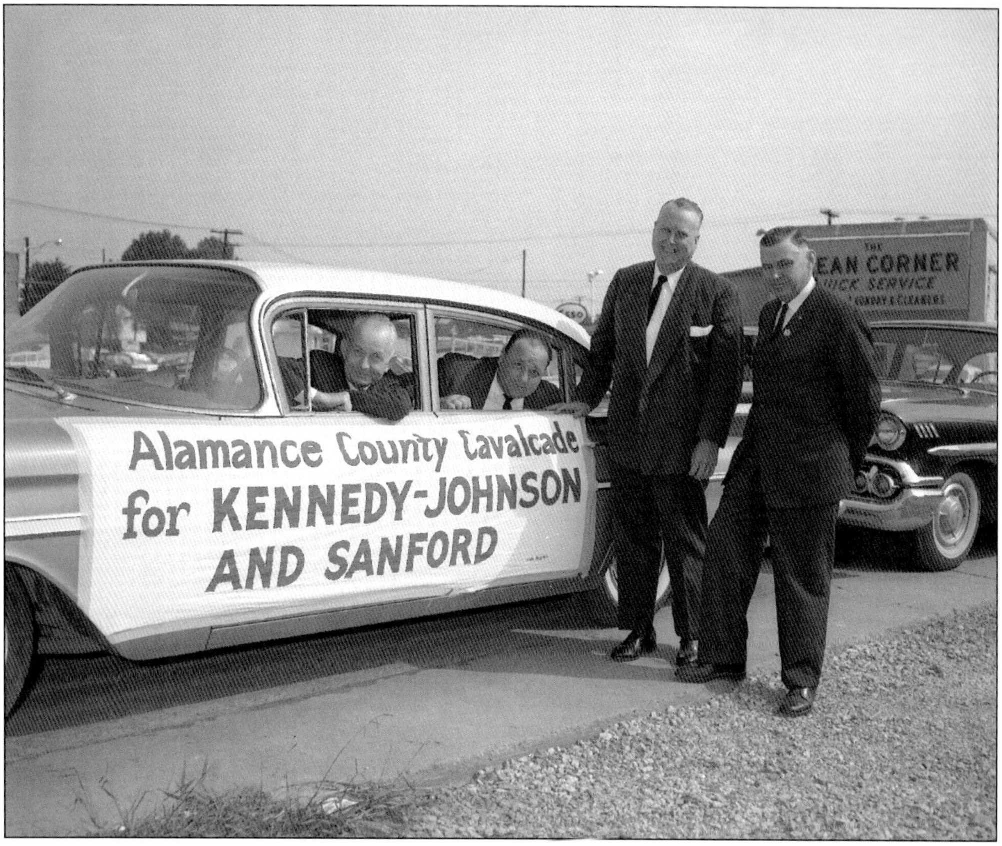

The rally at Greensboro-High Point Airport saw the Democratic faithful carpooling from adjoining counties. Edward J. McCauley, photographer for one of the leading newspapers in Alamance County, the *Burlington Daily Times-News*, took this photograph. (Photograph by Edward J. McCauley; courtesy of Wilson Library, University of North Carolina.)

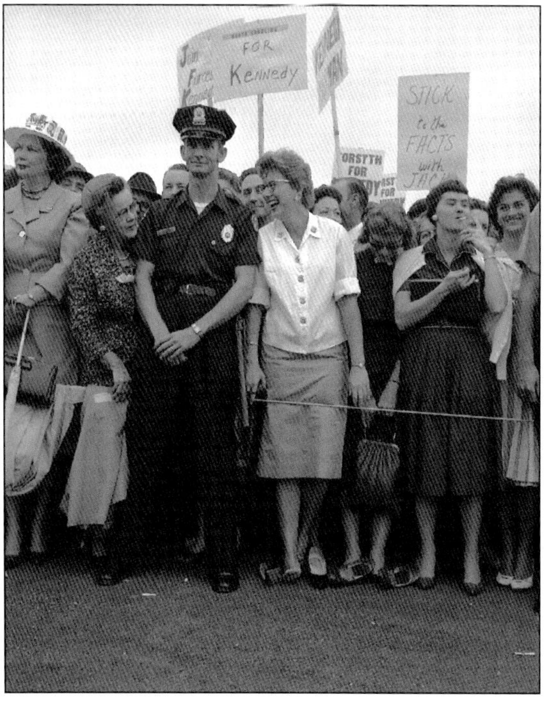

Conspicuous here is the divide between younger women, unabashed in their enthusiasm for Senator Kennedy, and the more mature women to the left of the officer, who are reserved and proper in expressing their support. (Photograph by Edward J. McCauley; courtesy of Wilson Library, University of North Carolina.)

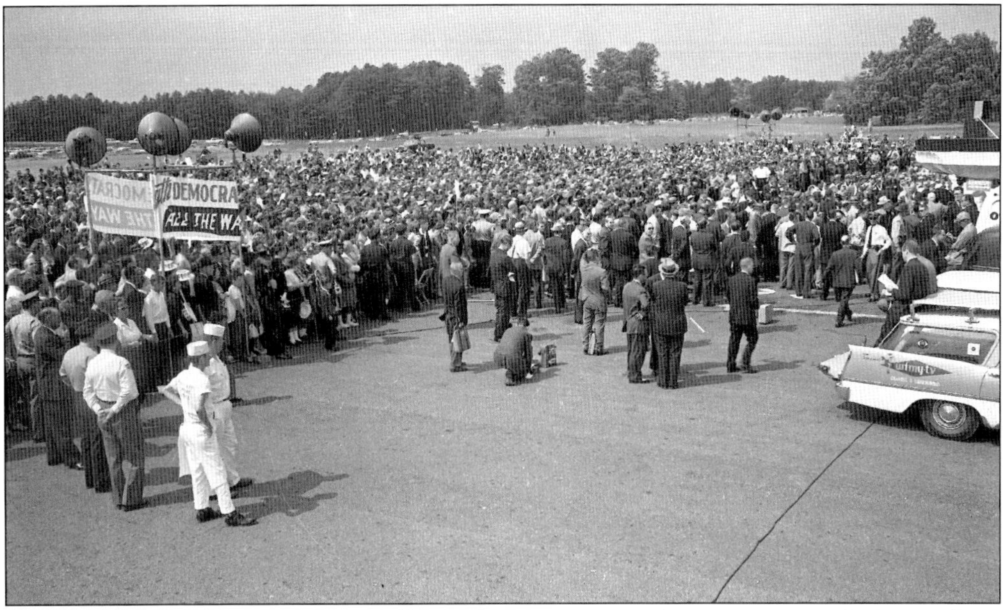

While the greater metropolitan area of Greensboro was massive by comparison with Greenville—even more so when adjoining cities, such as Winston-Salem in Forsyth County and High Point mostly in Guilford County, are included—the turnout for the Greensboro rally, estimated at 6,000 to 8,000, was smaller than the Greenville turnout. (Courtesy of the *News and Observer* and the North Carolina State Archives.)

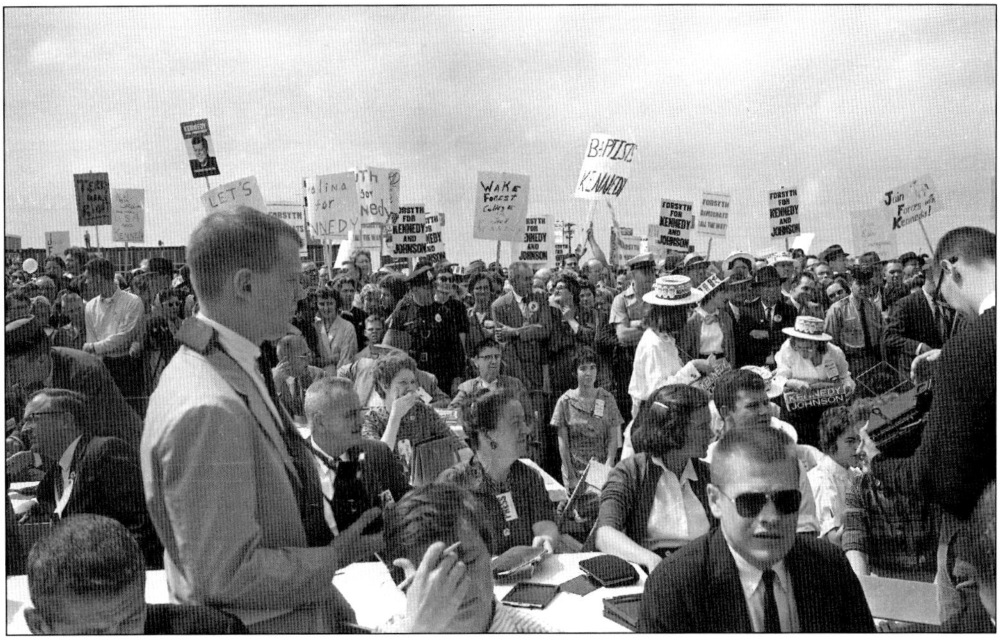

The press corps turnout was strong, but their placement in relation to the 6,000 to 8,000 members of the public attending made for crowded conditions, especially at midday. Senator Kennedy arrived in Greensboro late, in large part because he had arrived in Greenville late due to bad weather in Washington, DC. By mid-day, members of the press were eager for the rally to begin. (Courtesy of the *News and Observer* and the North Carolina State Archives.)

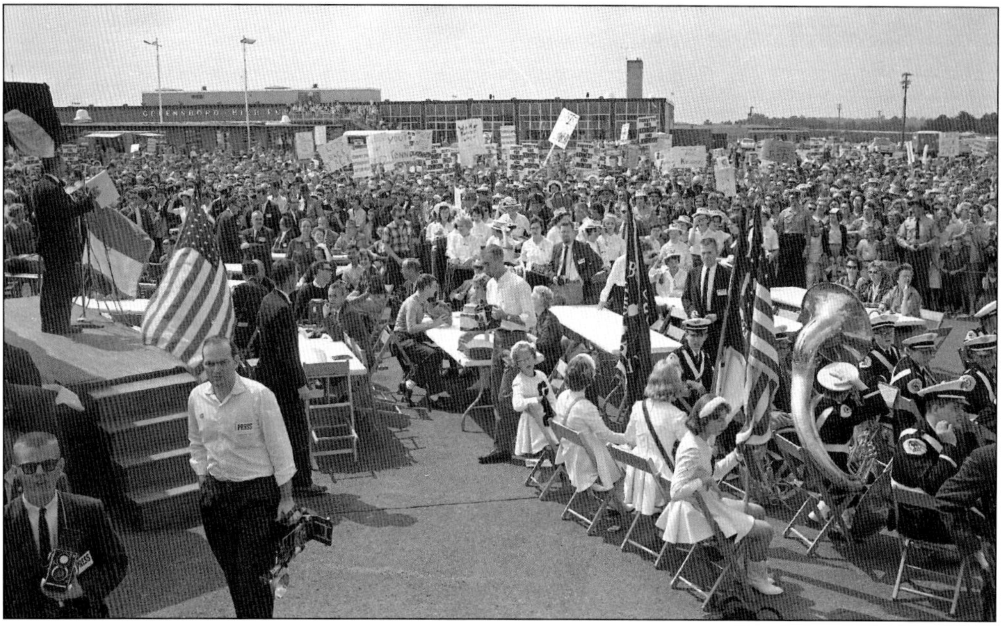

The Greensboro-High Point Airport, with its new passenger terminal, was a far finer facility than Greenville's small, unkempt airstrip. Edward Dragon, an advance man for the College Stadium rally, described the Greenville airport as "unused," adding that it "had been an auxiliary naval air station . . . [but that] there was nothing like a control tower there. The pilots landed on their own." (Courtesy of the *News and Observer* and the North Carolina State Archives.)

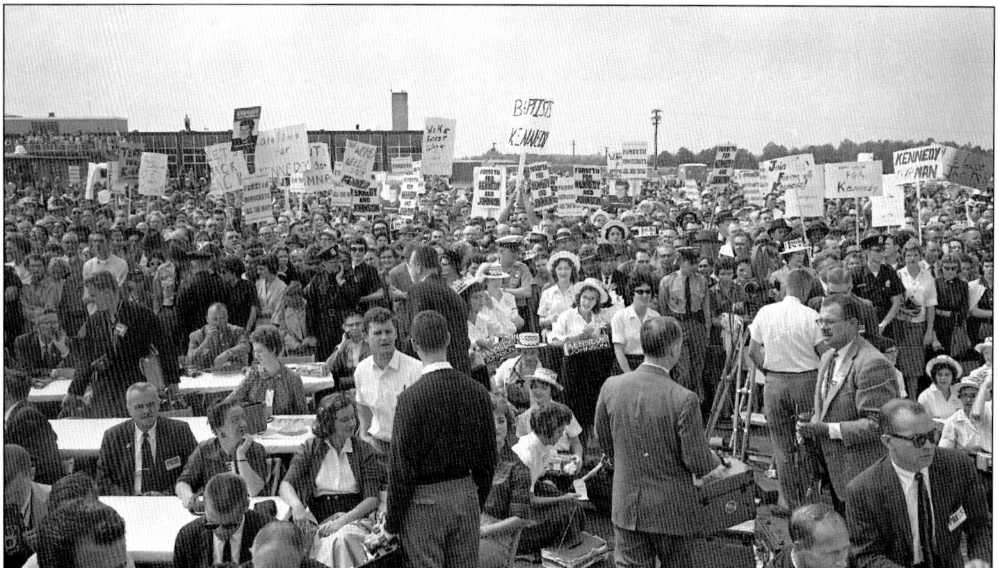

Signs such as "Baptists for Kennedy" and "Wake Forest College for Kennedy" signaled that Senator Kennedy's address before the Houston Ministerial Association on September 12 provided both a heartfelt defense of freedom of religion and a sincere expression of allegiance to the Constitution. Rebroadcast repeatedly, the Houston address convinced doubters that Kennedy would serve his country well. (Photograph by Edward J. McCauley; courtesy of Wilson Library, University of North Carolina.)

Senator Kennedy arrived in the *Caroline* after a short flight from Greenville. Although greeted by local dignitaries, Democratic political leaders, and municipal officials ready with keys to their cities, Kennedy was hardly "mobbed" at the Greensboro airport like he had been at Pitt-Greenville. The man wearing the hat in the photograph is one of Kennedy's bodyguards. (Photograph by Edward J. McCauley; courtesy of Wilson Library, University of North Carolina.)

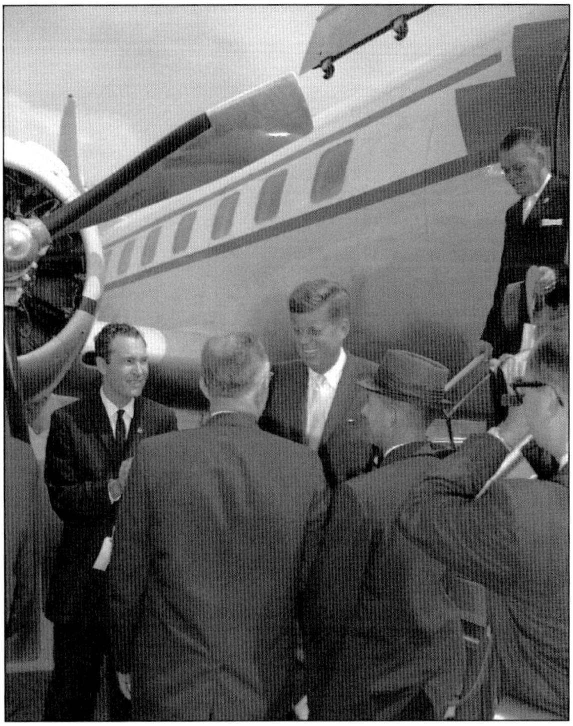

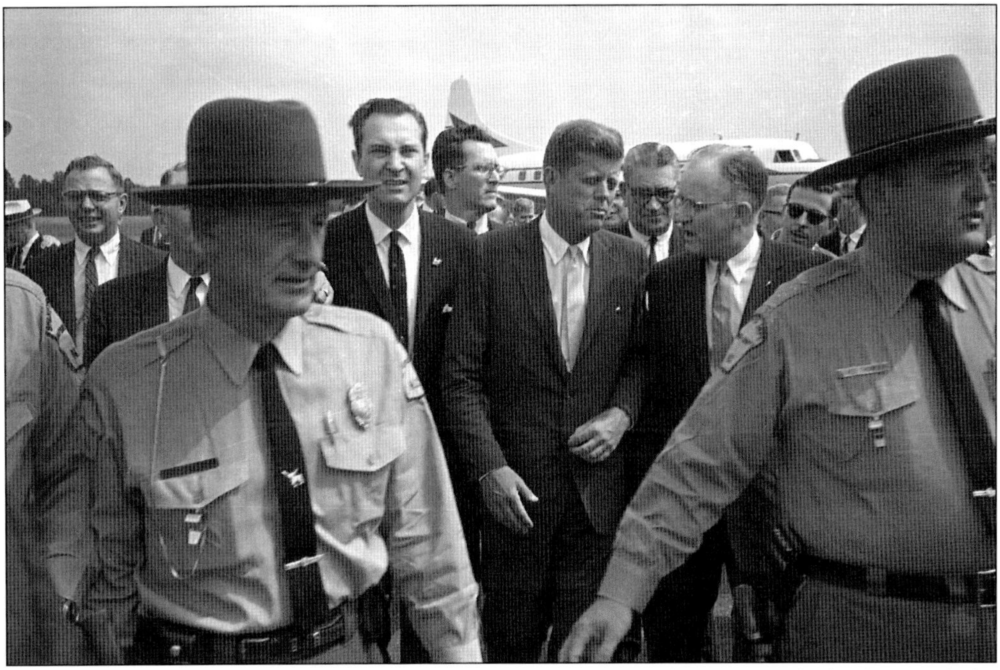

After landing, Senator Kennedy proceeded to the platform for the rally. In the background, the *Caroline* can be seen. The Greensboro rally was the quickest of the day. Vice Pres. Richard M. Nixon had staged a surprisingly successful rally in Greensboro Coliseum on August 17. Perhaps realizing that their rally would not exceed Nixon's, the Kennedy campaign staged a more modest stop. (Courtesy of the *News and Observer* and the North Carolina State Archives.)

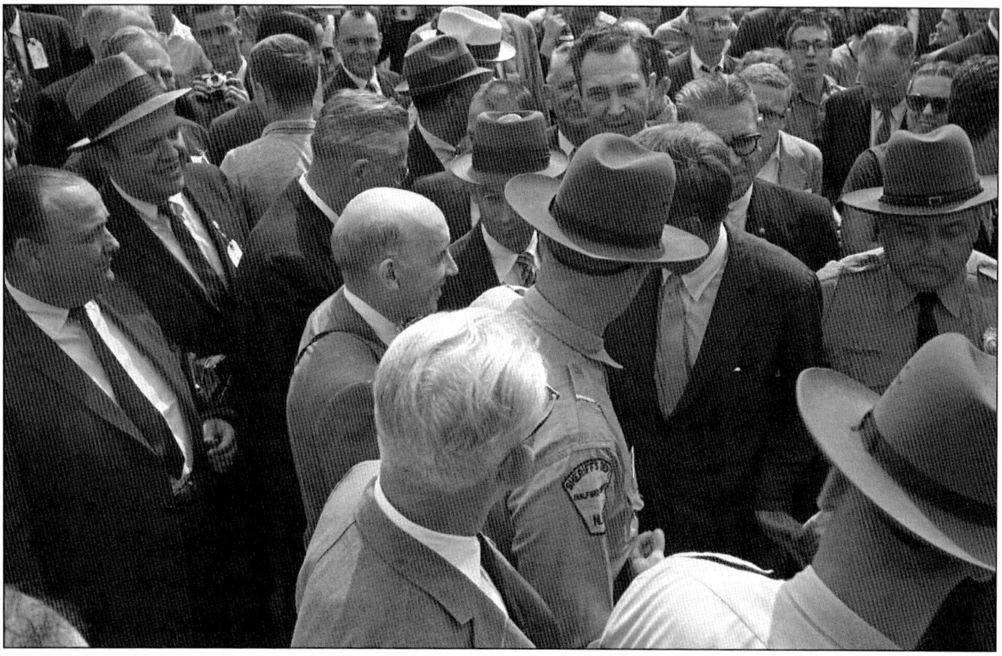

As Senator Kennedy approached the platform, the crowd around him thickened. Escorted by Guilford County deputies and accompanied by his bodyguard (the slight man left of Kennedy wearing a cap), Kennedy remained characteristically gregarious throughout his quick airport stop. (Courtesy of the *News and Observer* and the North Carolina State Archives.)

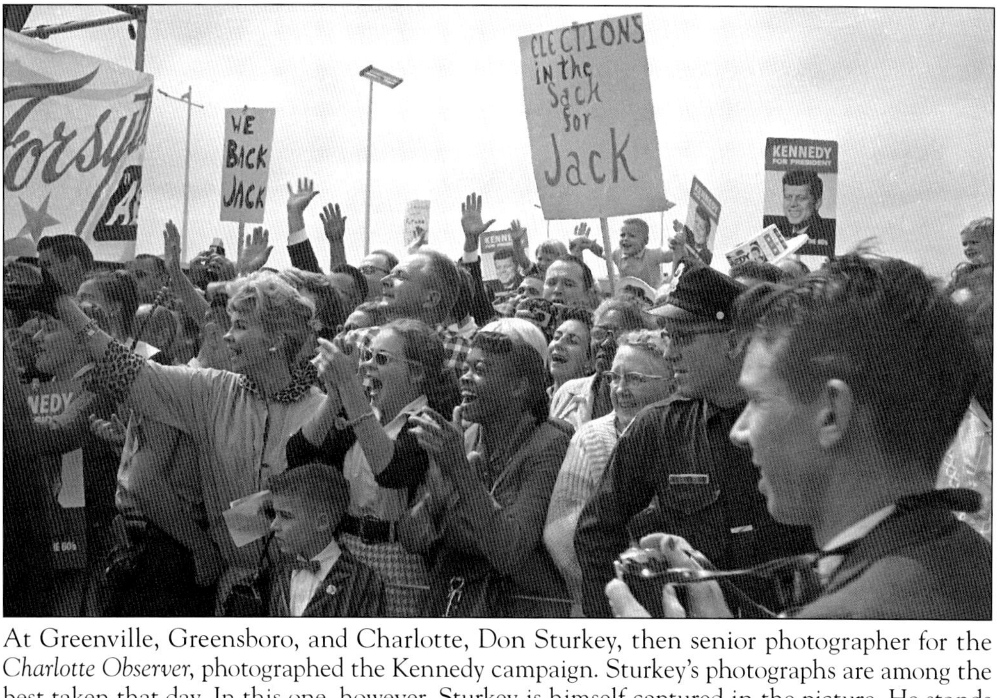

At Greenville, Greensboro, and Charlotte, Don Sturkey, then senior photographer for the *Charlotte Observer*, photographed the Kennedy campaign. Sturkey's photographs are among the best taken that day. In this one, however, Sturkey is himself captured in the picture. He stands looking toward a now excited crowd that sees Senator Kennedy approaching. (Courtesy of the *News and Observer* and the North Carolina State Archives.)

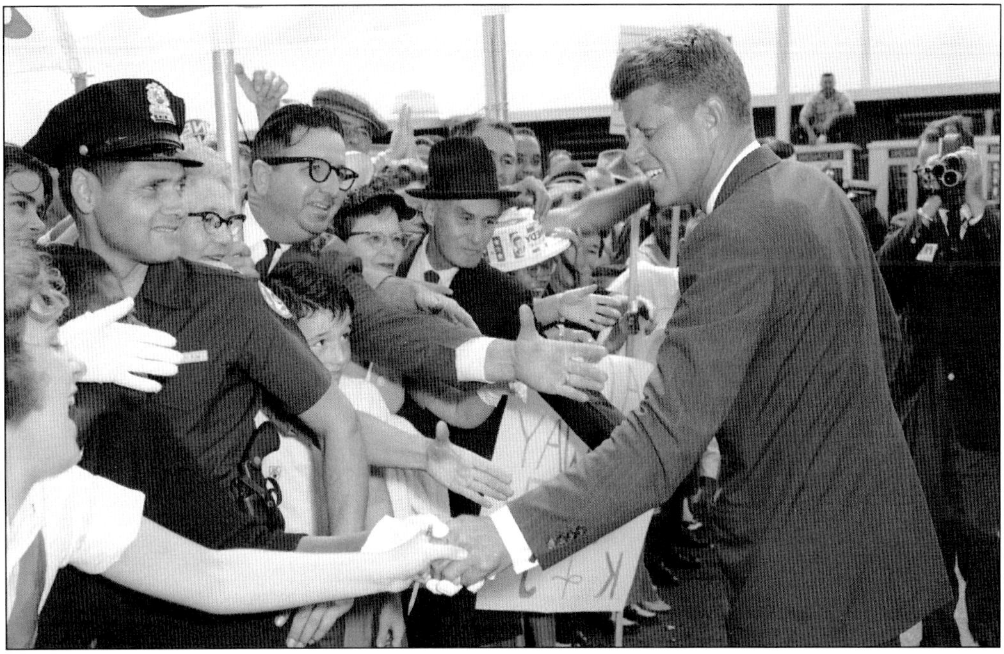

Throughout the day, Senator Kennedy remained fresh and well groomed, despite shaking hundreds of hands and greeting an ever-mounting number of excited North Carolinians. Here, Kennedy seems to be shaking two hands simultaneously. (Photograph by Edward J. McCauley; courtesy of Wilson Library, University of North Carolina.)

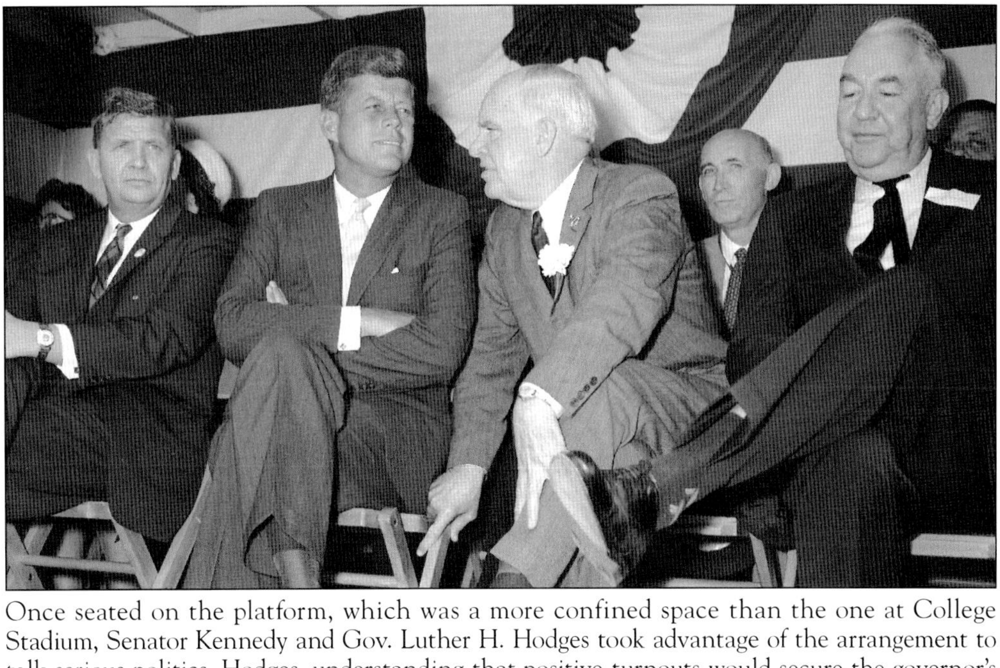

Once seated on the platform, which was a more confined space than the one at College Stadium, Senator Kennedy and Gov. Luther H. Hodges took advantage of the arrangement to talk serious politics. Hodges, understanding that positive turnouts would secure the governor's mansion for Sanford and possibly the White House for Kennedy, jockeyed for a post in the new administration. (Photograph by Edward J. McCauley; courtesy of Wilson Library, University of North Carolina.)

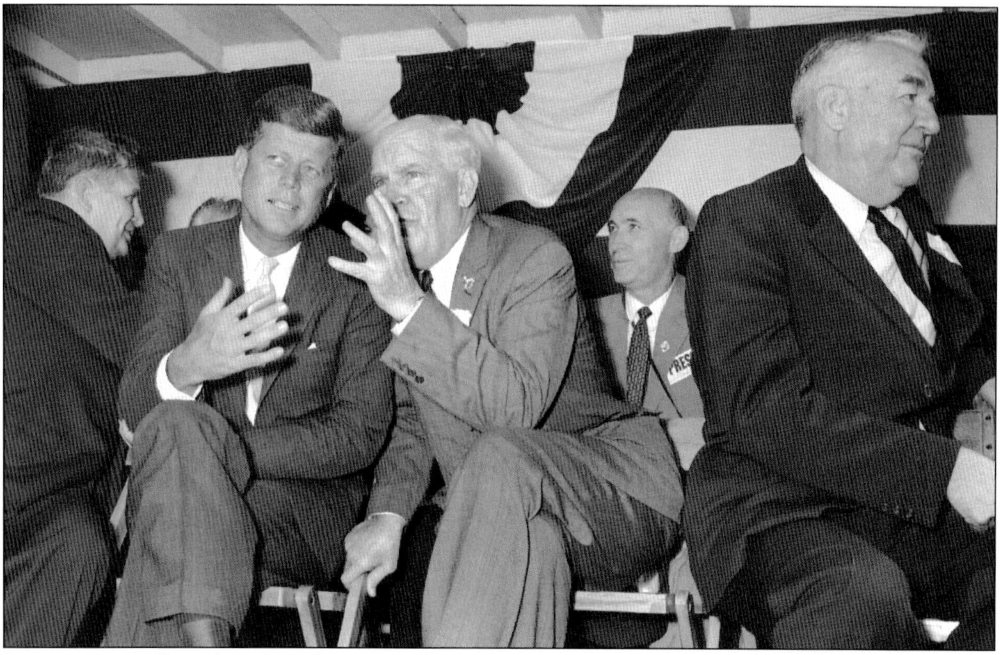

Senator Kennedy and Gov. Luther H. Hodges engage in a dynamic discussion while Sanford greets the press. Sen. Sam Ervin shares a moment with the junior senator from North Carolina, B. Everett Jordan, who is not included in this photograph, but seated to the right of Ervin. (Photograph by Edward J. McCauley; courtesy of Wilson Library, University of North Carolina.)

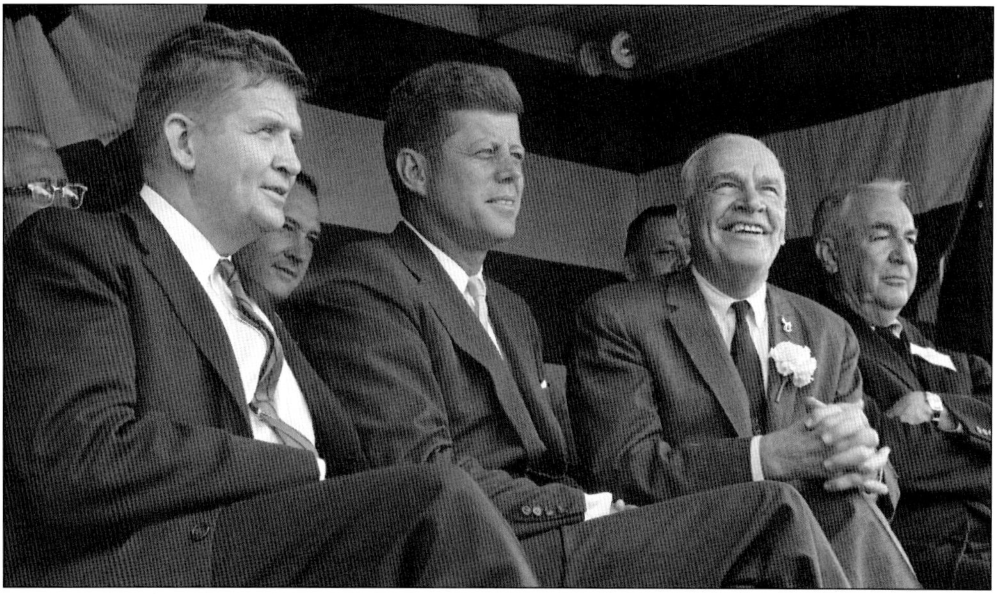

Governor Hodges's remarks to Senator Kennedy apparently had their impact. In his opening statements, Kennedy expressed pride in having the governor as a traveling companion, noting that Hodges "was generous enough to support me for the vice presidency in 1956, as did the majority of the North Carolina delegates." Tactfully, Kennedy did not recall the politics of the 1960 Democratic National Convention. (Photograph by Hugh Morton; courtesy of Wilson Library, University of North Carolina.)

Senator Kennedy shakes hands with a local Democratic leader as he rises to deliver his speech. (Photograph by Edward J. McCauley; courtesy of Wilson Library, University of North Carolina.)

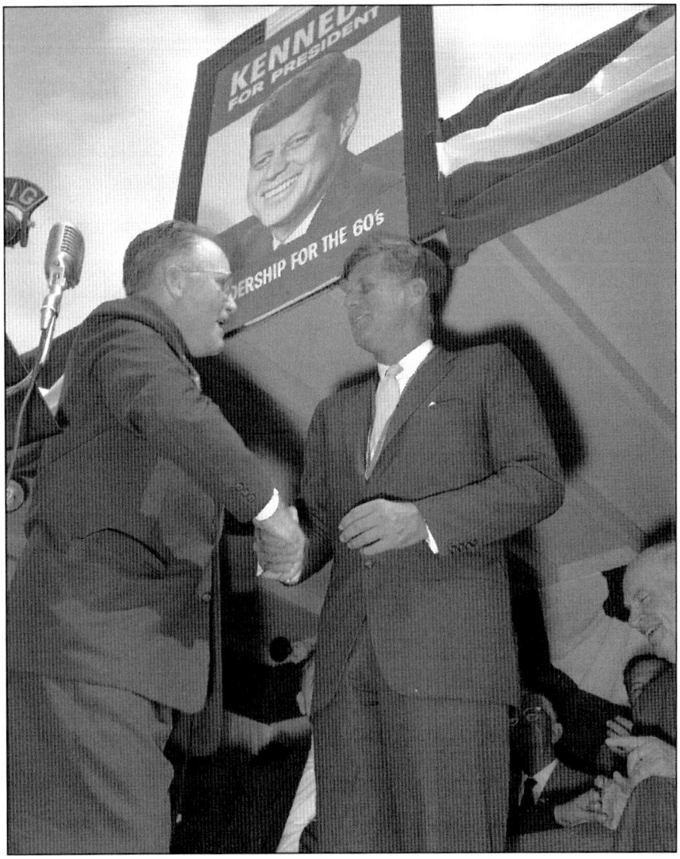

Senator Kennedy walks toward the microphones. In College Stadium, there had been a podium for him to rest his prepared remarks on, but in Greensboro on the tarmac platform, there was nothing more than an assemblage of microphones. (Photograph by Edward J. McCauley; courtesy of Wilson Library, University of North Carolina.)

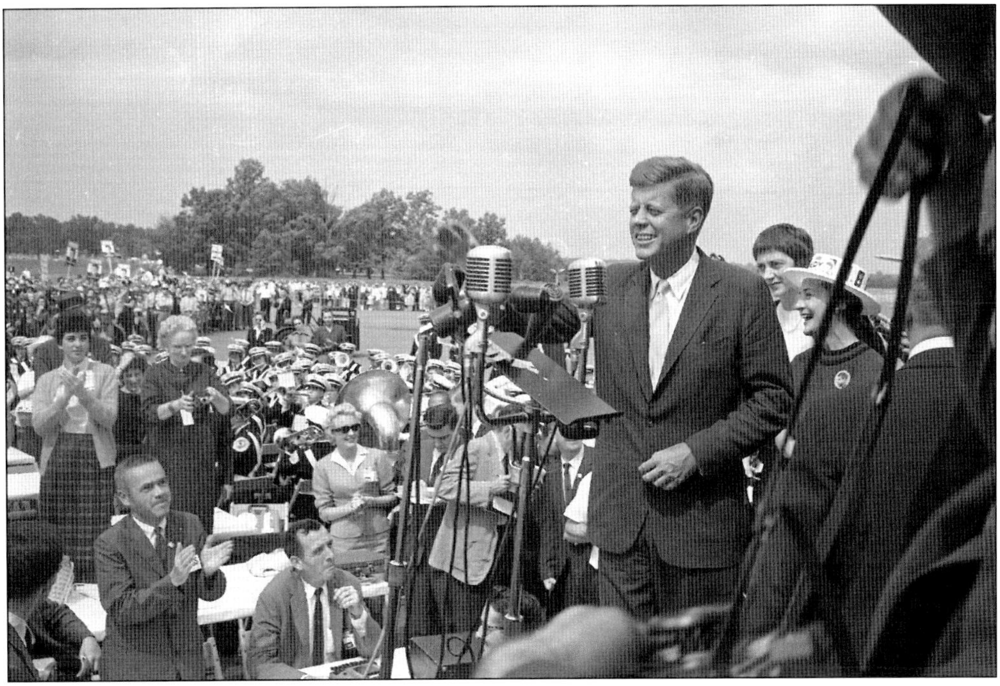

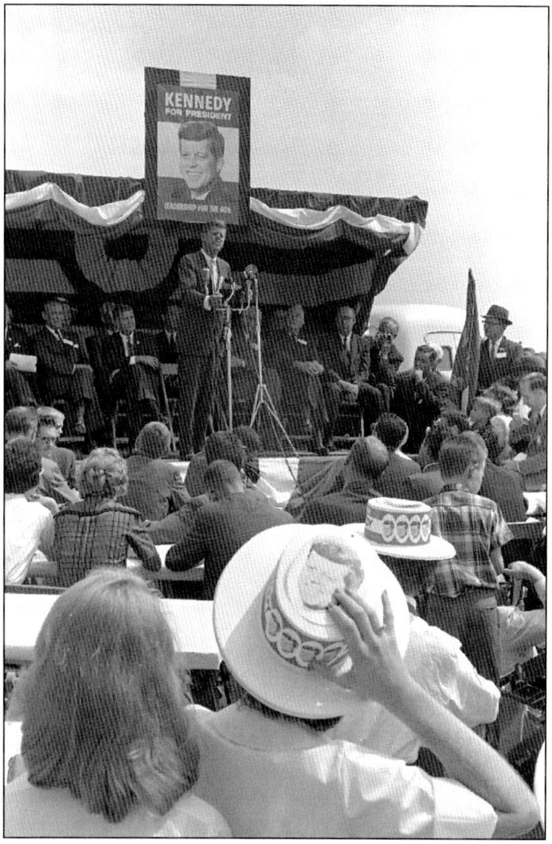

In Greensboro, a small group of "Kennedy Girls" wore signature white blouses and blue skirts with mock straw hats decorated with red, white, and blue "Kennedy for president" slogans. Compared to the ranks that Janice Faulkner had recruited at East Carolina College, however, the Greensboro contingent was modest. (Photograph by Don Sturkey, Wilson Library, University of North Carolina.)

Photographer Edward McCauley captured the Greensboro Airport rally from the rear of the crowd as Senator Kennedy spoke. The American Airlines plane provided transportation for the press corps. On the right is the tail of the *Caroline*. (Photograph by Edward J. McCauley; courtesy of Wilson Library, University of North Carolina.)

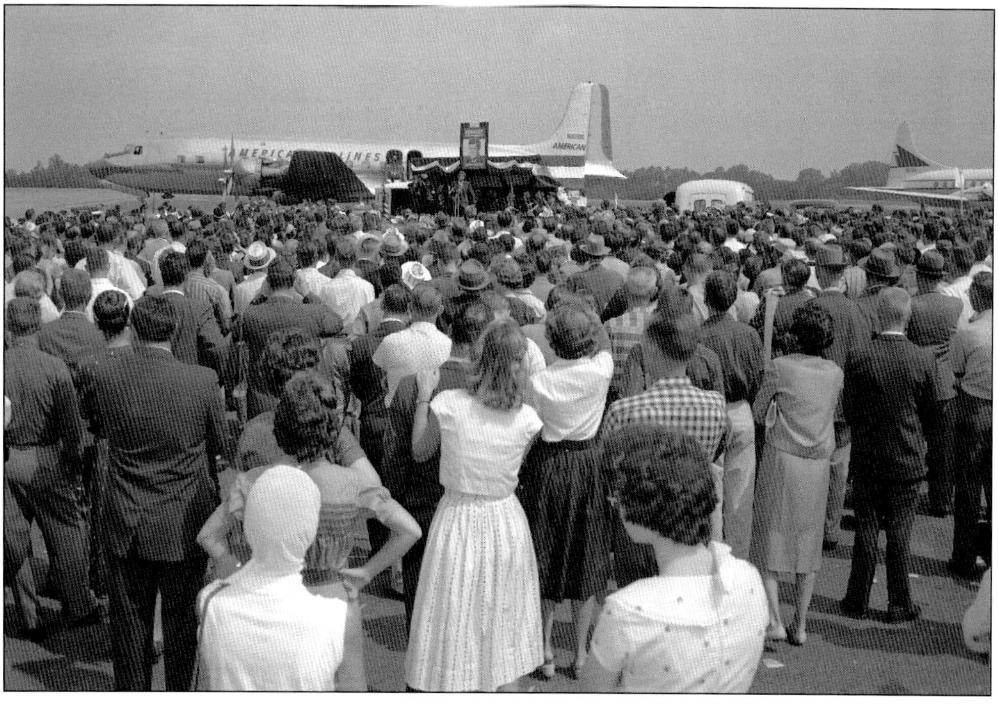

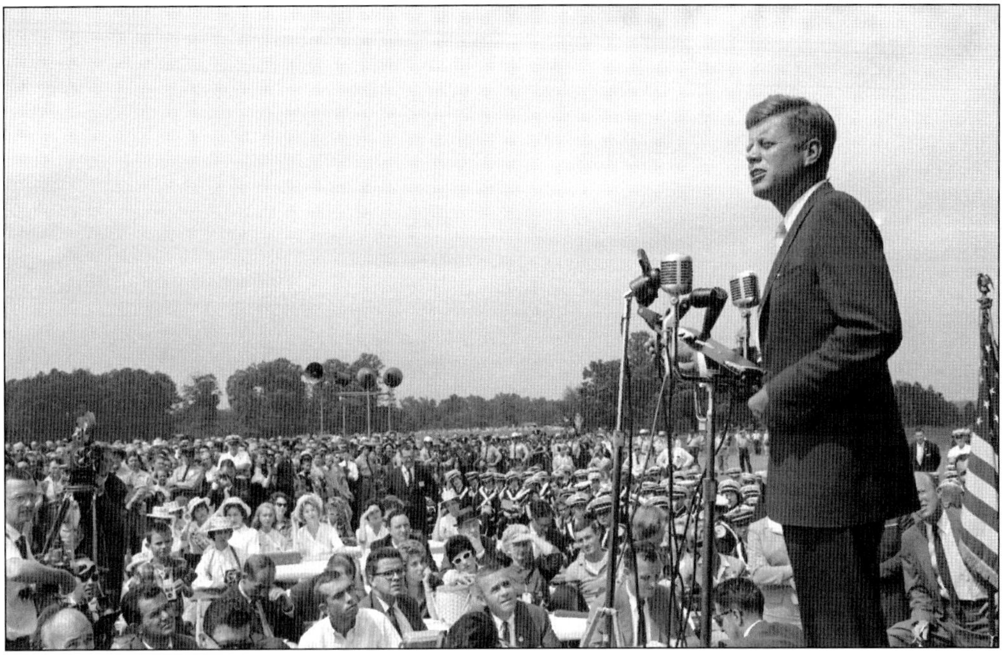

Much as he had in Greenville, Senator Kennedy's Greensboro address appealed to the Democratic heritage of leadership and how he came as the standard bearer of the party, intent on leading America and, in the process, leading the world forward as well. (Photograph by Hugh Morton; courtesy of Wilson Library, University of North Carolina.)

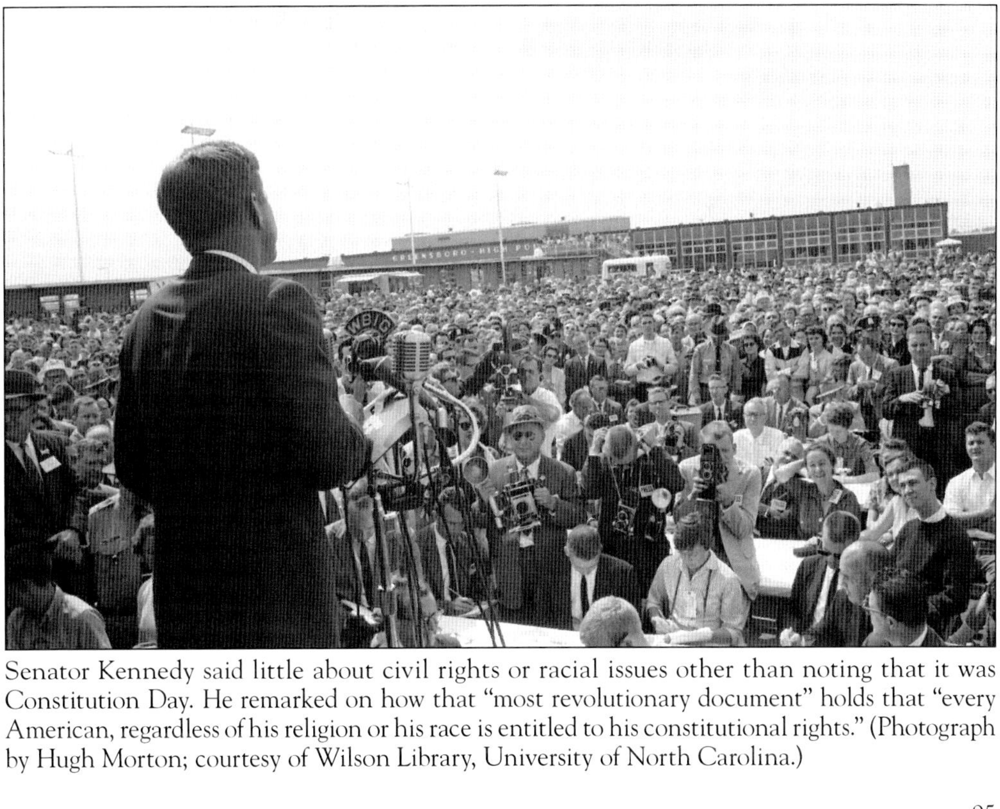

Senator Kennedy said little about civil rights or racial issues other than noting that it was Constitution Day. He remarked on how that "most revolutionary document" holds that "every American, regardless of his religion or his race is entitled to his constitutional rights." (Photograph by Hugh Morton; courtesy of Wilson Library, University of North Carolina.)

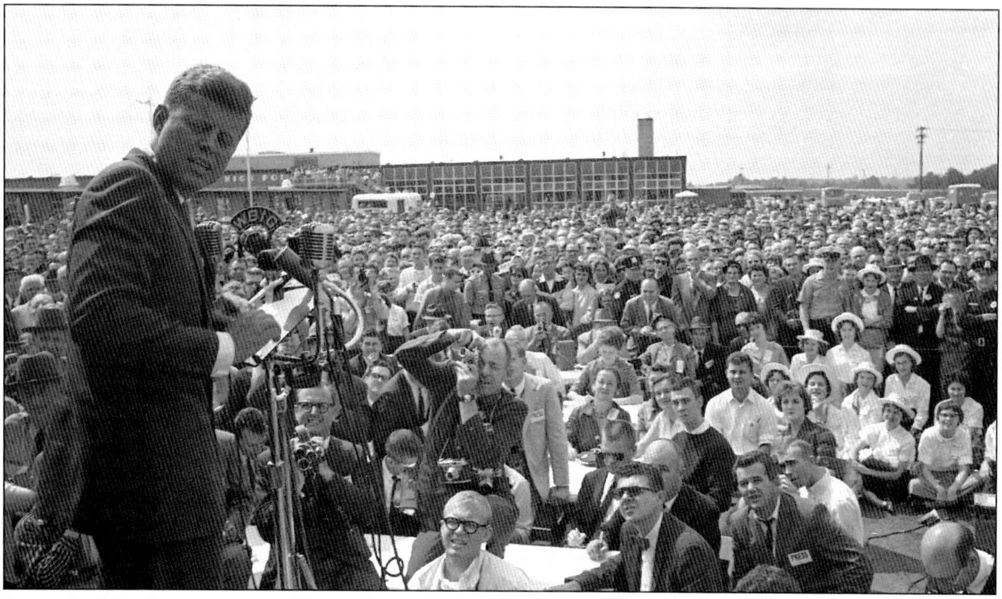

Instead of the farm program, Kennedy emphasized the need for America to produce more scientists and engineers, lest it fall further behind the Soviet Union. Kennedy's sense of urgency resulted partly from the Soviet Union's successful *Sputnik* satellite launch in 1957, an accomplishment the United States had yet to match in 1960. (Courtesy of the *News and Observer* and the North Carolina State Archives.)

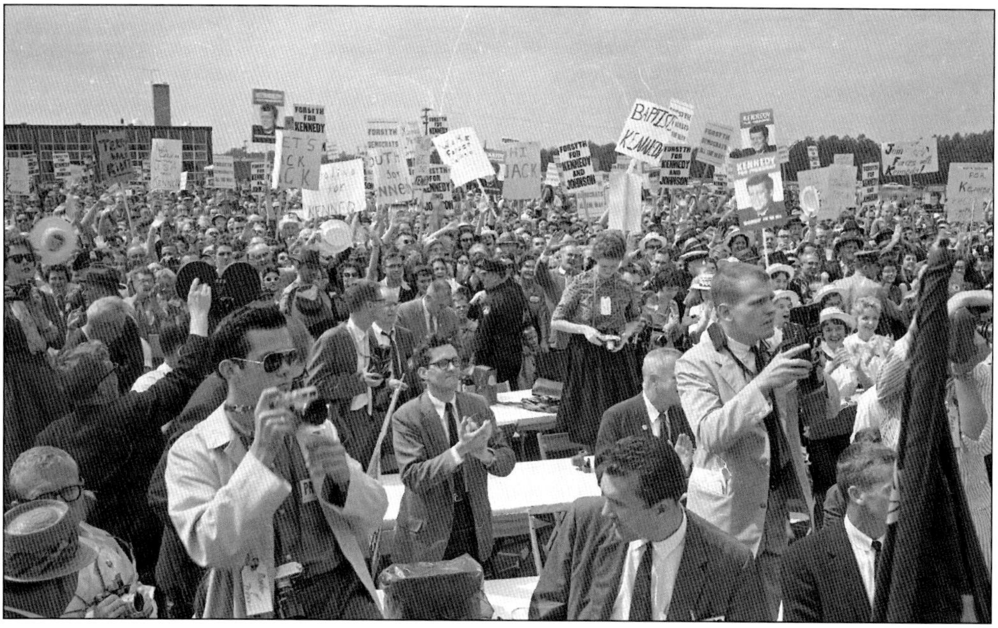

One sign in the crowd read, "Terry Was Right," alluding to Terry Sanford's decision to back Senator Kennedy at the Democratic National Convention. While that move upset many senior Democrats, Gov. Luther H. Hodges included, it resulted in the best interests for both Sanford and Hodges in the long run. Although the distance between Sanford and Hodges is evident in many photographs, they found common ground in Kennedy. (Courtesy of the *News and Observer* and the North Carolina State Archives.)

Seven

CHARLOTTE

From Greensboro, the *Caroline* flew to Asheville, but inclement weather forced the cancellation of the rally at McCormick Field. Once in Charlotte, Senator Kennedy sent a message to the disappointed Asheville crowd of approximately 5,000. Asheville might be bypassed, but Charlotte was another matter. The largest city in the Carolinas, the Queen City was as much a center of Southern Progressivism as it was a part of North Carolina. It was too major to miss.

The campaign arrived early at Douglas Airport and, with dark clouds looming, began the parade early. The route, therefore, was not as thick with supporters as might have been expected. Then again, Kennedy had visited Charlotte before, in 1959, speaking to the Charlotte Chamber of Commerce, just as he had spoken in Greensboro in 1956, addressing the Young Democratic Club of North Carolina.

Kennedy's speech in Charlotte before a crowd of 12,000 reflected the growing questions about the South's allegiance to the Democratic Party. Kennedy reminded his audience of North Carolina's close association with the Democratic Party and the progressive platform that Democrats consistently endorsed. Yet, far more than just political rhetoric, Kennedy's charisma made the rally a headline success.

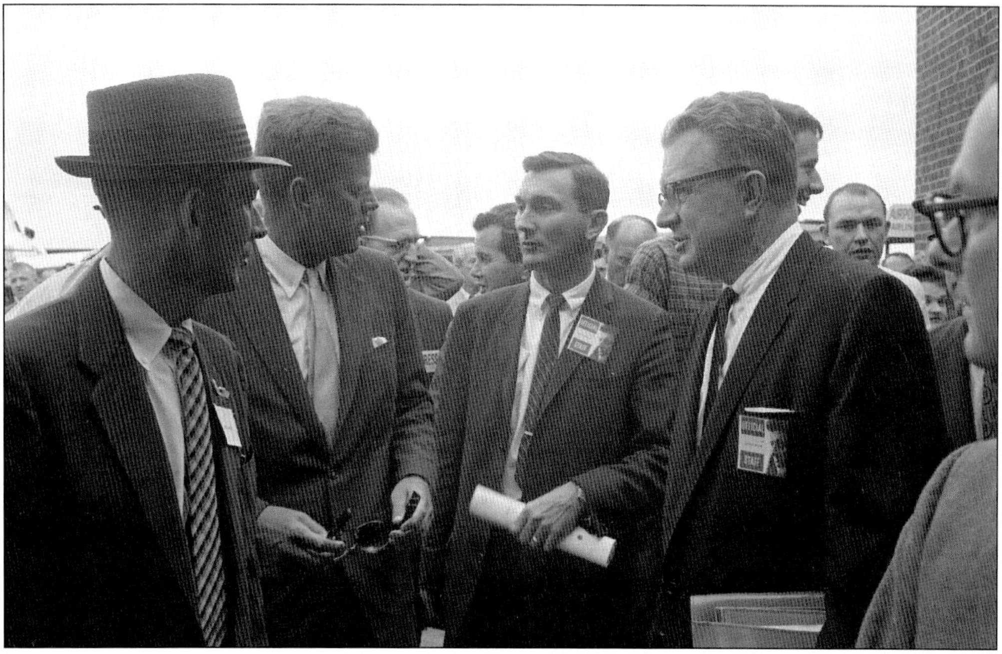

Senator Kennedy consults with Kenneth O'Donnell about the schedule for the remainder of the day. Wearing a hat on the left is Kennedy's bodyguard. O'Donnell, standing to the right of Kennedy, studied at Harvard with Robert Kennedy and later became one of his (Robert's) closest aides. (Photograph by Don Sturkey, Wilson Library, University of North Carolina.)

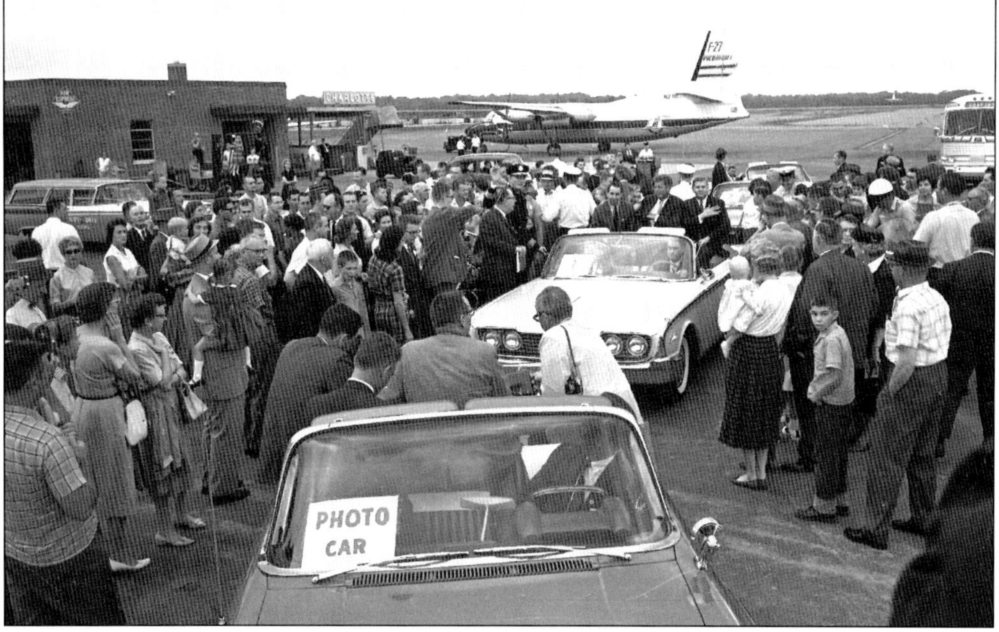

The motorcade leaves Douglas Airport. Seated in the Kennedy car are, from left to right, David Clark (Democratic candidate for the 10th Congressional District), Senator Kennedy, and Terry Sanford. Seated in the front seat—now wearing a white hat—is Gov. Luther H. Hodges. (Courtesy of the *News and Observer* and the North Carolina State Archives.)

Remnants of Hurricane Donna, which brought a "night of terror" into eastern North Carolina five days earlier, had yet fully to disperse. Rather than risk cancellation of the parade due to weather, the motorcade moved out a little early. (Courtesy of the *News and Observer* and the North Carolina State Archives.)

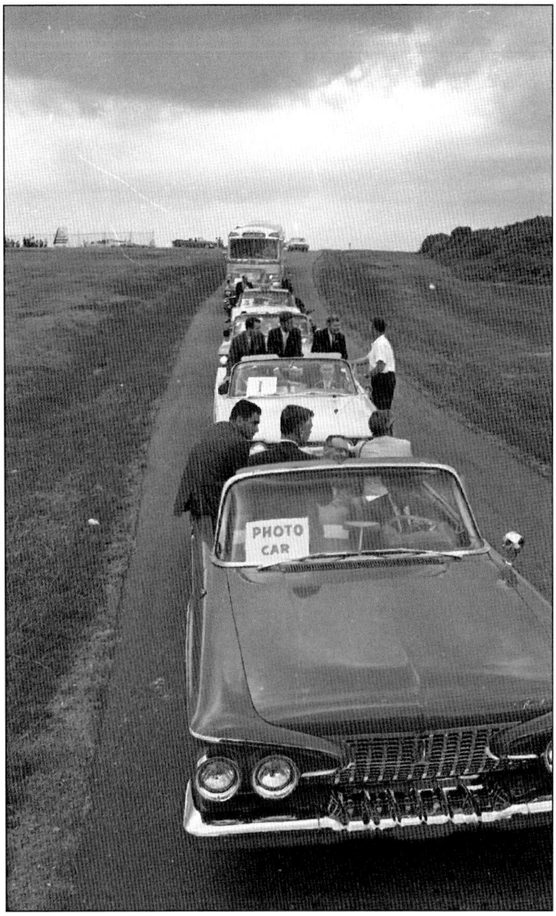

Given that Charlotte was the largest city in North Carolina and one of the most important in the Southeast, the turnout for the Kennedy parade was somewhat small. While the count was close, Vice Pres. Richard Nixon would receive more Charlotte votes than Senator Kennedy. (Courtesy of the *News and Observer* and the North Carolina State Archives.)

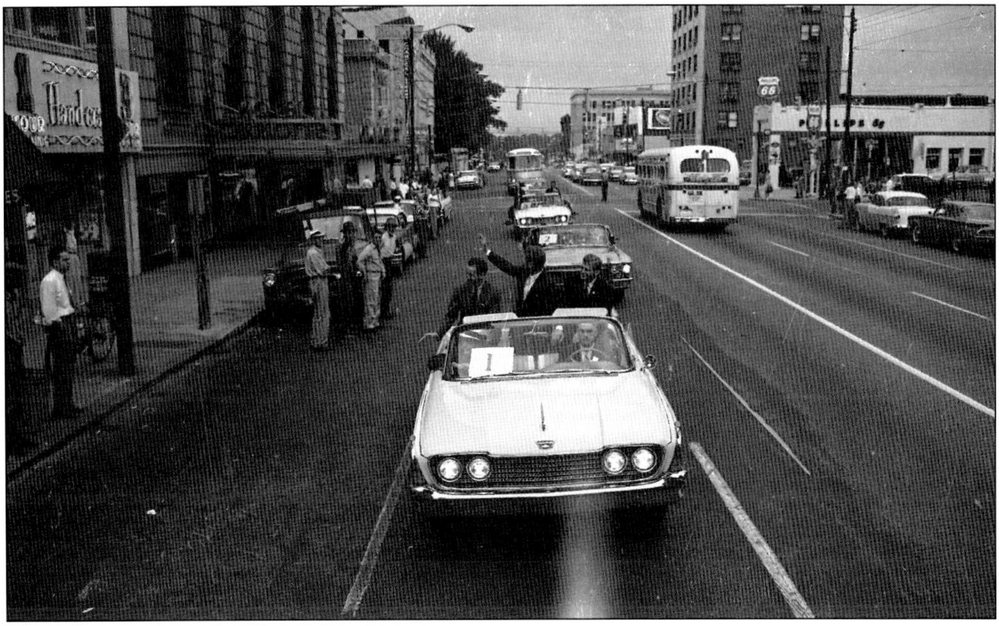

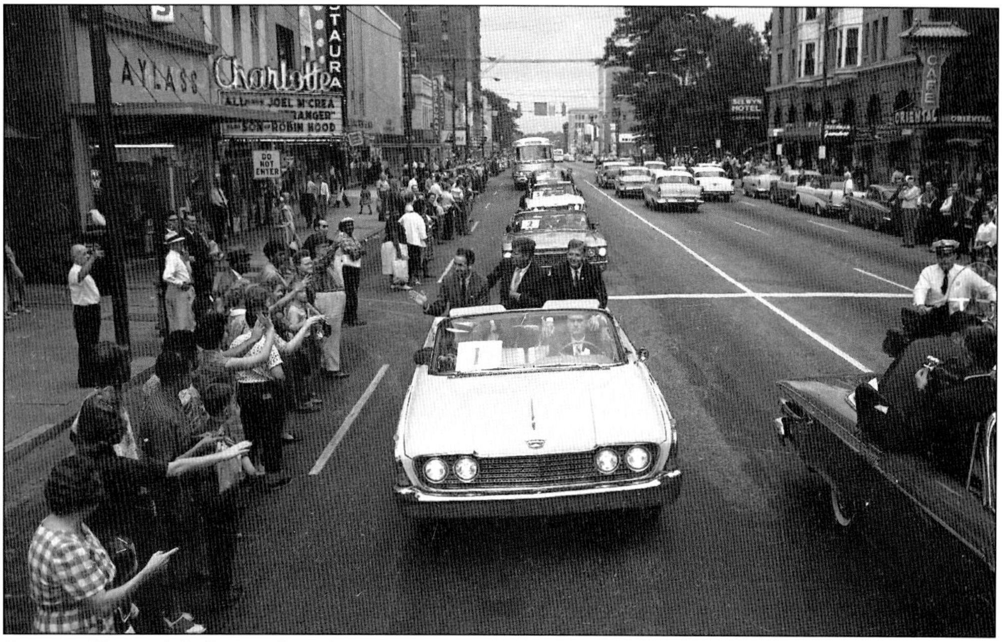

Senator Kennedy's September 17 campaign prompted Vice Pres. Richard M. Nixon to return to the South, specifically North Carolina and the Charlotte Coliseum. Nixon drew 13,000 people, packing the house and surprising many who still imagined the South to be solidly Democratic. (Courtesy of the *News and Observer* and the North Carolina State Archives.)

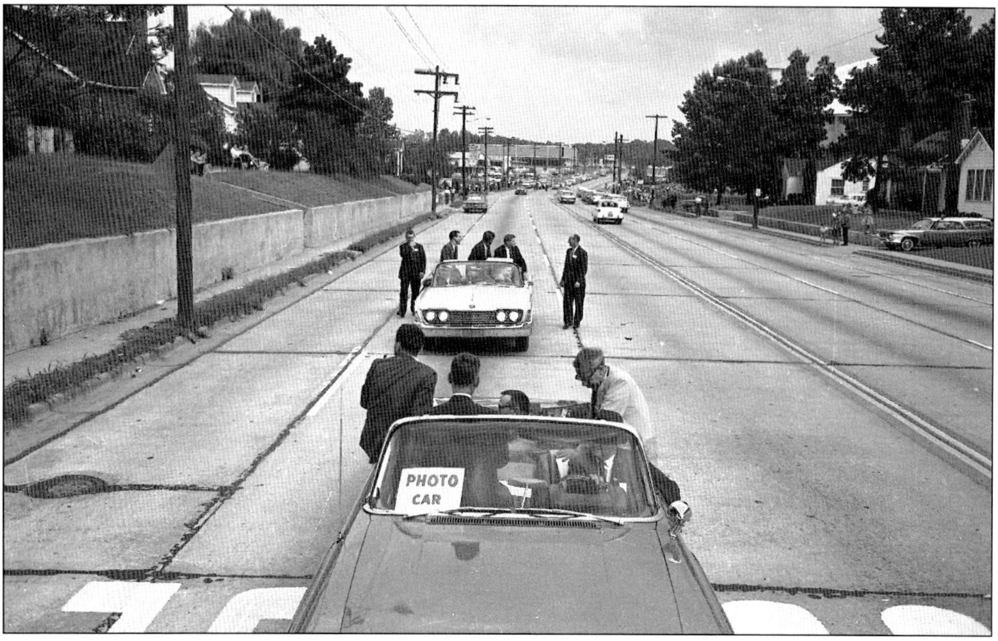

The motorcade paused before continuing to the Charlotte Coliseum, just a few hundred meters away. Lack of excitement was partly due to Senator Kennedy having visited Charlotte before. Also, Charlotte was more Republican than eastern North Carolina. (Courtesy of the *News and Observer* and the North Carolina State Archives.)

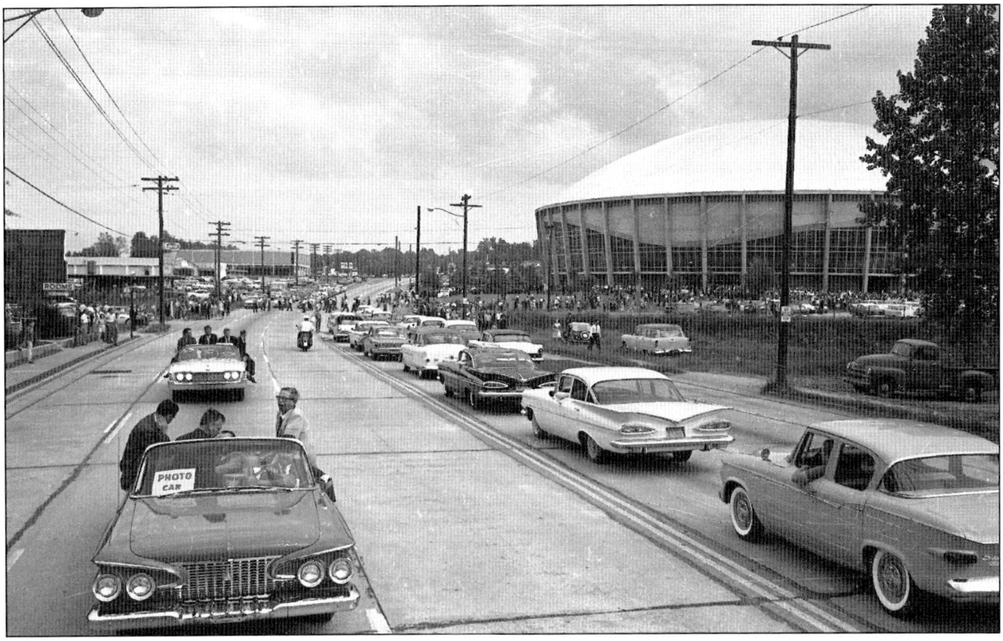

Charlotte Coliseum, today known as Bojangles Coliseum, opened in 1955 as Charlotte's premier venue for sports, popular culture, and entertainment. Back then, it was the largest unsupported steel dome in the world. The Kennedy motorcade seems almost unnoticed as people begin pouring into the facility. (Courtesy of the *News and Observer* and the North Carolina State Archives.)

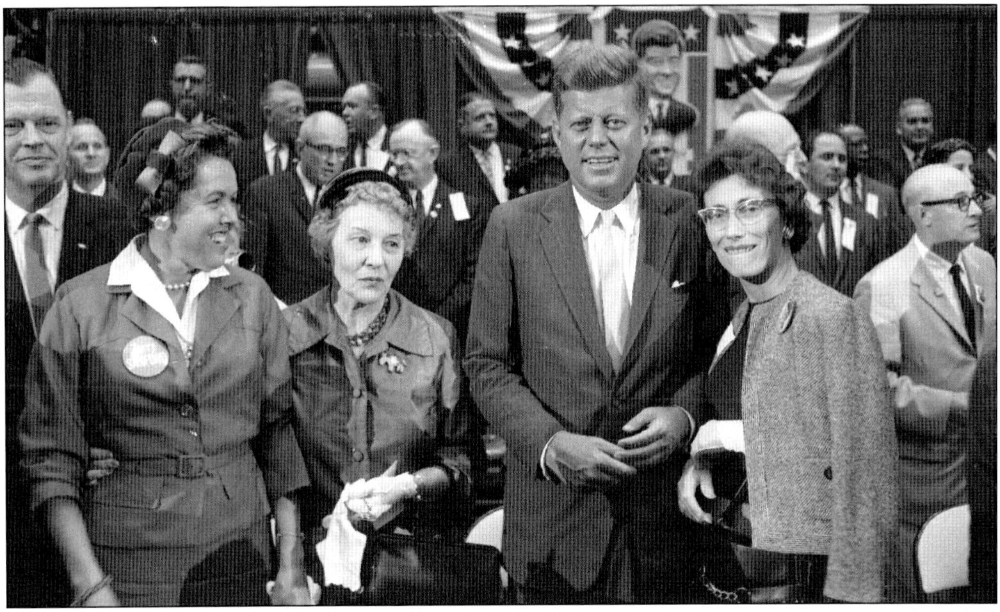

Senator Kennedy met with Charlotte's dignitaries and Democratic leaders. They are, from left to right, Mayor James S. Smith, Margaret Rose Sanford, Gladys Avery Tillett (an advocate of women's rights and a member of the North Carolina Democratic Party's Executive Committee), Senator Kennedy, and Doris M. Cromartie, a leader in the Democratic Women's Clubs of North Carolina and a loyal supporter of Terry Sanford. (Photograph by Don Sturkey, Wilson Library, University of North Carolina.)

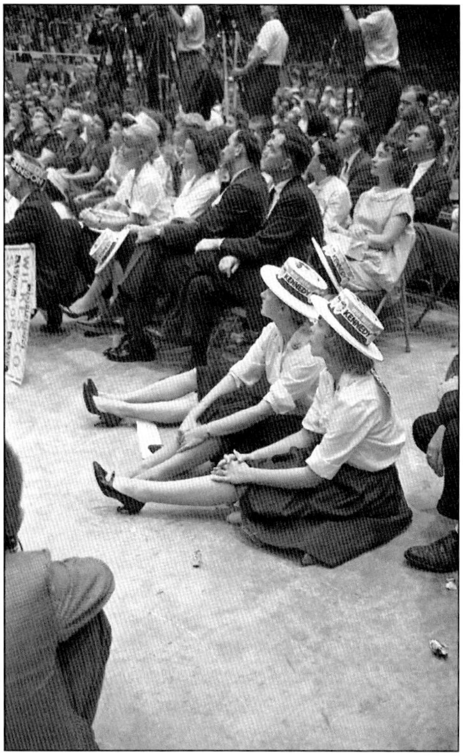

Charlotte Democrats organized approximately 100 young women into "platoons of Kennedy Girls" to help with the visit. Some 25 of these ladies, aged 21 to 22, were chosen to escort Kennedy. Yet another group being flown into Douglas Airport were featured on a float driven through town, the Charlottetown Mall, and then to the coliseum before Kennedy arrived. (Photograph by Don Sturkey, Wilson Library, University of North Carolina.)

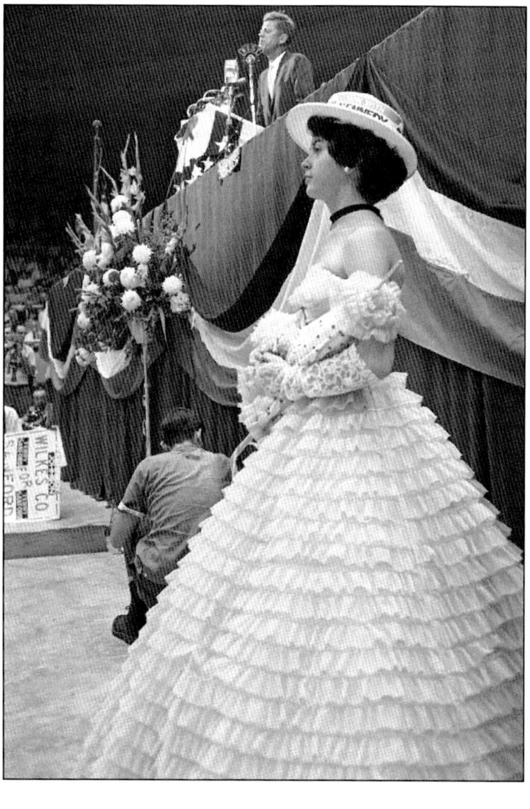

A distinctively Southern modification of the "Kennedy Girl" style seen at rallies took the form of a grand Southern belle replete with a fancy white parasol and Kennedy hat. (Courtesy of the *News and Observer* and the North Carolina State Archives.)

Kennedy reiterated the importance of the Democratic Party to North Carolina and North Carolina to the Democratic Party, recalling among other things North Carolina's contribution of three Democratic presidents to America's political tradition. (Photograph by Hugh Morton; courtesy of Wilson Library, University of North Carolina.)

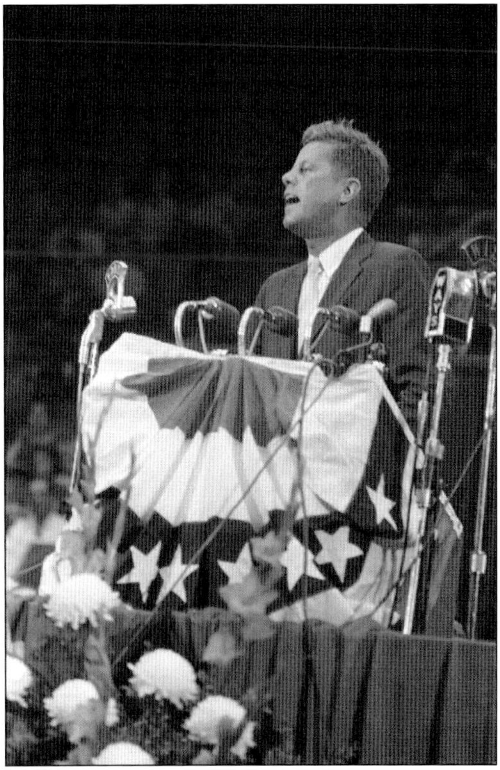

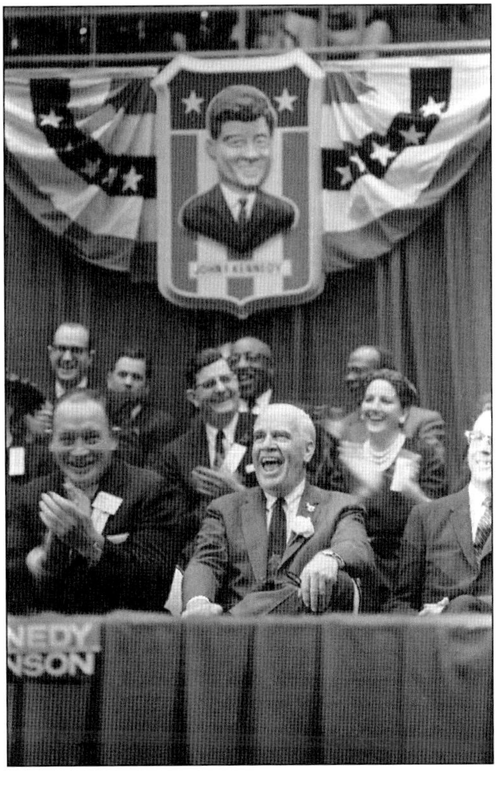

Evidently pleased with Kennedy's sense of humor, Gov. Luther H. Hodges enjoys a hearty laugh during the rally. Throughout the day, Kennedy hinted that if elected, he would continue to work with Hodges and seek Hodges's counsel. (Photograph by Hugh Morton; courtesy of Wilson Library, University of North Carolina.)

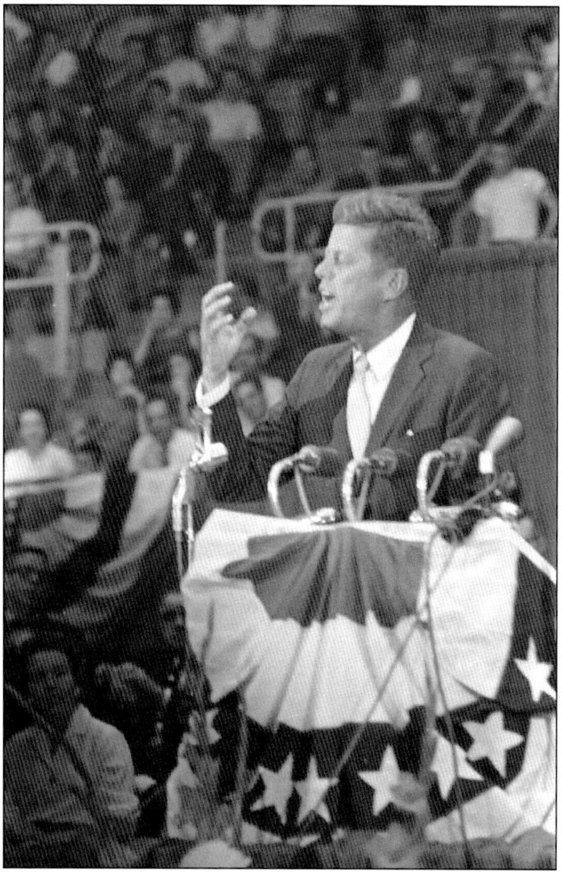

Kennedy's powerful oratorical style reflected the dynamism that he called for in government and national policy. He denounced Republican complacency that led the United States to being "second in space," to a sluggish rate of economic growth, and to an international image of indifference, if not stagnation. (Photograph by Hugh Morton; courtesy of Wilson Library, University of North Carolina.)

Senator Kennedy emphasized Cold War themes at every North Carolina rally. In Charlotte, he explained that the future would be "a difficult time" because as "the defender of freedom . . . only the United States stands between the Communists and world domination. Therefore, we must be prepared to bear our burdens." (Photograph by Hugh Morton; courtesy of Wilson Library, University of North Carolina.)

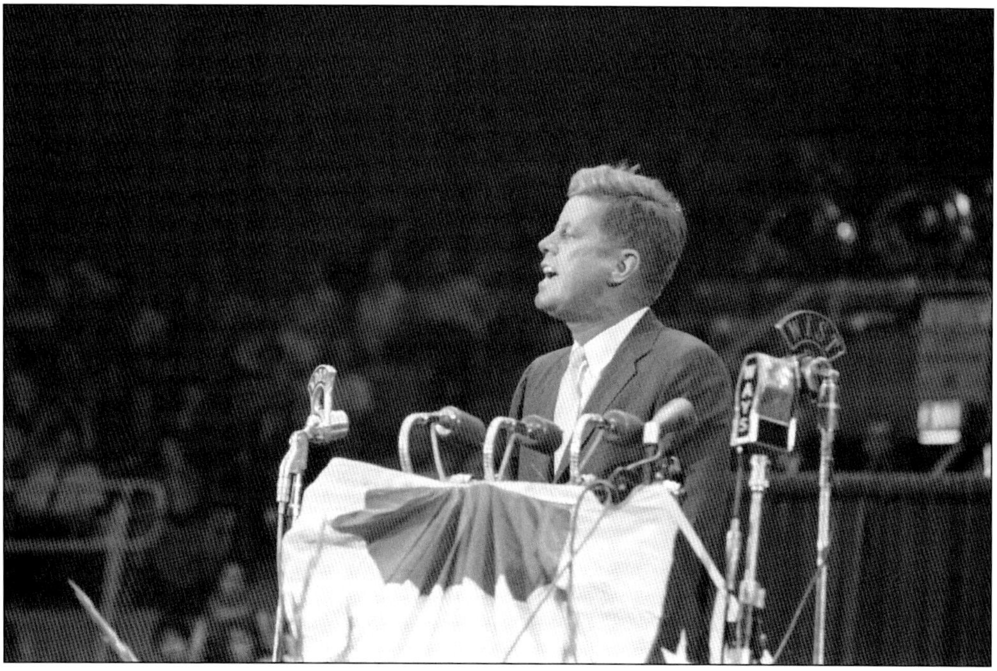

Eight

Raleigh

Senator Kennedy's North Carolina campaign concluded with a grand finale in Raleigh featuring dinner at the governor's mansion and an evening rally at Reynolds Coliseum. An early evening rain resulted in a smaller turnout, leaving the finale somewhat disappointing. Radio newscasts and evening newspapers covering the earlier rallies, plus the promise of a televised broadcast of the Raleigh rally statewide, contributed to a sense that the finale was anticlimactic. For many outside of Raleigh, however, the evening broadcast provided vicarious participation in the grandest day of the North Carolina political campaign season. By giving so much attention to North Carolina, Kennedy contributed significantly to his electoral success in the state. For North Carolinians at least, September 17 was a more decisive factor than the historic, but remote, televised presidential debates between Vice Pres. Richard Nixon and Senator Kennedy that began a week later.

Summarizing the day, Raleigh's *News and Observer* reported that the big event had been in eastern North Carolina, in Greenville, where excitement about the Kennedy campaign bordered on the ecstatic at every turn. Most likely, that was due to the historic significance the Kennedy visit had as the first ever by a presidential nominee in that small town. Moreover, considered in relation to eastern North Carolina, Kennedy's visit also had historic value: it was the first time in the 20th century a presidential nominee had devoted a campaign stop to that part of the state.

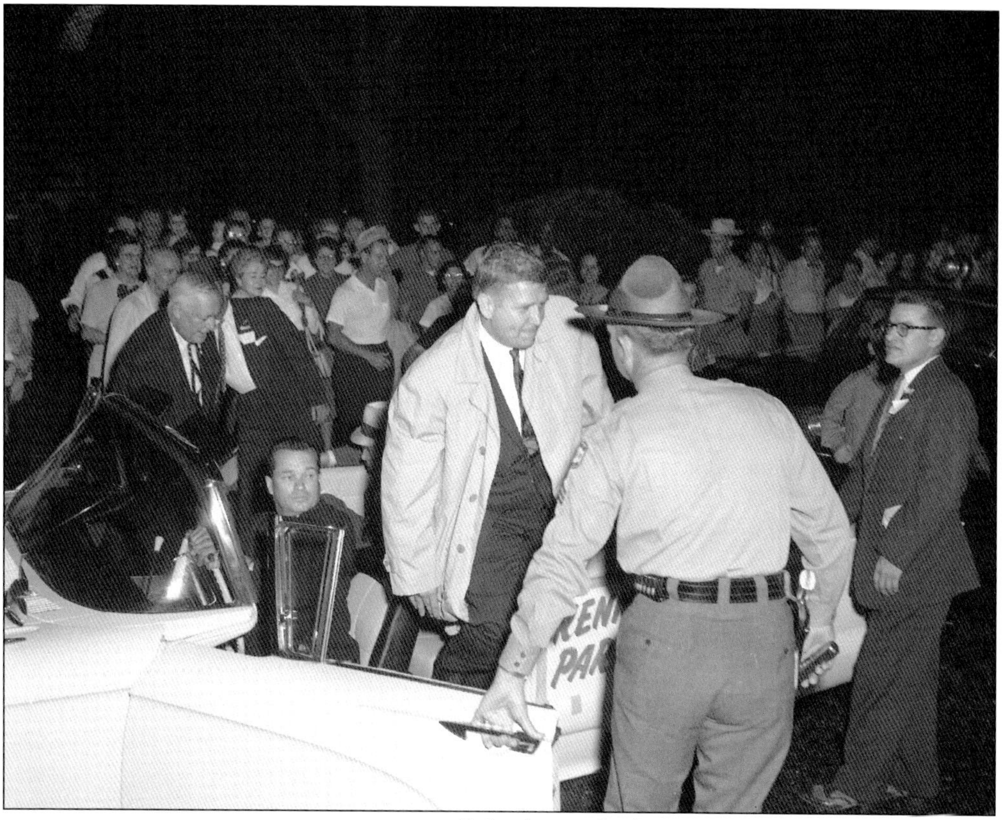

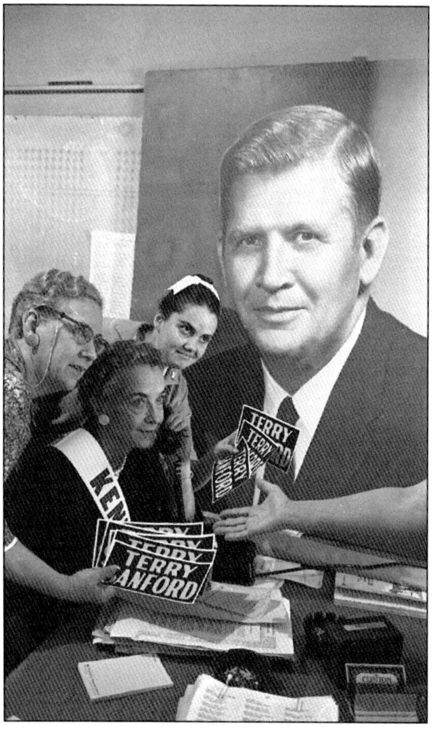

Raleigh was the last stop on Senator Kennedy's grueling, 12-hour air tour of North Carolina. As Terry Sanford exits the Kennedy motorcade car, his raincoat explains why so many seats in Reynolds Coliseum were empty. (Courtesy of the *News and Observer* and the North Carolina State Archives.)

North Carolina women were among the most dedicated and enthusiastic supporters of Terry Sanford and Sen. John Kennedy. In its coverage of the Kennedy campaign, the *Charlotte Observer*'s women's reporter contributed an entertaining piece about women's enthusiastic perception of the senator. (Courtesy of the *News and Observer* and the North Carolina State Archives.)

Kennedy hats were popular items for women of all ages at each of the North Carolina rallies. Typically, the Kennedy campaign made items like straw hats, pins, fliers, and even video copies of Kennedy's address before the Greater Houston Ministerial Association available to campaign organizers upon request. As the ladies reveal, the straw hats were plentiful in Raleigh. (Courtesy of the *News and Observer* and the North Carolina State Archives.)

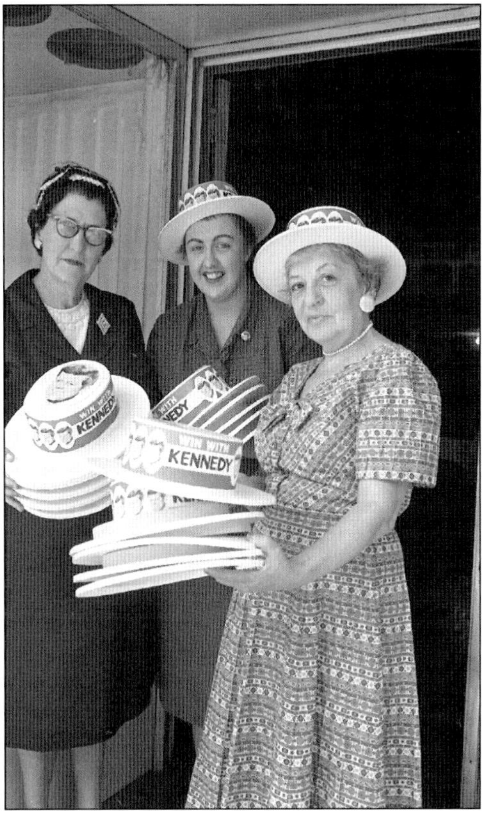

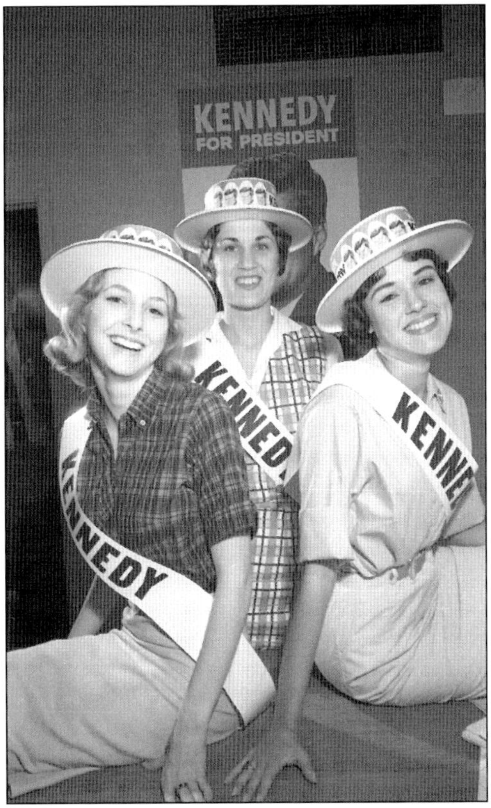

The Kennedy rally at Reynolds Coliseum, located on the North Carolina State College campus, had something of a collegiate character like that at East Carolina College earlier. Groups of Kennedy girls were conspicuous even in the more staid capital of Raleigh. Young women, such as these, were ready to play the part of adoring Southern belles supporting Kennedy. (Courtesy of the *News and Observer* and the North Carolina State Archives.)

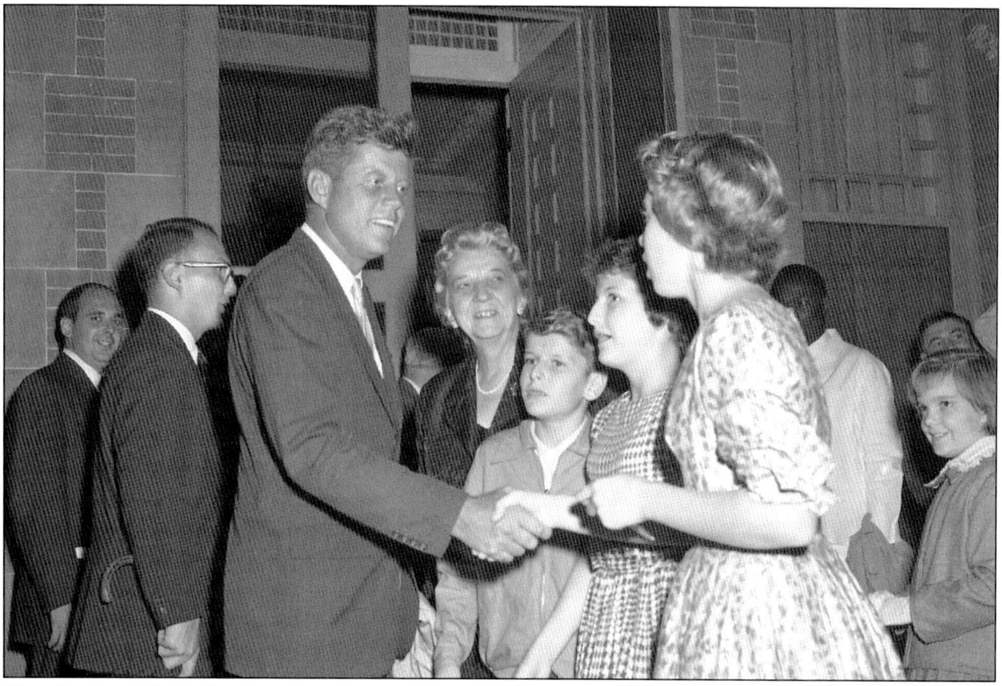

Gov. Luther H. Hodges's wife welcomed Senator Kennedy to the governor's mansion for dinner and a brief rest before the Reynolds Coliseum rally. While Reynolds Coliseum is on the North Carolina State College (now university) campus, the turnout was not the college crowd, but instead mature Raleigh and environs. (Courtesy of the *News and Observer* and the North Carolina State Archives.)

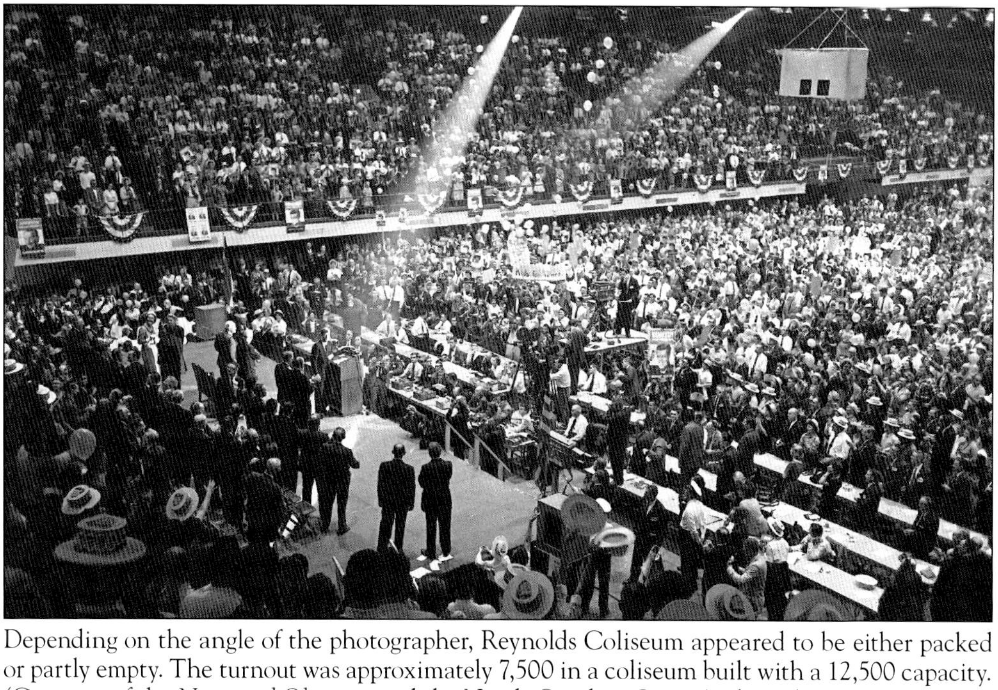

Depending on the angle of the photographer, Reynolds Coliseum appeared to be either packed or partly empty. The turnout was approximately 7,500 in a coliseum built with a 12,500 capacity. (Courtesy of the *News and Observer* and the North Carolina State Archives.)

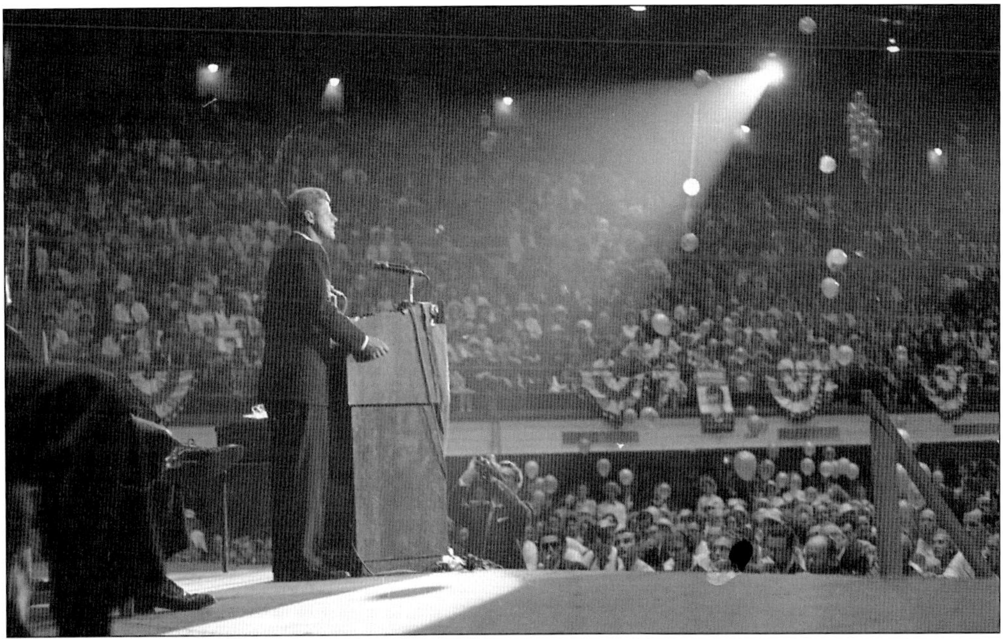

Senator Kennedy advanced his "New Frontier" rhetoric with an appeal to "a great son of North Carolina, Thomas Wolfe," who said, "I think the true discovery of America is before us. I think the true fulfillment of our spirit, of our people, of our mighty and immortal land, is yet to come." (Courtesy of the *News and Observer* and the North Carolina State Archives.)

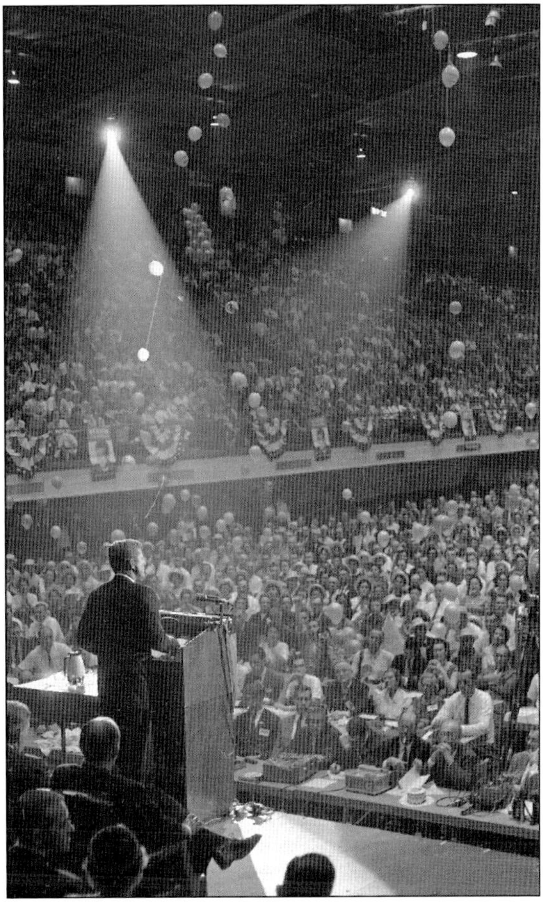

Senator Kennedy played to the Raleigh crowd by recalling the bravery of the 108 men who established the first English-speaking colony in the New World at Roanoke Island, North Carolina. He linked that theme with Massachusetts's Plymouth Rock, affirming the ties between the two regions that later worked together, birthing the Democratic Party and its contributions to the progressive American experience. (Courtesy of the *News and Observer* and the North Carolina State Archives.)

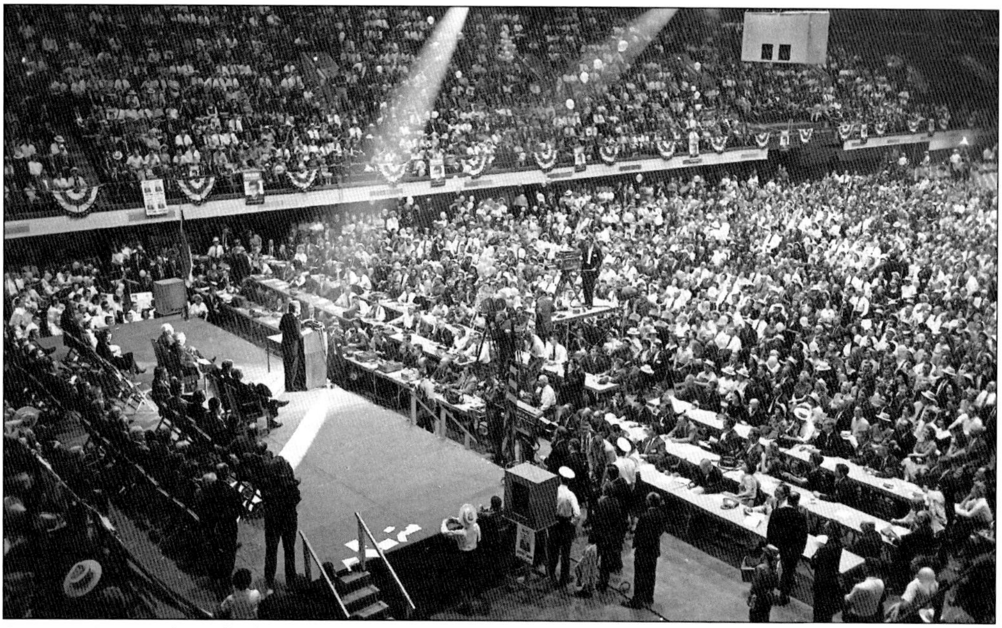

Senator Kennedy called for more economic growth, more military strength, more scientific advancement, and more leadership in world affairs, but sidestepped civil rights and the sit-ins that had defined much of the year in North Carolina. He concluded his address with praise for the South as "the land of Washington, who made our nation—of Jefferson, who shaped its direction—and of Robert E. Lee who, after gallant failure, urged those who had followed him in bravery to reunite America in purpose and courage." (Courtesy of the *News and Observer* and the North Carolina State Archives.)

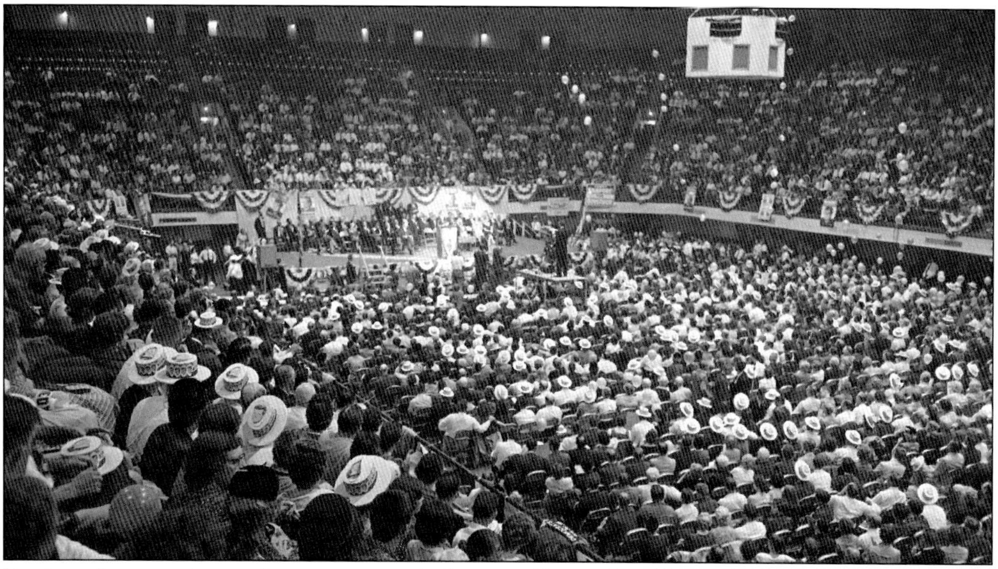

During the question and answer period, Senator Kennedy addressed religion, discarding his prepared remarks to offer a heartfelt response. He stated that his ideas on national strength and power should be of more concern for North Carolinians than "where I am going to go to church tomorrow." Applause followed. (Courtesy of the *News and Observer* and the North Carolina State Archives.)

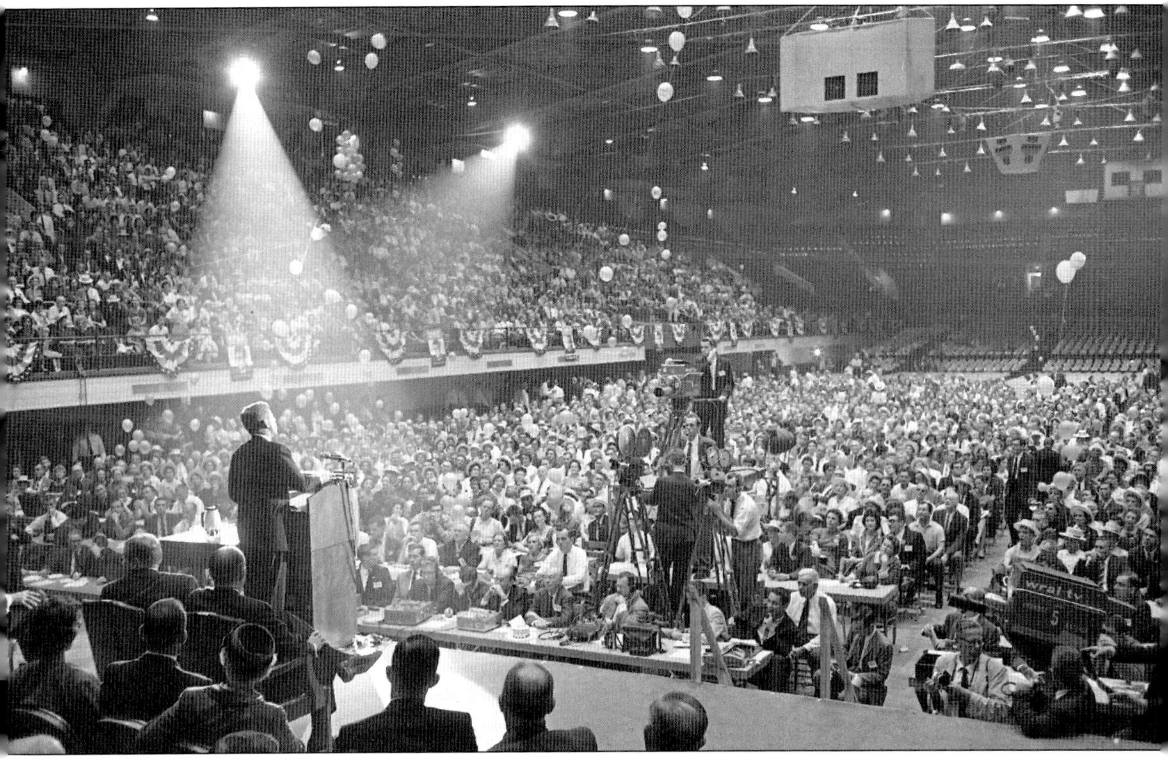

Despite the empty sections in the back, Senator Kennedy's rally at Reynolds Coliseum signaled the beginning of a new era in campaigning, one in which a photogenic, articulate candidate could, via television, sway a state even while speaking to a partially filled coliseum. On September 26, just over a week following the North Carolina campaign, Kennedy proved himself the master of this new campaign technology in the first of a series of historic nationally televised debates with Vice President Nixon. As Joe Steelman, a professor at East Carolina College, remarked regarding the first debate, "Kennedy figuratively mopped up the ground with Nixon in that first debate." While the personal touch in North Carolina made an enormous difference with the local people, it was also coupled with, and arguably climaxed by, a technology that signaled the wave of future campaigns. (Courtesy of the *News and Observer* and the North Carolina State Archives.)

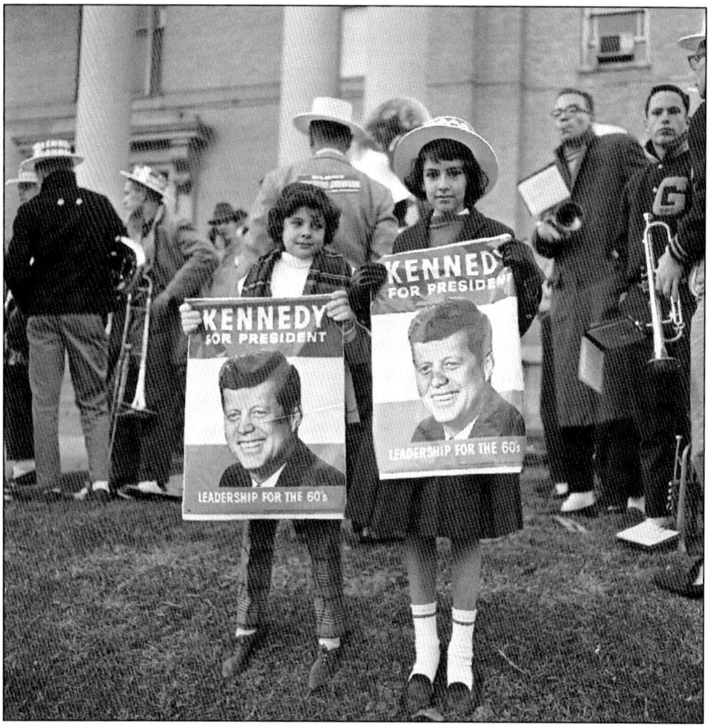

Two young girls are pictured campaigning for Kennedy late in the fall of 1960 in front of the Pitt County Courthouse in Greenville, North Carolina. Vice Pres. Richard Nixon campaigned in North Carolina twice—once in Greensboro and once in Charlotte. He never ventured into the eastern region of the state. (Courtesy of the *Daily Reflector* and J.Y. Joyner Library, East Carolina University.)

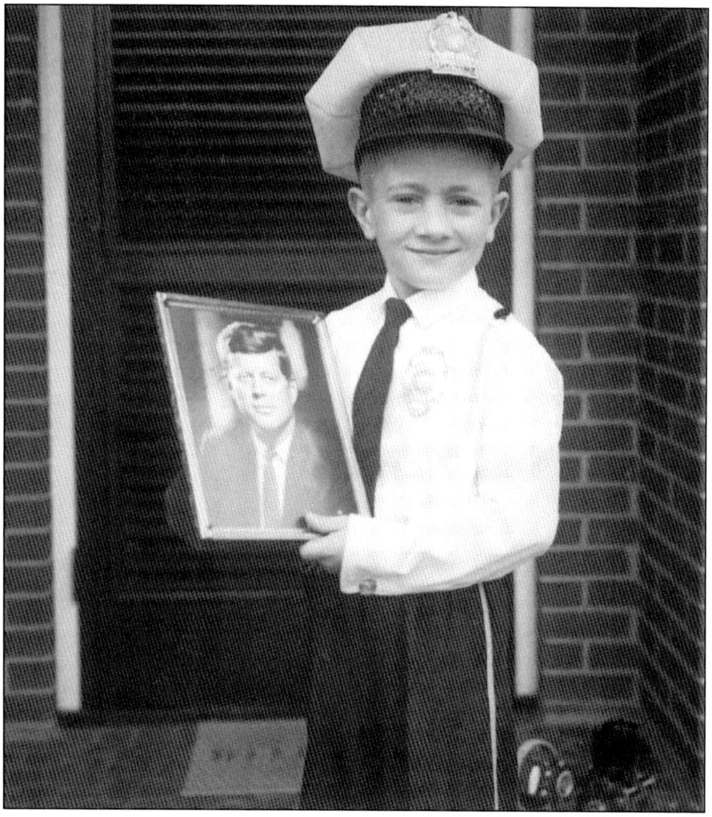

A young Farmville boy, Vance Daniels, displays a framed picture of the newly elected President Kennedy. Young Daniels had campaigned for Kennedy in 1960, despite a congenital heart defect. When Farmville mayor Charles Edwards wrote President Kennedy explaining Daniels's "lifelong ambition" to meet the president, Kennedy agreed to have Daniels for a visit at the White House. Rep. Herbert Bonner accompanied Daniels and his parents, Rev. and Mrs. Jack M. Daniels. (Courtesy of the *Daily Reflector* and J.Y. Joyner Library, East Carolina University.)

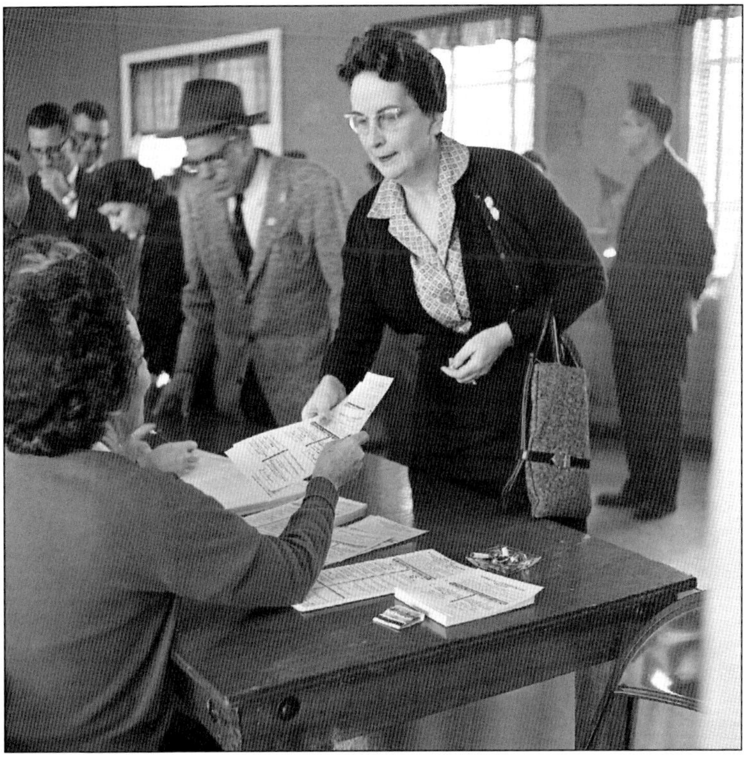

In every county of eastern North Carolina, Senator Kennedy prevailed by huge margins, in some cases with 75 percent of the vote or more. (Courtesy of the *Daily Reflector* and J.Y. Joyner Library, East Carolina University.)

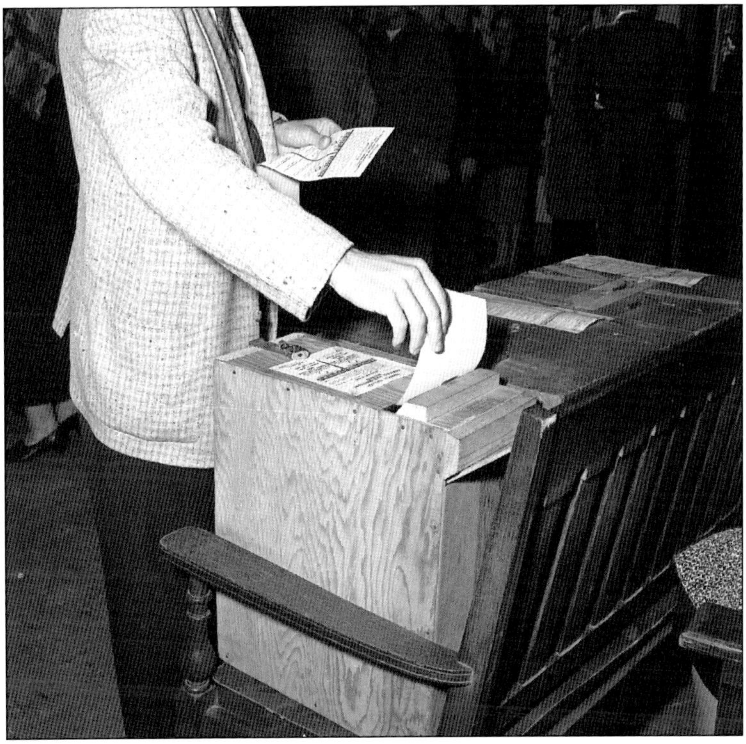

Eastern North Carolinians revealed that the anti-Catholic rhetoric that had targeted them and their often fundamentalist understandings of religion did not trump another form of deeply rooted fundamentalism, respect for religious freedom. (Courtesy of the *Daily Reflector* and J.Y. Joyner Library, East Carolina University.)

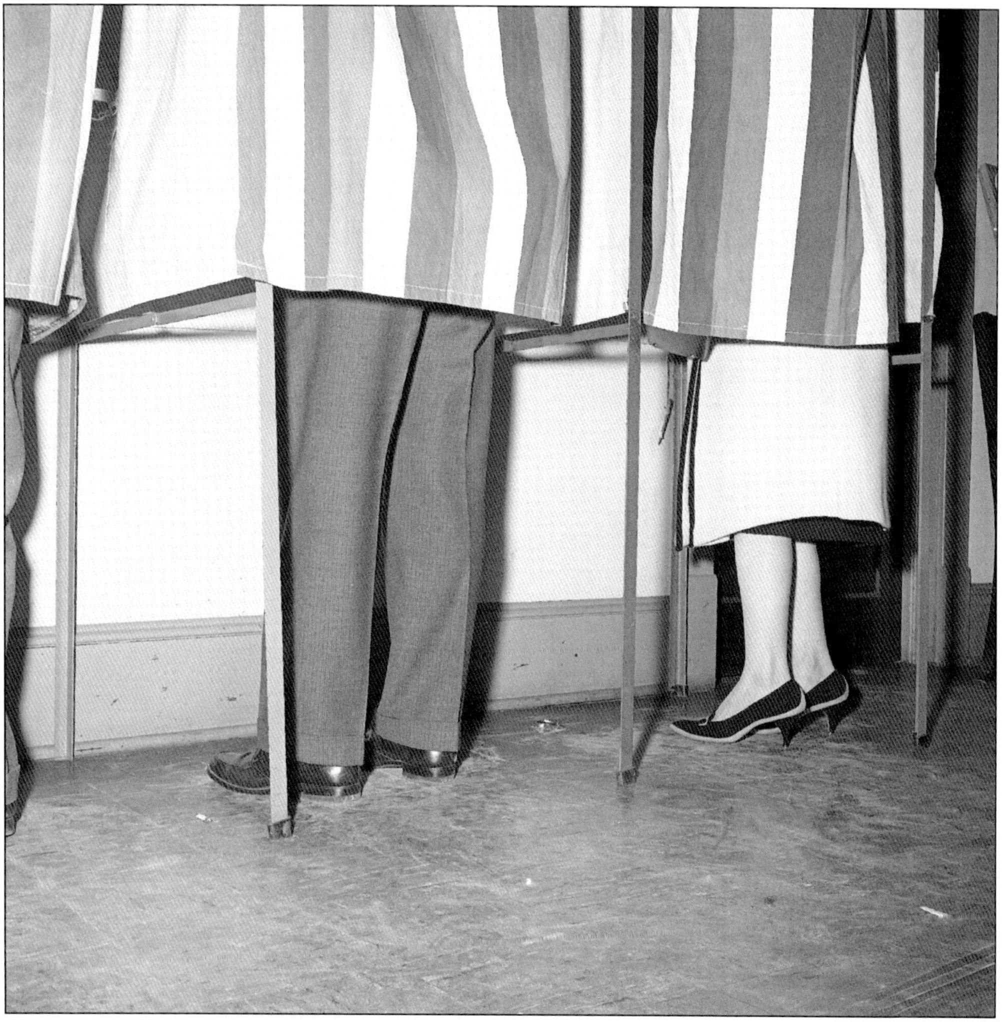

While the televised presidential debates might have been decisive factors in some areas, not all North Carolinians owned televisions and reception was not always ideal for those who did. Even if they watched the debates, Senator Kennedy's statewide campaign predisposed many to him. Kennedy carried the state with relative ease, securing 713,136 votes to Vice Pres. Richard Nixon's 655,432. In counties like Pitt County, where Kennedy campaigned and Nixon did not, Kennedy secured 12,526 votes to Nixon's 3,458. In Wake County (Raleigh), the vote was 26,050 to 18,436 in favor of Kennedy. In Mecklenburg County, where Nixon followed Kennedy with a rally packing Charlotte Coliseum, Nixon won (48,250 to 39,362), as he did in Guilford County where Nixon had earlier packed War Memorial Coliseum and Kennedy only staged an airport rally (41,357 to 30,486). Generally, Kennedy's margin of victory in eastern North Carolina was large, more than making up for the counties lost in the piedmont and west. (Courtesy of the *Daily Reflector* and J.Y. Joyner Library, East Carolina University.)

Nine

CELEBRATION AND TRAGEDY

In 1877, Gov. Zebulon B. Vance declared that October 12 be observed annually at the University of North Carolina "with appropriate ceremonies." On that date, the cornerstone of the first building on campus, Old East, had been laid. October 12 is now known as University Day, a time for celebrating the university's past and conceptualizing its future. North Carolina's governors traditionally have the honor of selecting featured speakers for the occasion. In 1961, Gov. Terry Sanford, a Chapel Hill alumnus, chose the newly elected president, John F. Kennedy. Over 32,000 people were present for the "golden moment" featuring the two young, progressive leaders.

While far grander with its academic pomp, University Day recalled Kennedy's appearance the year before at East Carolina College. The earlier event, however, was a campaign rally staged when Kennedy had yet to be elected president and Sanford was running for governor. On the one hand, East Carolina was a rural, normal school turned liberal arts college while Chapel Hill claimed to be the oldest state-supported institution of higher education in the nation. In many respects, East Carolina had pioneered, in a big way, the practice of politicizing a campus by hosting powerful statesmen and ambitious politicians. In 1961, for all the caps and gowns, chancellors and deans, honorary degrees and old school rituals, Kennedy's University Day address simply echoed, for many North Carolinians, the rally at East Carolina.

University Day also reflected the depth of Kennedy's relationship with North Carolina, the very bond that Leo Jenkins would allude to later by saying, "He was part of this campus." Kennedy's bond with the state made his tragic death a shocking blow to the hopes and dreams of many North Carolinians. Memorial services followed, revering the fallen leader and contributing to his future memory. Kennedy's North Carolina campaign then resulted in more than electoral victory. It created an unprecedented bond with a statesman, one that has not been matched since.

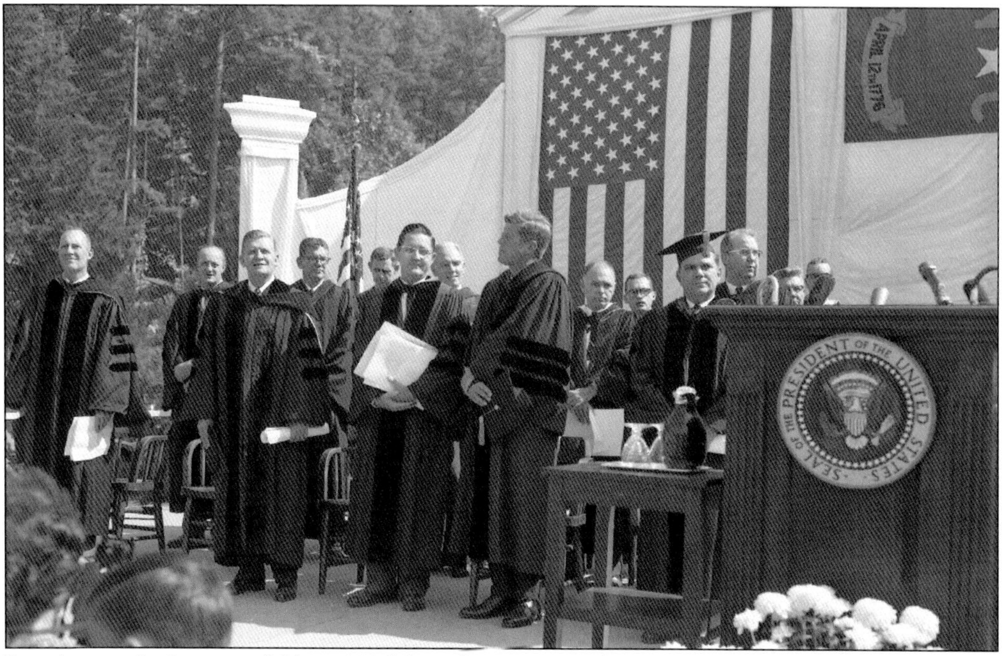

Few days in the history of Chapel Hill have been as grand as October 12, 1961, when Pres. John F. Kennedy addressed the University Day audience assembled in Kenan Stadium. Along with President Kennedy, Gov. Terry Sanford received an honorary degree. (Photograph by Roy Hardee; courtesy of J.Y. Joyner Library, East Carolina University.)

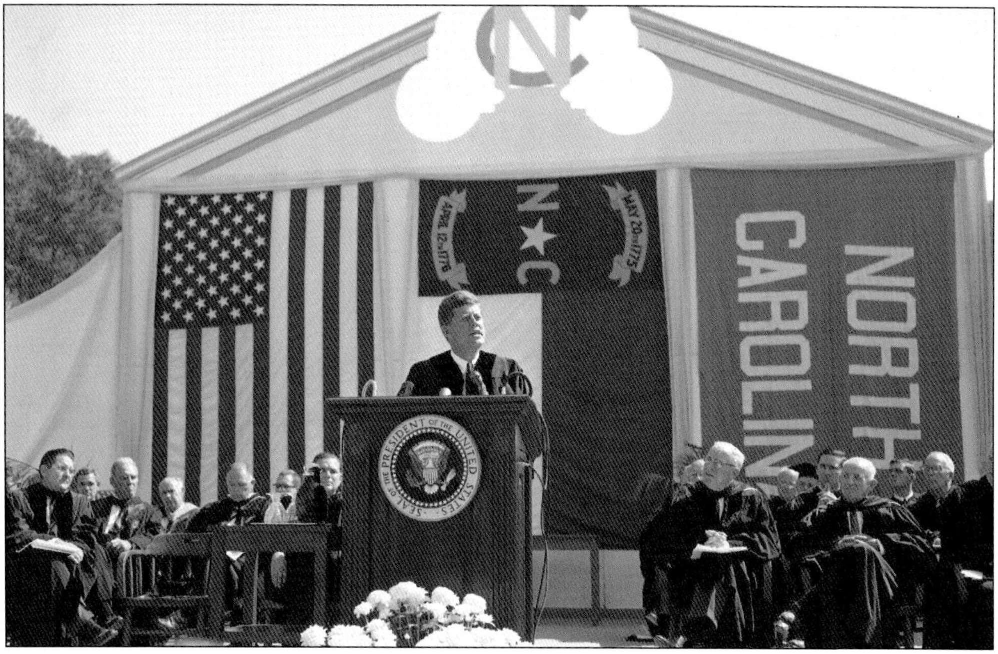

On the far left of the stage is William C. Friday, president of the University of North Carolina. To the right of the podium is former Gov. Luther H. Hodges, then secretary of commerce in the Kennedy Administration, and Franklin Porter Graham, former president of the university. (Photograph by Roy Hardee; courtesy of J.Y. Joyner Library, East Carolina University.)

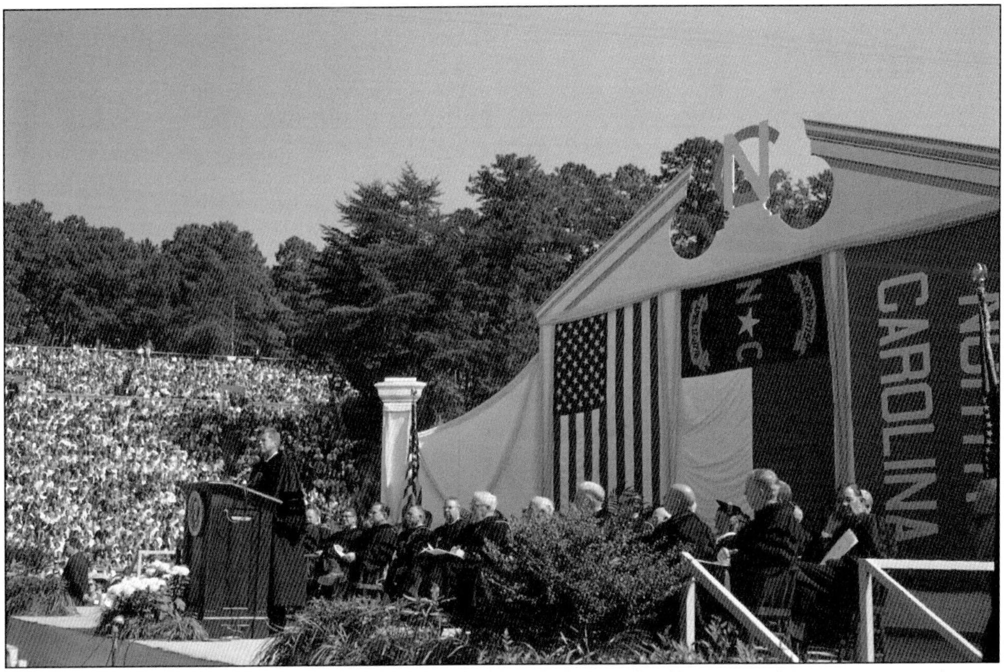

Dignitaries on the stage for University Day included a host of college presidents, provosts, deans, associate deans, and department chairs. (Photograph by Roy Hardee; courtesy of J.Y. Joyner Library, East Carolina University.)

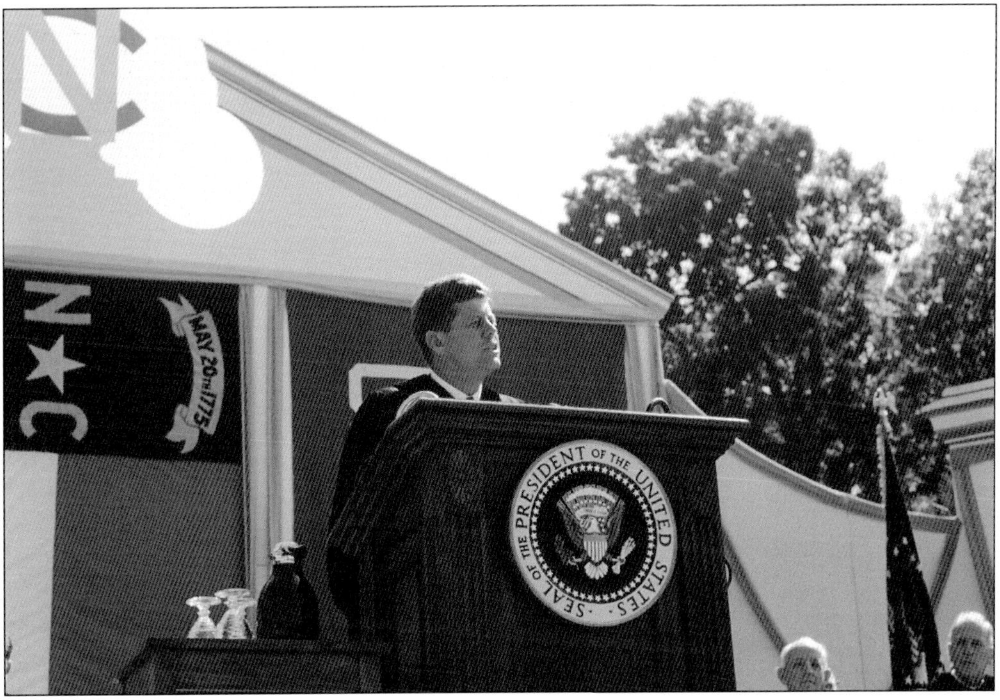

President Kennedy's University Day address continued many of the cold war themes that he had discussed while campaigning for the presidency. (Photograph by Roy Hardee; courtesy of J.Y. Joyner Library, East Carolina University.)

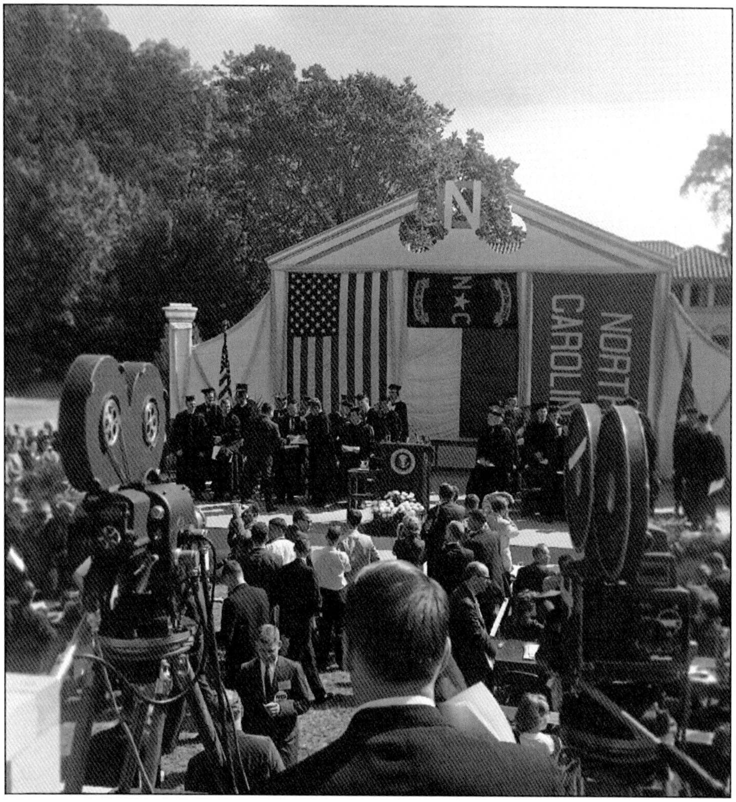

The University Day ceremony was videotaped with narration by Edward R. Murrow, a North Carolinian. When Pres. William J. Clinton spoke at the University Day ceremony in 1993, the film of Kennedy's University Day address was shown as part of the Kenan Stadium program. President Clinton claimed to have been inspired by President Kennedy. (Photograph by Roy Hardee; courtesy of J.Y. Joyner Library, East Carolina University.)

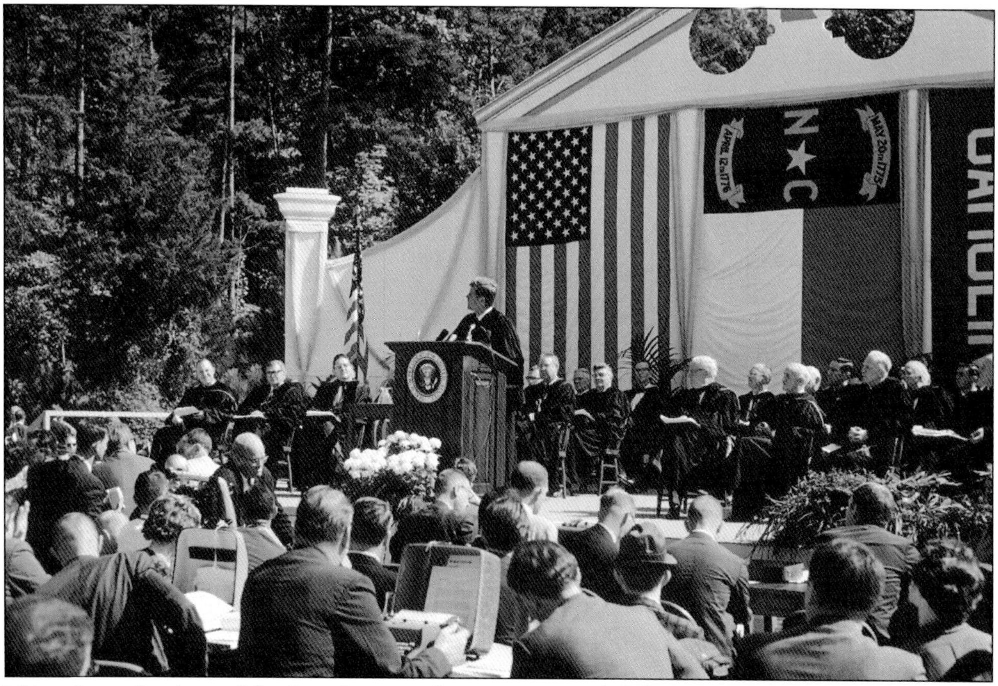

Using the technology of the day, a battery of newsmen recorded the major points President Kennedy made. (Photograph by Roy Hardee; courtesy of J.Y. Joyner Library, East Carolina University.)

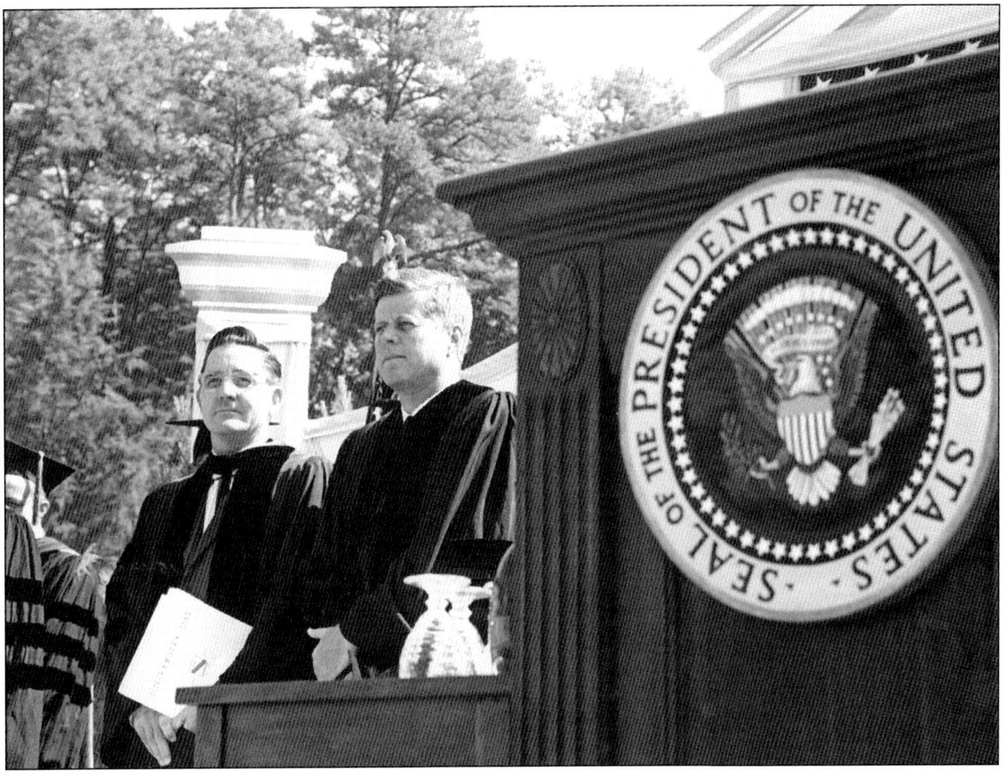

President Kennedy stands next to William Friday, president of the University of North Carolina. (Photograph by Roy Hardee; courtesy of J.Y. Joyner Library, East Carolina University.)

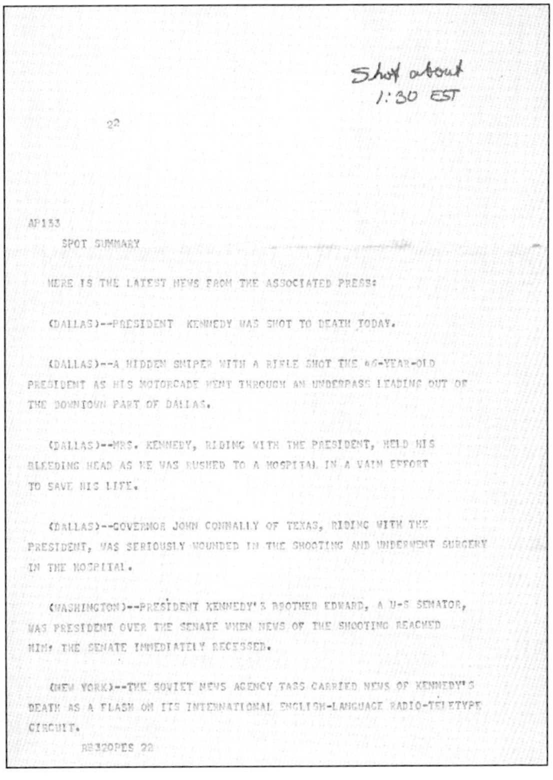

Shot about 1:30 EST

22

AP133

SPOT SUMMARY

HERE IS THE LATEST NEWS FROM THE ASSOCIATED PRESS:

(DALLAS)--PRESIDENT KENNEDY WAS SHOT TO DEATH TODAY.

(DALLAS)--A HIDDEN SNIPER WITH A RIFLE SHOT THE 46-YEAR-OLD PRESIDENT AS HIS MOTORCADE WENT THROUGH AN UNDERPASS LEADING OUT OF THE DOWNTOWN PART OF DALLAS.

(DALLAS)--MRS. KENNEDY, RIDING WITH THE PRESIDENT, HELD HIS BLEEDING HEAD AS HE WAS RUSHED TO A HOSPITAL IN A VAIN EFFORT TO SAVE HIS LIFE.

(DALLAS)--GOVERNOR JOHN CONNALLY OF TEXAS, RIDING WITH THE PRESIDENT, WAS SERIOUSLY WOUNDED IN THE SHOOTING AND UNDERWENT SURGERY IN THE HOSPITAL.

(WASHINGTON)--PRESIDENT KENNEDY'S BROTHER EDWARD, A U-S SENATOR, WAS PRESIDENT OVER THE SENATE WHEN NEWS OF THE SHOOTING REACHED HIM; THE SENATE IMMEDIATELY RECESSED.

(NEW YORK)--THE SOVIET NEWS AGENCY TASS CARRIED NEWS OF KENNEDY'S DEATH AS A FLASH ON ITS INTERNATIONAL ENGLISH-LANGUAGE RADIO-TELETYPE CIRCUIT.

RB320PES 22

Balinda Ferree was working in her father's radio station in High Point when a Teletype communicated that the president had been shot. Ferree realized the horrible but historic significance of the Teletype and saved it. In 2011, she and her husband, John, donated it to the Joyner Library, East Carolina University. (John and Balinda Ferree Teletype Collection, J.Y. Joyner Library, East Carolina University.)

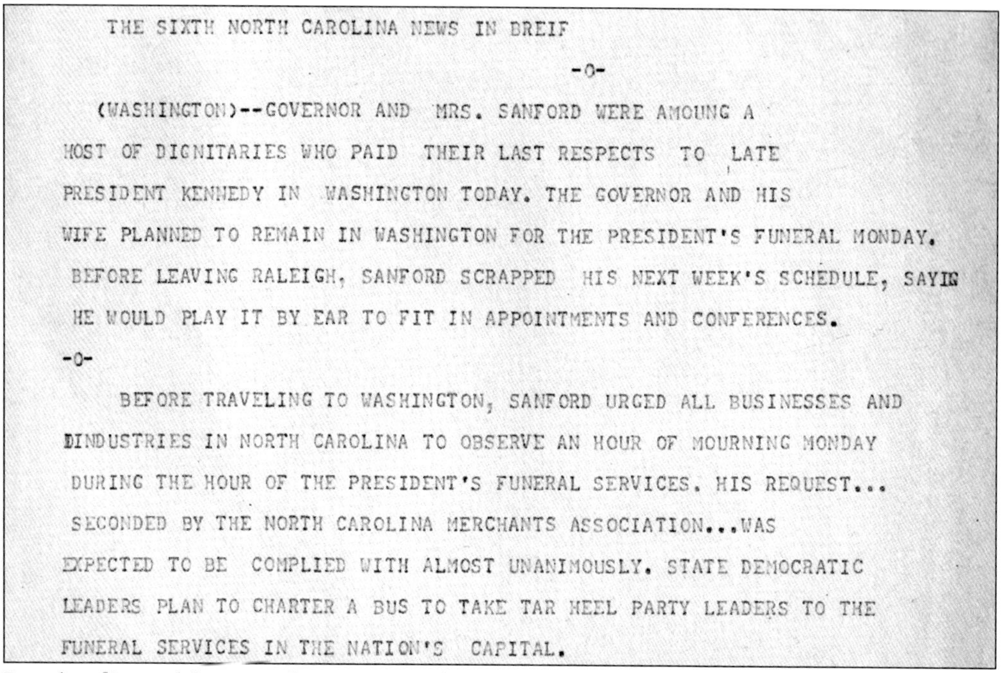
THE SIXTH NORTH CAROLINA NEWS IN BREIF

-0-

(WASHINGTON)--GOVERNOR AND MRS. SANFORD WERE AMOUNG A HOST OF DIGNITARIES WHO PAID THEIR LAST RESPECTS TO LATE PRESIDENT KENNEDY IN WASHINGTON TODAY. THE GOVERNOR AND HIS WIFE PLANNED TO REMAIN IN WASHINGTON FOR THE PRESIDENT'S FUNERAL MONDAY. BEFORE LEAVING RALEIGH, SANFORD SCRAPPED HIS NEXT WEEK'S SCHEDULE, SAYIN HE WOULD PLAY IT BY EAR TO FIT IN APPOINTMENTS AND CONFERENCES.

-0-

BEFORE TRAVELING TO WASHINGTON, SANFORD URGED ALL BUSINESSES AND BINDUSTRIES IN NORTH CAROLINA TO OBSERVE AN HOUR OF MOURNING MONDAY DURING THE HOUR OF THE PRESIDENT'S FUNERAL SERVICES. HIS REQUEST... SECONDED BY THE NORTH CAROLINA MERCHANTS ASSOCIATION...WAS EXPECTED TO BE COMPLIED WITH ALMOST UNANIMOUSLY. STATE DEMOCRATIC LEADERS PLAN TO CHARTER A BUS TO TAKE TAR HEEL PARTY LEADERS TO THE FUNERAL SERVICES IN THE NATION'S CAPITAL.

President Kennedy's personal secretary, Evelyn Lincoln, has written that Kennedy was considering Gov. Terry Sanford as a running mate in 1964. Sanford was never informed of this, however. Nevertheless, his sense of loss, both personal and political, resulting from Kennedy's tragic death was profound. (John and Balinda Ferree Teletype Collection, J.Y. Joyner Library, East Carolina University.)

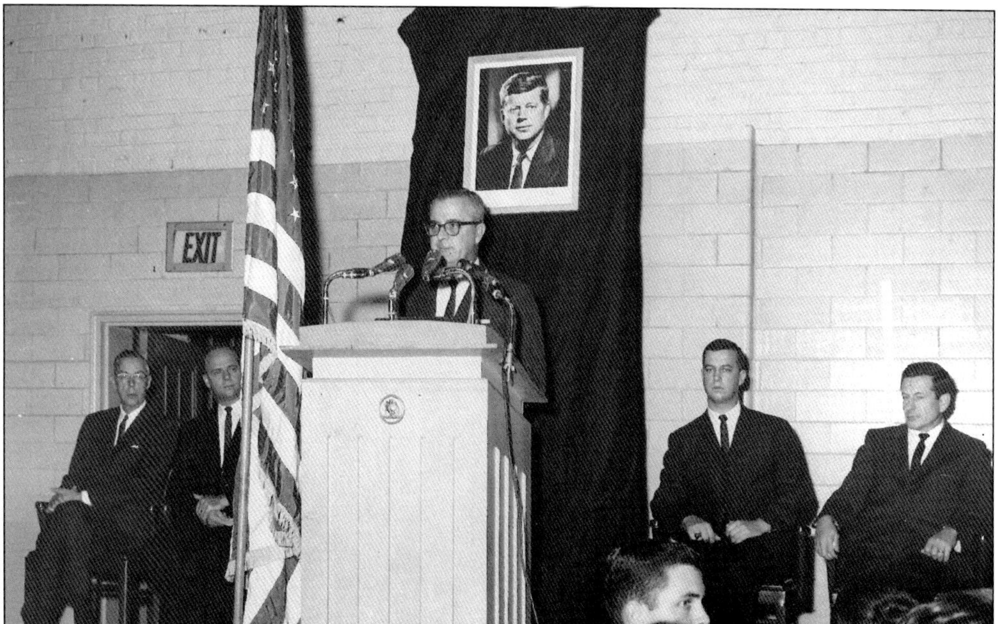

At East Carolina College, Pres. Leo W. Jenkins delivered a eulogy as part of a simple yet heartfelt memorial service, noting that Kennedy had been "part of this campus." (Courtesy of the *Daily Reflector* and J.Y. Joyner Library, East Carolina University.)

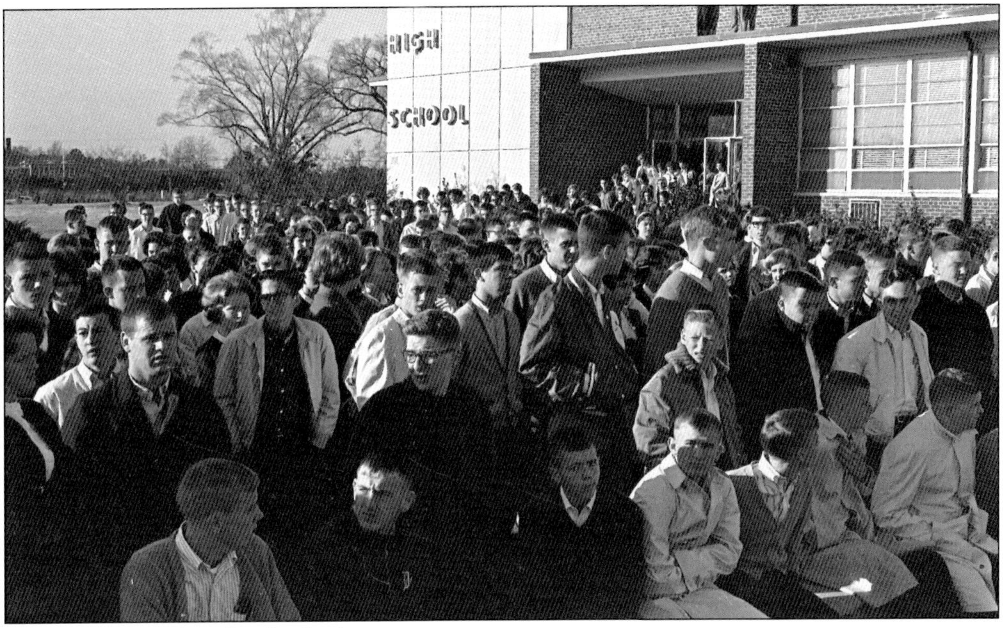

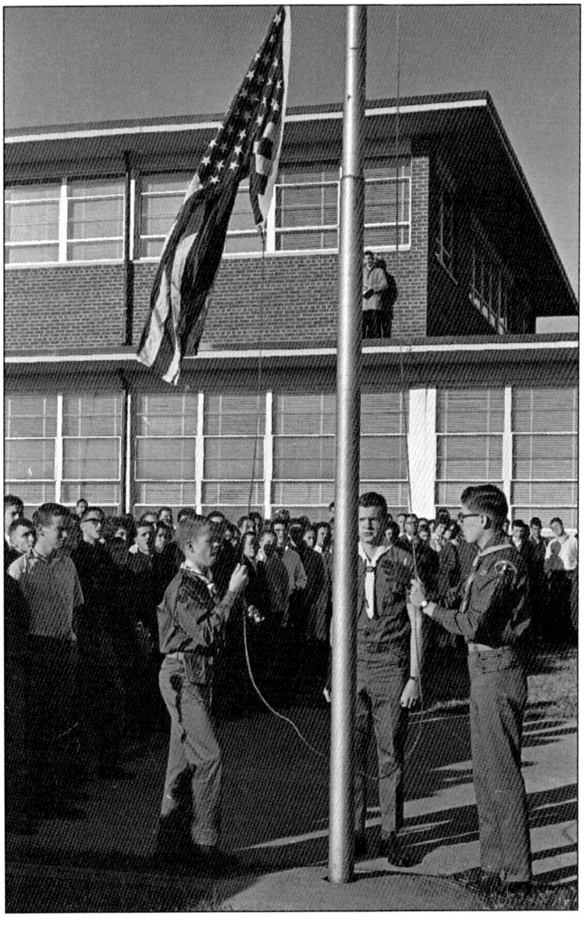

At J.H. Rose High School, which was located near College Stadium, a memorial service was held for the slain leader on the day of his burial, Monday, November 25, 1963. (Both, courtesy of the *Daily Reflector* and J.Y. Joyner Library, East Carolina University.)

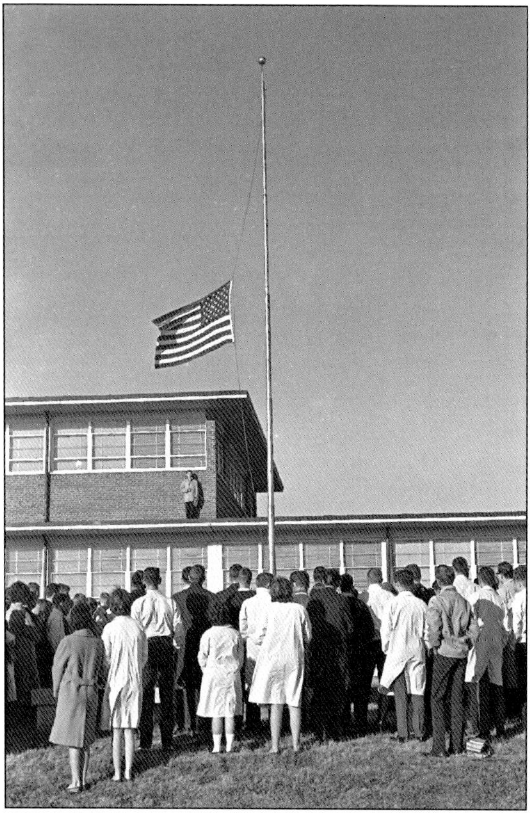

J.H. Rose, superintendent of the Greenville City Schools and namesake of the high school, was among those who had attended the Kennedy rally at East Carolina on September 17, 1960. (Courtesy of the *Daily Reflector* and J.Y. Joyner Library, East Carolina University.)

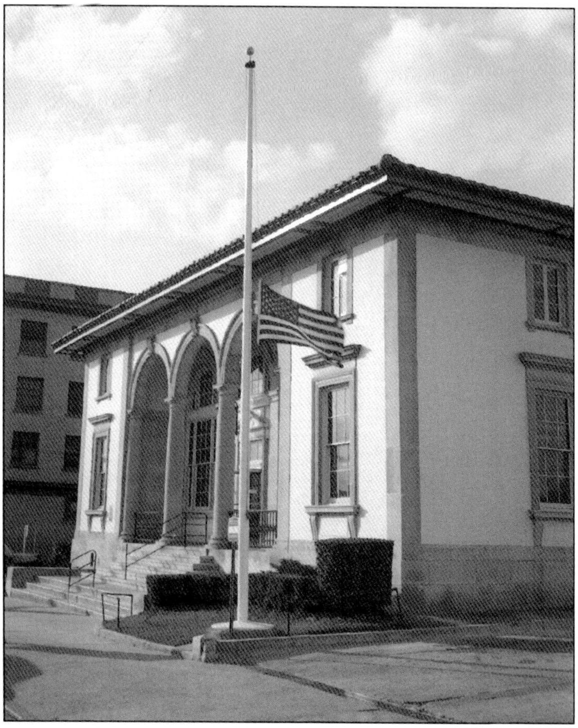

The US Post Office in Greenville flew its flag at half-mast for the late president. (Courtesy of the *Daily Reflector* and J.Y. Joyner Library, East Carolina University.)

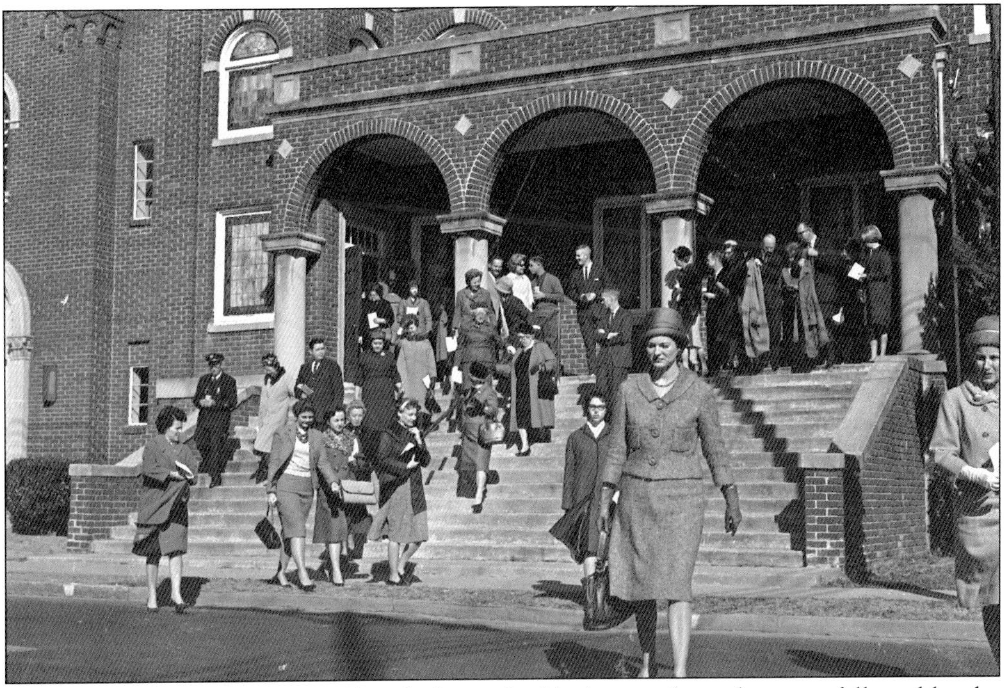

Greenville's First Presbyterian Church, located a block away from the route followed by the Kennedy motorcade during his visit to eastern North Carolina, also held a memorial service. Rev. Richard Gammon led the service. (Courtesy of the *Daily Reflector* and J.Y. Joyner Library, East Carolina University.)

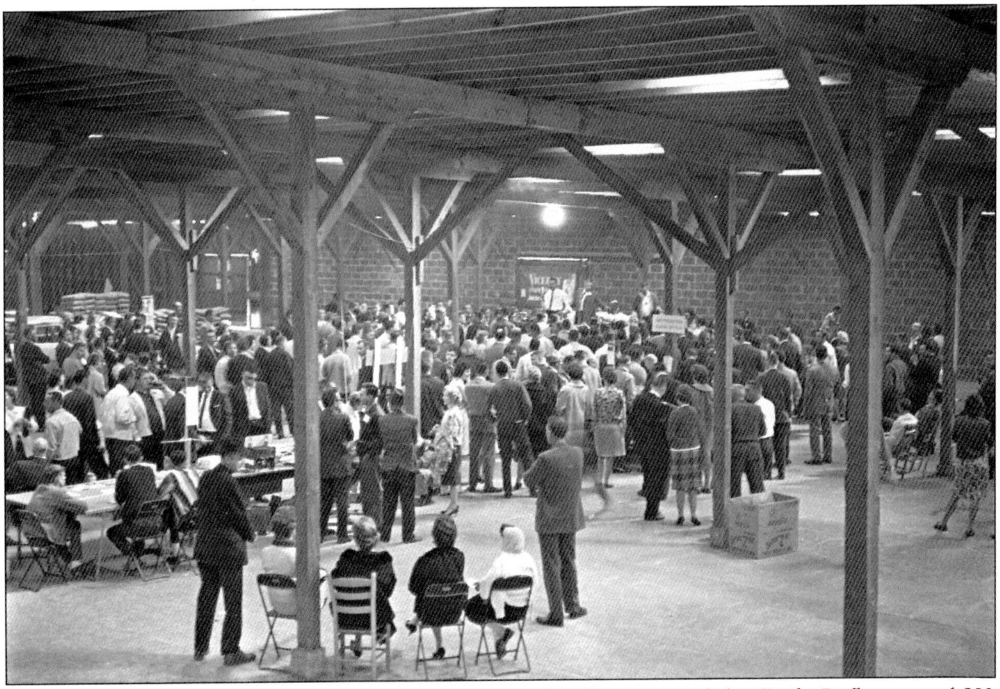

Farmers Warehouse held a brief service for Kennedy. (Courtesy of the *Daily Reflector* and J.Y. Joyner Library, East Carolina University.)

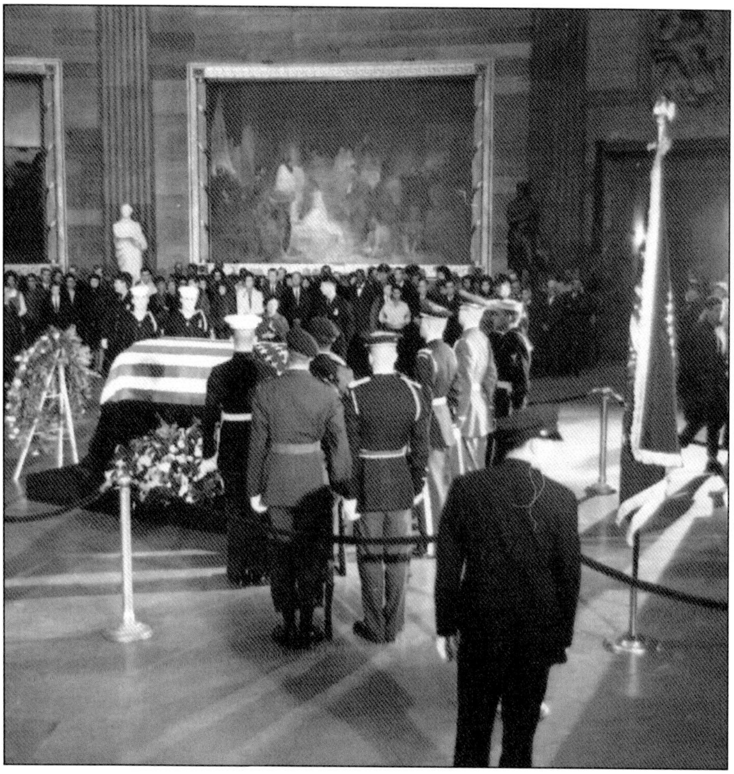

On Sunday, November 24, 1963, the day before the state funeral, the late President Kennedy's body lay in state in the US Capitol. (Photograph by Seth Muse; courtesy of J.Y. Joyner Library, East Carolina University.)

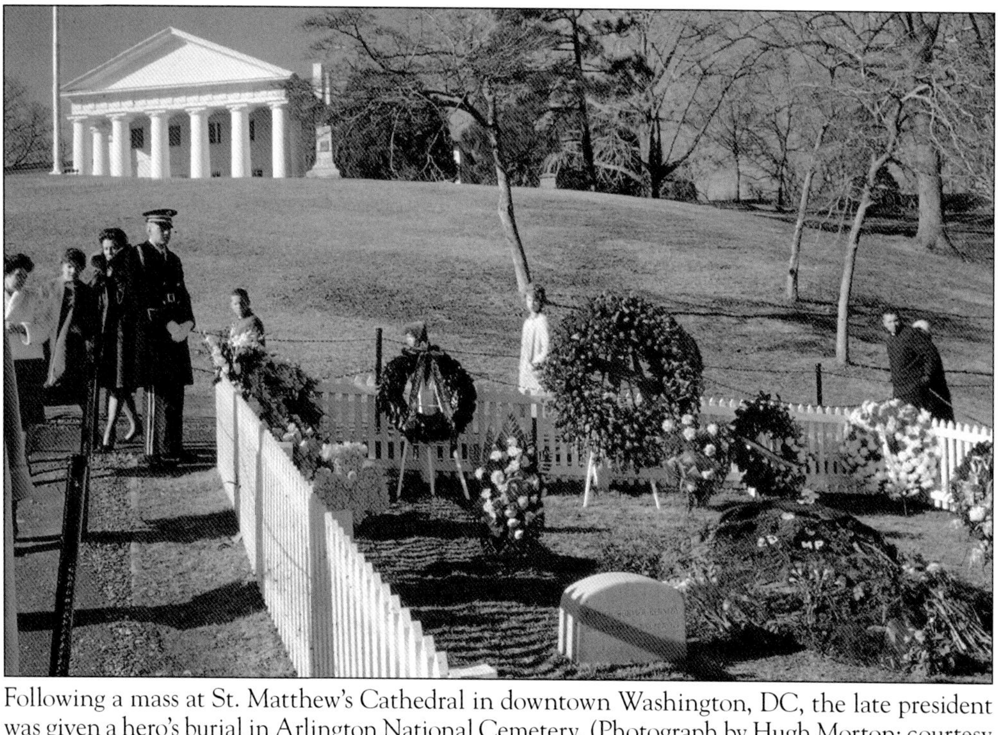

Following a mass at St. Matthew's Cathedral in downtown Washington, DC, the late president was given a hero's burial in Arlington National Cemetery. (Photograph by Hugh Morton; courtesy of Wilson Library, University of North Carolina.)

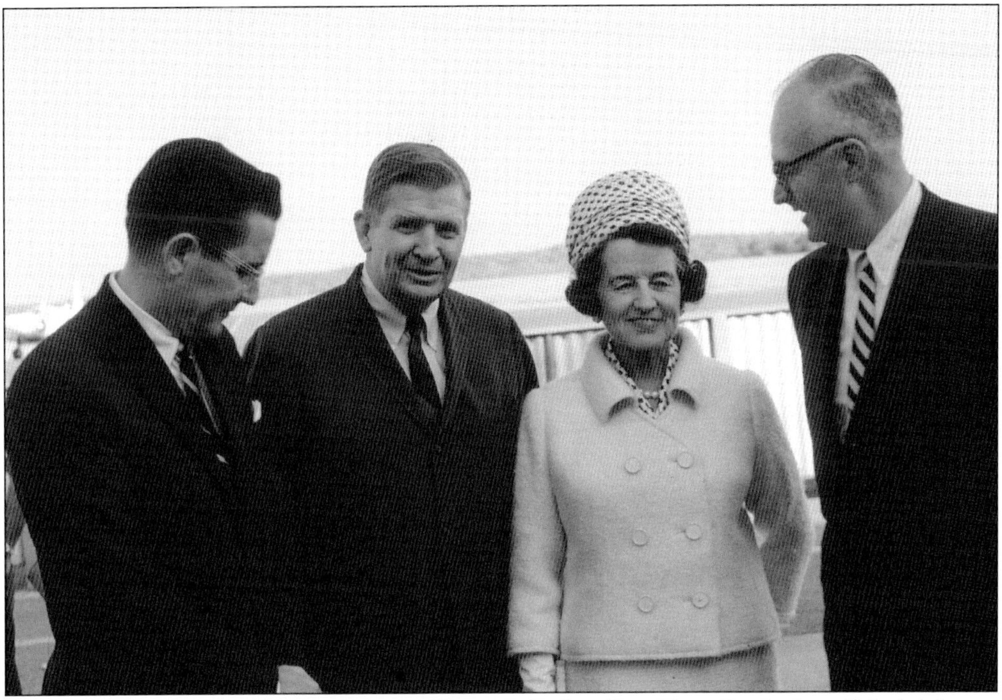

University of North Carolina president William C. Friday, Gov. Terry Sanford, and Hugh Morton (chair of the North Carolina Tribute to John Kennedy Campaign) welcome Rose F. Kennedy at the Raleigh-Durham Airport. She had flown in to participate in the North Carolina Tribute to John Kennedy held on May 17, 1964, in Chapel Hill at Kenan Stadium. (Courtesy of the Hugh Morton Collection, Wilson Library, University of North Carolina.)

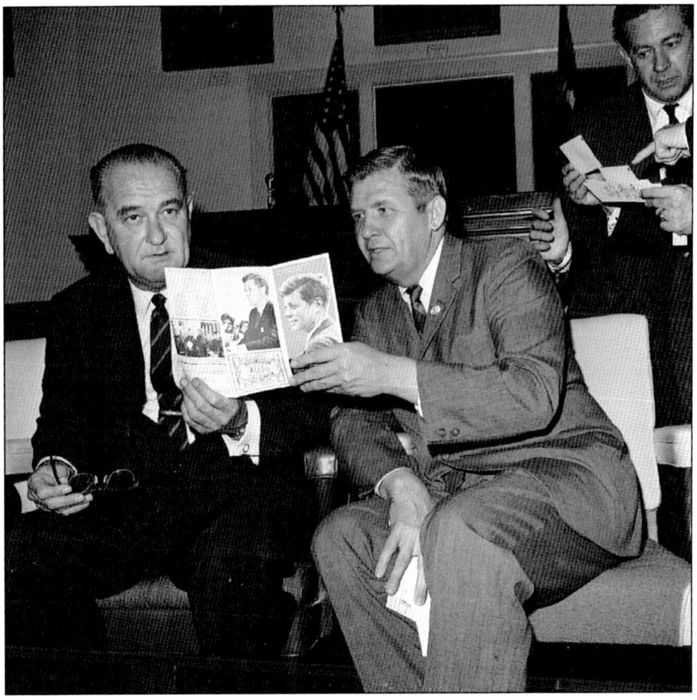

Gov. Terry Sanford and Pres. Lyndon B. Johnson display a copy of the program for the North Carolina Tribute to John F. Kennedy. Proceeds from ticket sales to the tribute, which featured Rev. Billy Graham delivering the main address, went toward North Carolina's contribution to the John F. Kennedy Library. (Photograph by Hugh Morton; courtesy of Wilson Library, University of North Carolina.)

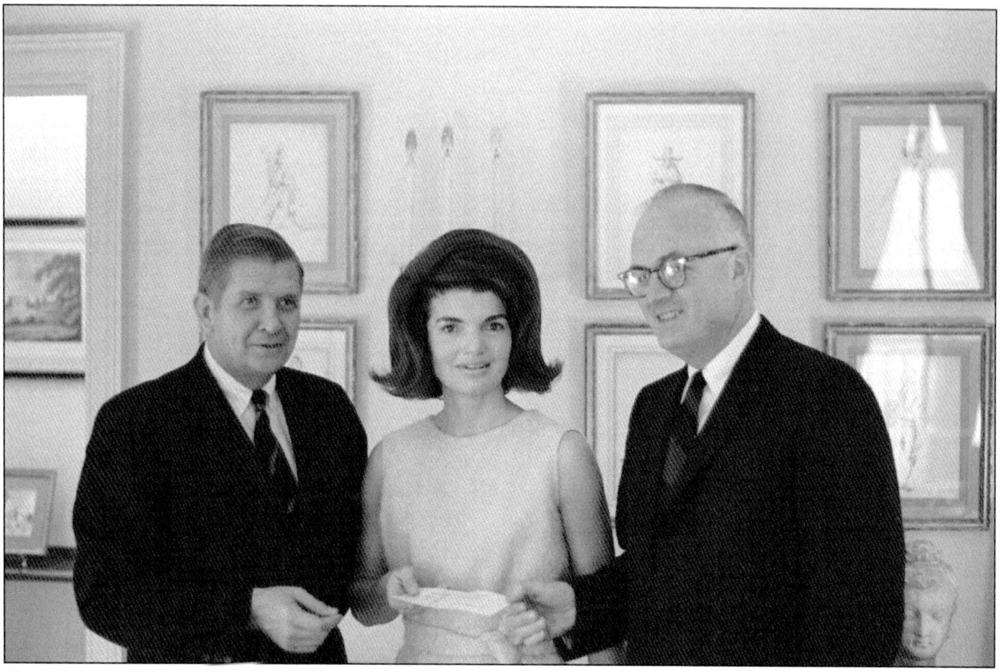

Gov. Terry Sanford and Hugh Morton present Jacqueline Kennedy with North Carolina's contribution, over $230,000, to the John F. Kennedy Library. (Courtesy of the Hugh Morton Collection, Wilson Library, University of North Carolina.)

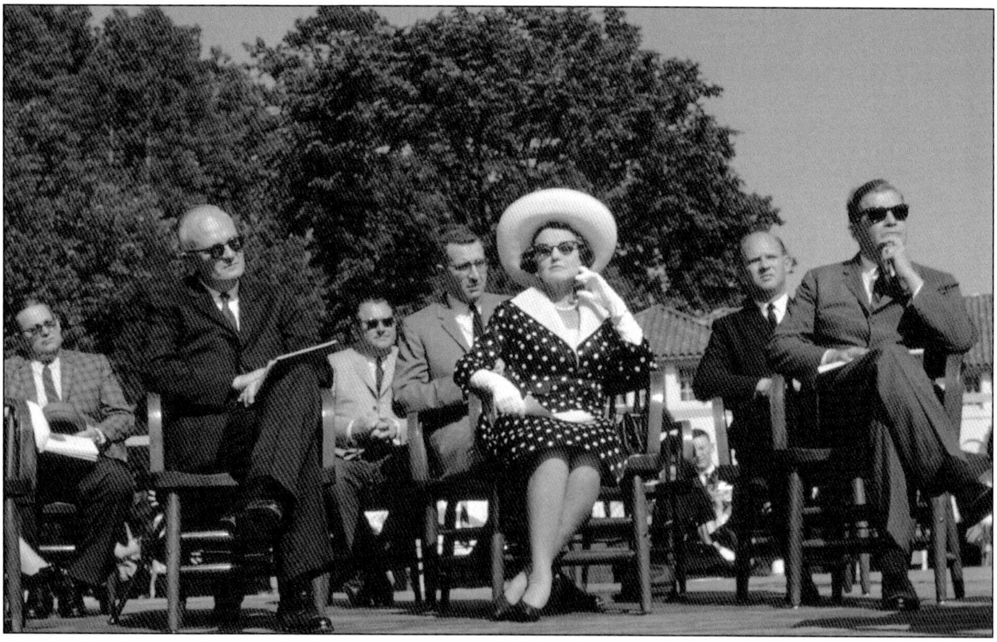

North Carolina's tribute to the late president was held on May 17, 1964, six months after Kennedy's death. The tribute, held in Kenan Stadium, featured Rev. Billy Graham delivering the main address. Former governor Luther Hodges, secretary of commerce for the Kennedy Administration, also spoke. From left to right are Hugh Morton, Rose Kennedy, and Gov. Terry Sanford. (Courtesy of the Hugh Morton Collection, Wilson Library, University of North Carolina.)

The late president's youngest brother, Edward Kennedy, also spoke at the Kenan Stadium tribute. Reportedly 12,000 people attended. (Courtesy of the Hugh Morton Collection, Wilson Library, University of North Carolina.)

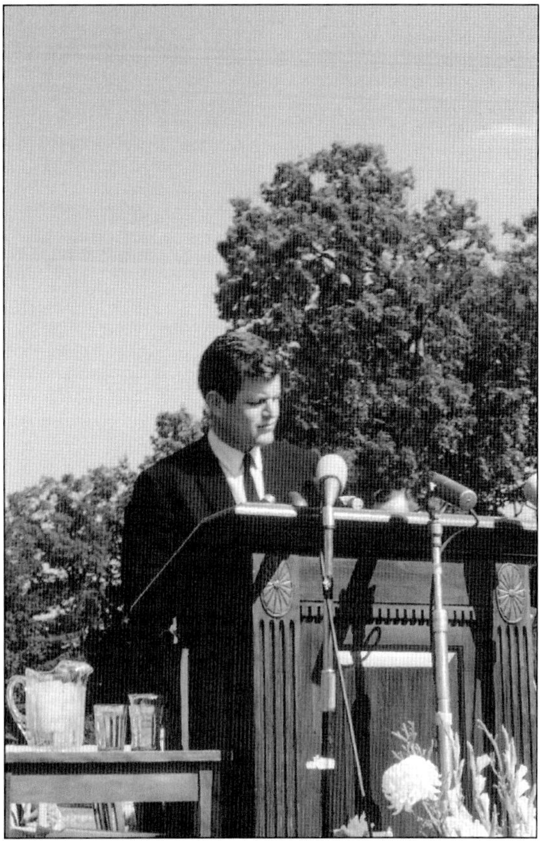

Rev. Billy Graham delivered the tribute at the North Carolina ceremony remembering the late president. Graham had publicly supported his longtime friend Richard M. Nixon in the 1960 election, but like so many Protestant clergy who once warned against the dangers of a Catholic president, supported President Kennedy in office. Kennedy's death hit those who had questioned his abilities all the harder. (Courtesy of the Hugh Morton Collection, Wilson Library, University of North Carolina.)

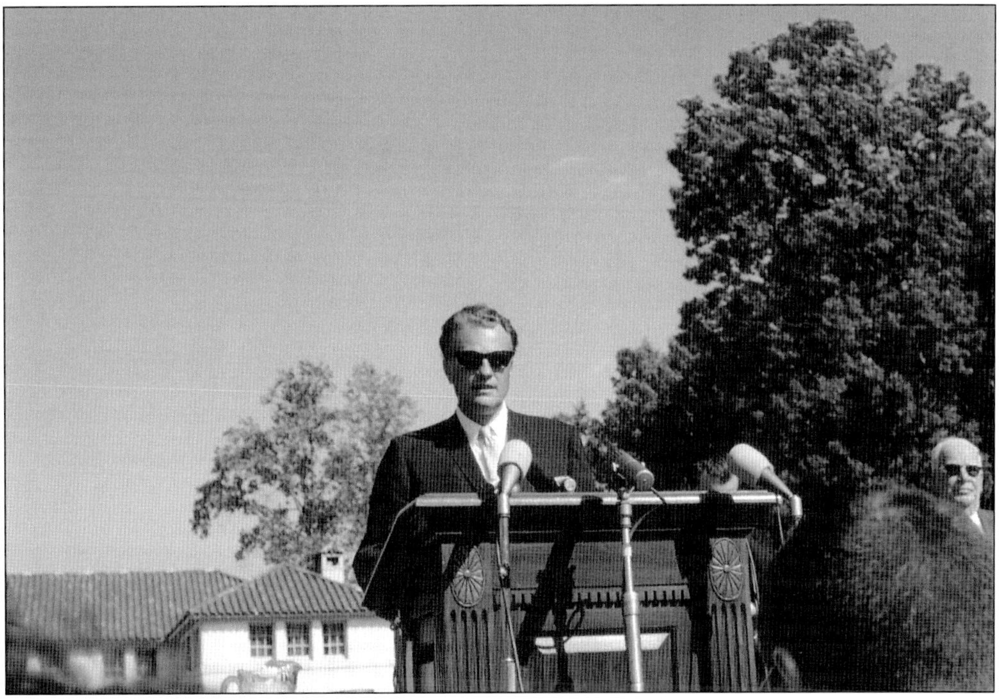